The Aztec Palimpsest

The Aztec Palimpsest

Mexico in the Modern Imagination

DANIEL COOPER ALARCÓN

The University of Arizona Press ✻ Tucson

The University of Arizona Press
Copyright © 1997
The Arizona Board of Regents
All Rights Reserved

♾ This book is printed on acid-free, archival-quality paper.
Manufactured in the United States of America
First printing

Library of Congress Cataloging-in-Publication Data
Cooper Alarcón, Daniel, 1961–
The Aztec palimpsest : Mexico in the modern imagination / Daniel
Cooper Alarcón.
p.   cm.
Includes bibliographical references and index.
ISBN 0-8165-1655-3 (cloth : alk. paper). — ISBN 0-8165-1656-1
(pbk. : alk. paper)
1. Mexico—Foreign public opinion.   2. Mexico—Description and
travel.   3. Mexico—In literature.   4. American literature—History
and criticism.   5. American literature—Mexican American authors—
History and criticism.   6. Mexican Americans—Ethnic identity.
7. Tourist trade—Government policy—Mexico.   8. Publicity.
I. Title.
F1216.5.C69   1997
972—dc21   96-45805
CIP

Publication of this book is made possible in part by the proceeds
of a permanent endowment created with the assistance of a
challenge grant from the National Endowment for the
Humanities, a federal agency.

This book is for
my mother and father,
my sister Susan,
and my Mexican family.

✿

"Consider this, señora," Don Enrique said. "You are transforming Amapolas into something more beautiful than it is."

   —Harriet Doerr, *Consider This, Señora*

＊

Simultaneously, however, this cultivation of an aesthetic ideal opens up a space for domination in the realm of concrete practice. When Mexico is removed by interpretation from the actual consequences of political and economic power, the capitalist and the archeologist can more readily go about their business.

   —David Spurr, *The Rhetoric of Empire*

＊

The very underdevelopment that exacerbates the resolution of political demands and frustrates economic aspirations is a potential asset in attracting tourism. Thus we have a paradox: nations which are veritable hellholes for most of their citizens are sold as "unspoiled paradises" to outsiders.

   —Linda K. Richter, "Political Instability and Tourism in the Third World"

Contents

Acknowledgments

A portion of this work was originally published as "The Aztec Palimpsest: Toward a New Understanding of Aztlán, Cultural Identity and History," *Aztlán* 19.2 (1988–90): 33–63. My thanks to editor Candelyn Candelaria for her help in bringing that article to the printed page.

I am grateful to my colleagues at the University of Minnesota and the University of Arizona for providing me with encouragement and criticism while I worked on this book. In particular, I thank Patricia Hampl, Michael Hancher, Peter Firchow, Arthur Geffen, Marty Roth, Kent Bales, Mario Montaño, Amy Kaminsky, Richard Carr, Thomas Reynolds, Charles R. Lewis, Shawn Gillen, John Mowitt, Larry Evers, Roger Bowen, Tenney Nathanson, Joan Dayan, Rudy Troike, Susan Hardy Aiken, Chris Carroll, Herbert N. Schneidau, Edgar A. Dryden, Annette Kolodny, Naomi Miller, Laura C. Berry, Ana Perches, and Jeremy Green. A special thank-you to John T. Irwin for his interest in and support of this project.

I also want to thank all of the graduate students with whom I have worked and whose insights enliven this study, in particular Alesia García, Donovan Gwinner, Eric Switzer, Ari Anand, Alicia Garza, Michelle Joffroy, and David T. Peterson.

Last and most, thank you Stephanie Athey for your tireless support and your boundless generosity, wisdom, and goodwill.

Introduction

While Cortés was at Coyoacán, he lodged in a palace with whitewashed
walls on which it was easy to write with charcoal and ink; and every morning malicious remarks appeared, some in verse and some in prose, in the
manner of lampoons. . . . As Cortés himself was something of a poet, he
prided himself on composing answers, which tended to praise his own great
deeds. . . . But the couplets and sentences they scrawled up became every
day more scurrilous, until in the end Cortés wrote: "A blank wall is a fool's
writing paper." And next morning someone added: "A wise man's too, who
knows the truth . . ."
   —Bernal Díaz, *The Conquest of New Spain*

✿

The events described in the story above, generated by suspicion
among Cortés's men that he had cheated them of their share of
Aztec gold, are emblematic of several points I wish to develop in
this book. First, the old adage that history is written by the conquerors is complicated here by a lack of consensus among them,
thus the competing versions of history presented in the anecdote
make the rejoinder "who knows the truth . . ." a problematic
statement at best and point toward common (mis)perceptions
about distinctions between history and myth, and history and literature. Second, we can also read this story as a dominant history
being challenged by those in a lesser position of power (i.e., Cortés's men) and, as such, as an example of counterhegemonic discourse, reminding us that challenges to hegemony often require
some degree of privileged agency.[1] Finally, the whitewashed walls
on which the texts can easily be inscribed and written over clearly
demonstrate that histories, although their authors may try very

hard to present them as monolithic, pristine texts, never emerge on a "blank wall" or tabula rasa. Díaz's history, like the wall he describes, is a complicated palimpsest, a site where texts have been superimposed onto others in an attempt to displace earlier or competing histories.[2] Significantly, such displacement is never total; the suppressed material often remains legible, however faintly, challenging the dominant text with an alternate version of events. Even when erasure appears total, important evidence of the textual removal remains that should prompt us to view the dominant discourse in a critical light, just as the walls of the Aztec palace transformed by the conquistadors into a blank slate remain a crucial marker of a silenced indigenous presence and suggest a ubiquitous but hidden wealth that generates the Spanish texts superimposed on them.

This process of erasure and superimposition resulting in a tangle of contentious and sometimes contradictory texts is characteristic of the production of Mexicanness, the object of this study. I begin with the premise that "Mexico" is a concept encompassing a broad geographic, social, and cultural terrain in historical flux, a concept that is as much the product of a complex network of discourses as it is a physical place.[3] Moreover, I believe that examination of these discourses (specifically, historiography, nationalist rhetoric, literature, literary criticism, and tourist propaganda) reveals an intense degree of interest as to how "Mexico" is defined and represented, not only by Mexicans themselves, but also by different ethnic and cultural groups in the United States and, to a lesser extent, Great Britain.[4] Not surprisingly, my notion that Mexicanness is produced through interdependent discourses manipulated in part by hegemonic groups has been strongly influenced by the work of Edward Said, in particular those theories put forward in *Orientalism* (1978). Building on the work of Michel Foucault, Said set out to show that discursive representation and political and economic dominion over groups different from one's own are intimately linked. More important, he demonstrated that the long-standing treatment of discursive representation as inherently separate from social institutions and material reality is one of the central pillars supporting such dominion. It is difficult to overstate the importance of Said's contribution. As José Rabasa puts it: "Orientalism (i.e., colonialism understood as a form of discourse) suggests a whole set of questions that point to how Europe systematically produced large portions of the non-European world, in our case the New World, through political, military, ideological, scientific, and imaginative kinds of writing and imagery" (*Inventing America* 10).

Thus, one of the goals of this study is to scrutinize the systematic production of Mexicanness in various discourses in order to reveal and understand the economic, social, and political interests driving it. Moreover, I seek to correct the erroneous but common assumption that Mexicanness is produced only by dominant or hegemonic groups. Here I have found it useful to apply Mary Louise Pratt's conceptualization of *transculturation*. The term implies a cultural interaction that forces us to consider the important role played by marginal or colonized peoples in the production of discourses about them. To quote Pratt: "Ethnographers have used this term to describe how subordinated or marginal groups select and invent from materials transmitted to them by a dominant or metropolitan culture. While subjugated peoples cannot readily control what emanates from the dominant culture, they do determine to varying extents what they absorb into their own and what they use it for" (*Imperial Eyes* 6).[5] But while it's important to recognize that marginalized groups may oppose, acquiesce to, or even collaborate with the institutionally driven production of their "selves" by hegemonic groups, we need to go a step further and remember that, as in a palimpsest, an indigenous discourse precedes those (super)imposed on it, one that is never completely erased. Therefore, the types of Mexicanness produced by Mexicans and Mexican Americans occupy crucial sites of analysis in this study and are situated against one another in ways that reveal neglected areas of inquiry: for example, the disturbing parallels between many Chicano configurations of

Mexico and their Anglo counterparts, and the relationship between Mexicanness and tourism as a form of neocolonialism actively promoted by Mexicans themselves.

To return to my original premise, it is possible to speak of two networks here: a discursive network producing Mexicanness, and a network of divergent interests seeking to manipulate that discursive network. In order to examine how the different social groups comprising the network of interests manage the discursive network for specific political agendas, I offer the palimpsest as a theoretical paradigm through which the construction and representation of cultural identity can be foregrounded as an object of study. As already noted, a palimpsest is a site where a text has been erased (often incompletely) in order to accommodate a new one, and it is this unique structure of competing yet interwoven narratives that changes the way we think of cultural identity and its representation, as well as enabling an examination of history, cultural identity, ethnicity, literature, and politics *in relationship to each other*, providing a new vantage point on the relationship of the United States and Mexico at a time when these two nations are more intimately linked than ever.

The examination of the production and utility of Mexicanness has proven to be a challenging project, particularly in terms of coverage, and I have limited the scope of my investigation to three specific areas of inquiry that are interconnected in significant ways but have received little cross-disciplinary scrutiny: Chicano nationalism, English-language literature about Mexico (focusing on prose), and Mexican touristic discourse. While there have been excellent studies within each of these three principal areas of investigation, historically they have been treated as isolated topics. By examining them in relation to one another, as I do here, we see how these three discourses are inextricably bound together and how a critical approach that treats them as a network is crucial to understanding their wide-ranging social implications. In the following paragraphs I outline my investigation and elaborate on the problems in existing scholarship that it addresses and seeks to correct.

Significantly, each of the three discourses produces Mexicanness for a non-Mexican audience, most often one in the United States. Part 1 examines the relationship between Mesoamerican histories, Mexicanness, and Chicano nationalism. More specifically, it examines the ways in which the historical production and revision of the Mesoamerican myth of Aztlán proved useful to the architects of Chicano nationalism during the heyday of the Chicano movement, but then paradoxically helped to fragment the movement soon after its period of greatest success.[6] In this section we see the vital role that the creation of a paradisal Mexican space played in both Aztec empire building and Chicano civil rights struggles; but more important, we see how a lack of attention to the palimpsestic historical production of the Aztlán narrative has contributed to misconceptions about the nature of Mesoamerican histories and Chicano cultural identity. Until very recently, it was rare for Chicano studies scholars to criticize Chicano nationalism or the Mexicanness it produced as a means of legitimating Chicano presence in the United States. Building on the important work of Angie Chabram, Rosa Linda Fregoso, J. Jorge Klor de Alva, and Alex Saragoza, I demonstrate how one of the unfortunate consequences of this unquestioning allegiance to Chicano nationalism has been the lack of a critical paradigm for Chicano cultural identity that can accommodate *intra*cultural differences. Moreover, I show that by familiarizing ourselves with the historical production of the Aztlán narrative prior to its appropriation by Chicano nationalists, we witness a demonstration of a theoretical model that not only can accommodate intracultural differences but is also capable of responding to the provisional and rapidly shifting nature of cultural identities. Furthermore, this model enables us to read in new and provocative ways the colonial discourse that shaped the production of Mexicanness, as I demonstrated above in my reading of the story of Cortés at Coyoacán. In short, the palimpsest becomes a valuable tool for identifying attempts to revise and control Mexican myth, history, and culture, as well as a viable model for understanding Chicano cultural identity. Perhaps most important, however, part 1 details the intricate relationship between historical inquiry, historiography, and cultural nationalism, a relationship that demands a paradigm like the palimpsest that can accommodate interwoven narratives.

We can similarly apply the insights of critical studies of colonialism and theories of the Other to the production of Mexicanness in English-language literature, a field that has received little scholarly attention and none at all through these important theoretical lenses. Thus part 2 of this book considers the production of Mexicanness by Anglo and Chicano writers in terms of recent critical thinking on discursive representation. Furthermore, despite the pioneering work of Cecil Robinson, Benjamin Keen, Ronald Walker, and Drewey Wayne Gunn, there exists a considerable body of literature produced by Anglo writers since 1980 that has received no attention in terms of the production of Mexicanness and which I examine closely because it raises important questions about the relationship of postmodernism and cross-cultural writing.[7] In terms of the Chicano literary tradition, scholars have consistently focused on the ways Chicano literature produces Mexicanness in order to solidify a Chicano identity, while neglecting the potentially negative impact of such production on Mexicans and Mexican culture, another problem addressed here.

Just as Aztlán emerged from Chicano nationalist discourse as a crucial imaginary Mexican space, so too do these distinct literary traditions construct other influential Mexican myths, most notably the myth of Mexico as Infernal Paradise (a phrase coined in 1946 by Malcolm Lowry, whose novel *Under the Volcano* [1947] occupies a prominent place in this literary tradition and has been extremely influential in the development of the Infernal Paradise myth). I examine recurrent figures, tropes, and representations (e.g., the frequent insistence that Mexico is "timeless") and their evolution in order to consider their wider social implications and to read them as clues to the political agendas they support. For example, I contend that the rise of Manifest Destiny in the United States and that country's subsequent imperial thrusts into Mexico were to a certain extent encouraged and made possible by the literature in this tradition. This relationship is clearly visible in Richard Henry Dana's 1840 memoir, *Two Years before the Mast,* one of the most popular American texts of the nineteenth century. In it, Dana represents Mexican territory in attractive terms (focusing on its wealth of natural, exploitable resources) while representing the Mexicans in pejorative ones (lazy, slow-witted, lascivious—in short, undeserving of such wealth).

Or, to give a more contemporary example, if timelessness becomes part of a Mexican mystique through its historical reinscription in English-language literature and subsequently becomes a quality actively searched for by tourists visiting Mexico, we are confronted with the paradox articulated by Linda K. Richter: namely, that serious social problems in Mexico remain unattended because they have become part of the "authentic" Mexicanness the tourist pays to see. My approach is to challenge the assumptions of the texts supporting these myths, to disrupt them and ask questions of them they prefer not to address. I argue that rather than give us a set of "truths" about Mexico, the texts provide us with both comforting and frightening fictions that serve a number of different political and economic purposes. In these middle chapters, the interconnectedness of the three principal areas of investigation becomes clear: not only is the Infernal Paradise gradually invested with a liberating mystique similar to that attributed by Chicano nationalists to Aztlán, but a devotion to Aztlán encourages some Chicano authors to reinscribe Mexico as Infernal Paradise and to reproduce other troubling forms of Mexicanness.

This interdependence is also central to the book's third and final part, which examines how the kinds of Mexicanness produced by Anglo and Chicano writers have been put into the service of the Mexican tourist industry. Fascinating problems abound here, particularly in terms of transculturation: economic incentives encourage the reinscription of Mexican stereotypes by Mexicans themselves, who dramatize and perform popular narratives for the tourist; tourist advertisements and propaganda seek to ground an "authentic" Mexicanness in reality, while Mexican communities revise their collective sense of themselves in response. Part 3 both documents these phenomena and discusses their far-reaching implications.

To sum up, this study amplifies and extends the small number of existing analyses of Mexicanness into new theoretical realms, examining the relationship of the different discursive traditions surrounding Mexico to systems of power. It tracks and delineates the markedly interdependent and systematic historical production of Mexicanness in a variety of discourses, and locates them in relation to one another, correcting the prevailing tendency to treat them as isolated topics. I also seek to challenge the notion that the Mexicanness produced by Chicanos and Mexicans is inherently unproblematic. Thus, the cross-cultural and interdisciplinary approach employed here distinguishes this study from previous scholarly work. Perhaps most important, this study shows how the Mexicanness produced by different discourses has been used by the Mexican tourist industry in ways that clearly illustrate the dangerous repercussions of the myth that reality exists independently of its discursive representations.

Part One

Chicano Nationalism
and Mexicanness

Chapter One

✡

Toward a New Understanding of Aztlán and Chicano Cultural Identity

In this study, I have conceived of the palimpsest as a metaphor with three primary functions. First, it is used to understand constructions of Mexicanness as a series of interdependent erasures and superimpositions; second, it is used to underscore the complicated, transcultural nature of colonial discourse in order to insist on a new way of analyzing it, as well as to identify practices in opposition to it; and finally, the palimpsest is offered as a paradigm for Chicano cultural identity.[1] Those familiar with the concept of the palimpsest most likely encountered it within the disciplines of classical studies or archaeology, where it is used to describe a parchment or stone text that has been erased, defaced, or partially removed in order to make room for a new inscription. For example, in her study of Mesoamerican writing systems, Joyce Marcus notes that in pre-Columbian Mexico, the Mixtecs frequently created palimpsests to satisfy a ruler's demand that he be inserted into royal genealogies to which he didn't belong or to appropriate the accomplishments of earlier rulers as his own. Such historical revisions were carried out by covering the bark records with lime sizing and then repainting them with new text (149–50). Significantly, in pre-Columbian Mesoamerica the erasure of old text and its replacement with new was *always* politically motivated. Marcus observes that "Mesoamerican writing was both a tool and a by-product of this competition for prestige and leadership positions" (15). Above all, it was "*a tool of the state*" (xvii;

emphasis in original). Thus, modern scholars have studied palimpsests to gain a better understanding of the intricate relationship between language, writing, political power, and empire in pre-Columbian Mesoamerica. It would be a mistake of major proportions, however, to assume—based on its association with older civilizations—that the palimpsest is solely an archaic concept. On the contrary, it holds the key to understanding the construction of Mexicanness and the domination and exploitation such construction has historically supported and that continues today. Such understanding, however, requires thinking of the palimpsest in a broader, metaphorical sense. If we remember that the definitive characteristic of the palimpsest is incomplete erasure and superimposition, and if we begin to look for this characteristic in uncharacteristic sites, we begin to locate the palimpsest as the nexus of power, empire, and discourse. The conquest and colonization of Mexico provide many instances of this characteristic process. The Spaniards strategically pursued a policy of *partial* cultural erasure because many indigenous institutions could be molded to fit their imperial design. It is no accident that Spanish cathedrals were built on top of razed Aztec temples or that indigenous historical accounts were rewritten under the supervision of Spanish missionaries. José Rabasa notes that the ruins of Tenochtitlán (the Aztec capital destroyed during the Spanish siege of 1521) assumed a crucial function, simultaneously symbolic and practical, for the nascent Spanish colony—namely, it acted as a blueprint for the capital of New Spain:

> On the ruins of the ancient city, Mexico City arises and retains indelible traces of the ancient order for the present. This transformation of reality may be likened to a palimpsest where the text of the conquered furnishes and retains its formal structure in the text of the conqueror. It is not the explorer's accidental and fortuitous mushrooming of colonial entrepôts on a landscape that murmurs an extraneous language. The *fuerat,* the had-been of Tenochtitlán, retains a ghostlike presence in a mnemonic deposit of information about the land despite the city's destruction. (*Inventing America* 101)

More important, Rabasa concludes that in this palimpsest, in the ghostlike original text, is a discourse that runs counter to and opposes colonization. Michel de Certeau makes a similar point and offers the syncretic practices of the Mesoamericans as a useful example:

> For instance, the ambiguity that subverted from within the Spanish colonizers' "success" in imposing their own culture on the indigenous Indians is well known. Submissive, and even consenting to their subjection,[2] the Indians nevertheless often *made of* the rituals, representations, and laws imposed on them something quite different from what their conquerors had in mind; they subverted them not by rejecting or altering them, but by using them with respect to ends and references foreign to the system they had no choice but to accept. They were *other* within the very colonization that outwardly assimilated them; their use of the dominant social order deflected its power, which they lacked the means to challenge; they escaped it without leaving it. The strength of their difference lay in procedures of "consumption." To a lesser degree, a similar ambiguity creeps into our societies through the use made by the "common people" of the culture disseminated and imposed by the "elites" producing the language. (xiii)

Significantly, de Certeau uses the palimpsest as a metaphor for this kind of tactical, oppositional practice by a group confronted with the strategic productions of a dominating institution, and I propose to use it in a similar way, as both a tool that enables a critique of existing models of Chicano cultural identity and history, and as a trope that allows a deeper understanding of cultural identity and history. To demonstrate its potential, I will sketch out two main avenues of inquiry that necessarily overlap.

The first considers the Mesoamerican and colonial histories from which Chicano nationalists of the 1960s derived the political symbol Aztlán without fully realizing the complexity or intertextuality of the historical narratives the symbol invoked. Aztlán was celebrated by Aztec mythology as the Aztecs' ancient homeland, their utopic place of origin somewhere to the north of

Tenochtitlán. Michael Pina observes, "Although this myth is pre-
served for contemporary peoples in a number of primary sources
that were composed early in Mexico's colonial period, . . . most
Chicanos are unaware of the narrative contents of these texts"
(38). As a result, Chicanos are at a crucial juncture vis-à-vis Mesoamerican history, one that appears to offer a choice between two
paths only, both of them political cul-de-sacs. The first, as Genaro
M. Padilla and Gloria Anzaldúa have noted separately, continues
the Chicano and Mexican nationalist tendency to romanticize
the past; the other choice, usually resulting from a negative reaction to such nostalgia, rejects the past, particularly the mythic
past, as irrelevant to the concerns of the present.[3] Both approaches
are flawed; we must approach the Mesoamerican past with interdisciplinary study that considers the diversity of Mesoamerican
cultures and the implications of intracultural differences such as
class, gender, and sexuality—especially as more and more scholars come to grips with the present-day diversity of Mexican and
Chicano cultures.

As Alex M. Saragoza notes in his important assessment of Chicano historiography, the conceptualization of Chicano history for
the most part has failed to take into account the diversity of the
Chicano experience "from its beginnings," and instead has emphasized a collective Chicano experience that minimizes class,
gender, and regional differences while romanticizing the past.
While some recent interdisciplinary scholarship in this arena has
made important strides,[4] much of the general perception of Mesoamerica, and even much historiography, continues to derive from
a narrow, positivist, Eurocentric perspective that distorts and over-
simplifies the Mesoamerican cultures, whose complexity we are
only beginning to grasp.[5] The increasing recognition of Mesoamerican cultures as multilingual and multiethnic, and the consideration of Mexican culture as the product of a much more
complicated *mestizaje* than a simple Spanish/Indian dichotomy,
holds significant implications for discussions of Mexican and

Chicano identity and will require interdisciplinary consideration.[6] Just as Annette Kolodny has noted in regard to literary history, scholars of Mesoamerican cultures must break out of their tightly compartmentalized departments if they wish to deal with social issues and concerns that have no respect for academic boundaries. Thus, the palimpsest is offered here as a model of textual superimpositions and territorial remappings; its inherently shifting and overlapping boundaries make it a model well suited to interdisciplinary study. It is also a model capable of challenging attempts to draw clear boundaries between myth and history, a problem that has plagued Mesoamerican studies in particular. Furthermore, the palimpsest's structure of interlocking, competing narratives has the advantage of preventing a dominant voice from completely silencing other voices, thus encouraging scholars to recognize and consider diversity. In short, I believe that adopting the palimpsest as a conceptual and historical tool will allow scholars to move toward a more complicated and ultimately more valuable notion of Mesoamerican, Mexican, and Chicano history.

This chapter's second major area of critique centers on Aztlán and its changing relationship to Chicano communities. As a durable political symbol of Chicano cultural nationalism, Aztlán has been linked to and used to legitimate Chicano identity.[7] However, critics of el Movimiento have criticized the ideology symbolized by Aztlán as monolithic and unresponsive to many of the members it sought to encompass. Angie Chabram and Rosa Linda Fregoso, for example, argue that Chicano nationalism conceived of Chicano identity in "a static, fixed, and one-dimensional formulation" that "failed to acknowledge our historical differences in addition to the multiplicity of our cultural identities as a people" (205). Drawing on their work, Saragoza echoes their conclusion, saying that for too long the notion of a collective experience has dominated Chicano studies, fueled by the residue of the Chicano nationalist movement (7), a concept that requires rethinking, particularly in regard to class and gender—and, I would add, to such other important cultural differences as sexuality, language use, and political and religious affiliations.

Saragoza's and Chabram and Fregoso's arguments are strengthened by the admitted failure of social scientists and historians to create models of Chicano ethnicity based on ethnic commonalities. Susan Keefe and Amado Padilla, for example, are forced to concede that "from our data we are not able to specify with precision the characteristics that describe Chicano culture, since even in the area of language use some Chicanos are fluent in Spanish while others are monolingual in English." They conclude that "a multidimensional model of cultural change and persistence is required in order to account for the variations within the ethnic minority group, in different spheres of social action, and for different cultural traits" (195).[8]

Building on the work of Saragoza, Fregoso and Chabram, and Norma Alarcón, I will argue here that Aztlán has been used to obscure and elide important issues surrounding Chicano identity, in particular the significance of intracultural differences. I will also argue, however, that Aztlán has the potential to be remade into the kind of multidimensional model that Keefe and Padilla call for, a model to examine precisely the issues that Aztlán has been used to evade in the past. Among the neglected issues related to Chicano identity are (1) the disturbing tendency to focus only on the relationship between Chicano communities and the dominant Anglo culture, at the expense of any discussion of the complex, diverse character of Chicanos and their relationships with other ethnic groups; (2) the tendency to focus on the Southwest, minimizing the attention paid to Chicanos who live in other geographic regions;[9] (3) competing claims to the Southwest—which Aztlán is often intended to be synonymous with—by Native Americans, Asian Americans, and African Americans; (4) the ongoing dialectic between Chicano and Mexican culture(s) and the effects on those culture(s) of continued Mexican emigration to the United States; and, as the work of Norma Alarcón suggests, (5) the complex interrelationship of subjectivity, agency, and privilege.[10]

How to respond to these issues is an important question. In her essay addressing internal differences in the women's movement, Chela Sandoval theorizes that the power of dominant groups stems from mobile networks, which require nondominant groups to develop an "oppositional consciousness which creates the opportunity for flexible, dynamic, tactical responses," and "a self-conscious flexibility of identity and political action" (66). I propose recognizing Aztlán as a palimpsest in order to make of it a more sophisticated model that can address the neglected issues outlined above and to create a paradigm for understanding Chicano identity that is at once fluid, overlapping, and inherently provisional, and thus one that moves toward the flexible, versatile model Sandoval calls for—one that may help us answer the difficult questions currently being raised about cultural identity. This chapter, then, is my initial attempt at using the palimpsest as such an interdisciplinary model.

The Second Departure from Aztlán

We did not, in fact, come to the United States at all. The United States came to us. We have been in America a long time. Somewhere in the twelfth century our Aztec ancestors left their homeland of Aztlán, and migrated south to Anahuac, "the place by the waters," where they built their great city of Mexico-Tenochtitlan. . . . Aztlán was left far behind, somewhere "in the north," but it was never forgotten. Aztlán is now the name of our Mestizo nation, existing to the north of Mexico, within the borders of the United States. Chicano poets sing of it, and their *flor y canto* points toward a new yet very ancient way of life and social order, toward new yet very ancient gods.
  —Luis Valdez, "La Plebe"

Even when the romanticizing of the past, as well as the present cultural identity, is exposed as a self-serving illusion and corrected by those social critics, historians, or political theorists whose view of social relations remains dispassionately fixed upon material forces in society, the mythic element that permeates the popular consciousness may not easily be exorcised as useless trivia since it has come to assume a life of its own in the group's imagination.

—Genaro M. Padilla, "Myth and Comparative Cultural Nationalism"

✳

Perhaps the most enduring legacy of the Chicano movement, the legend of Aztlán has been an important rallying point for a people who often feel dislocated, not only from Mexican and Anglo American society, but from each other as well. In their critique of the movement, Chabram and Fregoso account for the symbol's initial appeal and longevity:

> Twenty years ago, the Chicano student movement created a space where an alternative cultural production and identity could flourish. . . . Aztlán, the legendary homeland of the Aztecs, claimed by Chicano cultural nationalism as the mythical place of the Chicano nation, gave this alternative space a cohesiveness. Chicano identity was framed in Aztlán. And, Aztlán provided a basis for a return to our roots, for a return to an identity before domination and subjugation—a voyage back to pre-Columbian times. In its most extreme cases, Aztlán was said to be located in the deepest layers of consciousness of every Chicano, an identification which thereby posited an essential Chicano subject for cultural identity. (204–5)

But this focus on Aztlán is now being questioned and scrutinized, both within and outside the academy. Stripped of its historical implications, quarantined in utopic myth, Aztlán increasingly appears to be an empty symbol to many Chicanos, one that does not unite so much as divert those who do not wish to consider the very real differences of region, gender, class, sexuality, language, and *mestizaje* within Chicano communities. Fregoso and Chabram comment that

> the shortsightedness of Chicano studies intellectuals was that they assumed that the construction of their own self representations as subjects was equivalent to that of the totality of the Chicano expe-

rience, and that this shared representation could be generalized in the interest of the entire group. . . . How else could we explain the fact that an ahistorical "Aztec" identity would fall on the deaf ears of an urban community versed in the rhythms of disco, *conjunto* music and *boleros*? By recuperating the mythic pre-Columbian past and formulating this as the basis of our shared identity, Chicano academic intellectuals of the post-colonial condition failed to see that cultural identities have histories, that they undergo constant transformation and that far from being etched in the past, cultural identities are constantly being constructed. (206)

Their point is well taken. As conceived by the Chicano nationalists of el Movimiento, Aztlán was posed as a monolithic narrative into which all Chicanos were to write themselves, regardless of their intracultural differences. Instead, as Chabram and Fregoso point out, a fluid, continuously changing narrative or model is needed, one that is adaptable to the myriad possibilities of Chicano identities, which are in constant flux. For these reasons, Chabram and Fregoso prepare to leave behind Aztlán as a symbol; but perhaps this second departure is premature. After all, Aztlán bears all of the characteristics that Chabram and Fregoso attribute to cultural identities: it has a complicated history, it has undergone repeated transformation, and, far from being etched in the past, Aztlán is continuously being remade. I believe that when understood as a palimpsest, Aztlán ceases to be ahistorical and insists upon an examination of the past, a study that will reveal not only the complexity of Aztlán, but of the Mesoamerican history that was used as a resource by Chicano nationalists. Not only must we recognize the decreasing value of the ahistorical symbol Aztlán for a changing, diversifying Chicano community, we must also consider why only this sliver of the mythic pre-Columbian past was recuperated and transformed into a modern-day rallying point. Aztlán as palimpsest immediately changes the way we look at the past and the sources from which we have derived our notions of the past, thus offering new resources and new avenues of investigation. To demonstrate, I turn to the Mesoamerican past—that alternative space created by scholarship that has become so controversial—and trace some of the attempts to control it, in order to examine its significant implications for Chicanos today.

The Aztec Palimpsest

Between us and the pre-Columbian city and its symbols stand not just time and wear, distance and cultural diversity, and renewal within a tradition of wisdom, but also the conquest of Mexico and the invention of the American Indian . . . . [S]cholars encountering this fragmented situation and the enigmatic Quetzalcoatl have attempted to design and redesign the symbol's significance according to their theories of culture, religion, civilization, and Indians.

—Davíd Carrasco, *Quetzalcoatl and the Irony of Empire*

✿

Any discussion of Mesoamerican history is complicated by the intricate nature of the early primary sources. The letters and chronicles of the Spanish conquistadors and colonizers view and represent Mesoamerica through a Western, Christian lens. As for the indigenous texts, Susan Gillespie points out that although strong oral and written traditions were practiced for many years, not many of the pre-Conquest Mesoamerican "books" survived the Conquest, and the existence of Aztec books from the pre-Conquest era remains controversial. The pre-Conquest texts that have proven most valuable to ethnohistorians have been the surviving architecture and artifacts (S. Gillespie xvii–xli).

The scarcity of indigenous books from the pre-Conquest eras is an indication of the scope of the Spaniards' colonial and missionary ambitions. Ironically, the Aztecs, like many Mesoamerican peoples, had a tradition of assimilating the religious practices of other cultures, and the delight with which the early Spanish missionaries claimed rapid and widespread conversion of the Mesoamericans to Catholicism quickly turned to frustration as the natives' syncretic tendencies surfaced. Furthermore, the similarity between certain indigenous religious practices (often closely associated with the culture hero Topiltzin Quetzalcoatl) and Christian beliefs and rites fascinated and confused the missionaries (S. Gillespie xxviii–xxxv). Two schools of thought developed to explain these parallels: either earlier missionaries had preceded the Spanish priests (Diego Durán believed it was no one less than Saint Thomas),[11] or it was the devil's handiwork. Both schools came to the same conclusion: Mesoamerican history needed to be recovered to solve the mystery and to more effectively convert the Mexicans.[12] The Catholic priests began the difficult process of finding survivors of the Mesoamerican elite who could recreate the historical records that, ironically, had been destroyed in the name of the true faith.

Although few in number, the written and pictographic documents, or codices, produced by these historical recovery efforts under the supervision of the Spanish clergy are a major source of information for Mesoamerican scholars. That said, it is important to note the special types of problems involved in working with the codices, for they are not so much individual texts as elaborate palimpsests, and the superimposed material is no small obstacle. As Davíd Carrasco puts it, "It is clear that a thick Spanish, colonial, Christian gloss has been brushed across the ideas, beliefs, symbols, and dramas of ancient Mexican culture." However, the gloss does not completely obscure the indigenous material: ". . . significant segments of authentic pre-Hispanic culture can be discerned and understood in an illuminating fashion. Through the gloss, indigenous images and patterns show themselves in an engaging manner" (12).

José Rabasa furthers Carrasco's observation by noting the subversive quality of the "indigenous images and patterns" in the following passage from book 12 of the *Historia general de las cosas de Nueva España*, also known as the *Florentine Codex*, the impressive Aztec history dictated by older members of the Aztec elite to younger Mesoamerican scholars under the supervision of Fray Bernardino de Sahagún:

> And Moctezuma thereupon sent [and] charged the noblemen, whom Tziuacpopocatzin led, and many others besides of his officials, to go to meet [Cortés] between Popocatepetl and Iztac tepetl, there in Quauhtechcac. They gave them golden banners, precious feather streamers, and golden necklaces.
>
> And when they had given them these, they appeared to smile; they were greatly contented, gladdened. As if they were monkeys they seized upon the gold. It was as if their hearts were satisfied, brightened, calmed. For in truth they thirsted mightily for gold; they stuffed themselves with it; they starved for it; they lusted for it like pigs.
>
> And they went about lifting on high the golden banners; they went moving them back and forth; they went taking them to themselves. It was as if they babbled. What they said was gibberish. (*Florentine Codex* 13:31)

Rabasa astutely cites this passage as an example of counterdiscourse within a text supervised by a dominant colonizing culture. It is what Mary Louise Pratt calls an autoethnographic text, "a text in which a people undertake to describe themselves in ways that engage with representations others have made of them. . . . [T]hey involve a selective collaboration with and appropriation of idioms of the metropolis or the conqueror. These are merged or infiltrated to varying degrees with indigenous idioms to create self-representations intended to intervene in metropolitan modes of understanding, and are addressed to both colonizer and colonized" ("Contact Zone" 35). Drawing on the work of Angel María Garibay, Rabasa argues that the Aztec authors embedded indigenous literary conventions within the dominant genre in order to critique the Spaniards:

> From all appearances the syntactical doubling of metaphors is a characteristic trait of prehispanic poetry. Whereas the Franciscans

would comply with the moral outrage expressed in this passage, they would not express it as such. The fixation on gold, as revealed in its monotonous repetition in the text, implies a native view wherein the Europeans are mocked ("like monkeys," "like pigs") and wherein gold is seen as a lowly object of desire. . . . [I]ts doubling of metaphors actually upturns and makes redundant any pursuit of a figurative meaning as it marks an insistence on expression over content. Paraphrasing Deleuze and Guattari, we might add that just as the Spaniards become pigs and monkeys, so the pigs and monkeys become Spaniards. Thus the characterization of the Spaniards as savages, *popolcas* (those who cannot speak Nahuatl), gains intensity with their animal behavior and the suggestion that they eat gold. The attributes *teule* [god] and *popolca* do not contradict each other but reinforce each other with the image of an uncouth god that brings about the destruction of culture; after all, the Spaniards melt down artifacts in order to devour gold. ("Dialogue as Conquest" 152–53)

Rabasa's interpretation suggests another important idea: not only are these early primary sources palimpsests because of the interwoven cultural expectations and literary traditions they contain, they are also written over each time a scholarly interpretation of them is attempted (including my own). Furthermore, the layers of dominant and subversive texts are not limited to those in which the indigenous, oppressed people are given some degree of direct input into the construction of history.[13] We can also use the palimpsest as a trope to identify competing histories within texts written by authors who do not intend to give the natives a voice. Consider the following passage from Bernal Díaz: "The lord of Tacuba said that in his house at Tacuba, about twelve miles away, he had some gold objects, and that if we would take him there he would tell us where they were buried and give them to us. Pedro de Alvarado and six soldiers, myself among them, took him there. But when we arrived he said he had only told us this story in the hopes of dying on the road, and invited us to kill him, for he possessed neither gold nor jewels. So we returned empty-handed" (410). This is a brilliant example of the power of storytelling to open up a space for counterdiscourse. By creating a story that he knows will fascinate the Spaniards, the Lord of Tacuba is able to influence the shape of Díaz's narrative and become a participant in it, so that for the time it takes to travel twelve miles the power relationship has been slightly altered. When he can no longer sustain his narrative and reveals his position as author, the Lord of Tacuba literally disappears from Díaz's account. But although Díaz considers the ultimate fate of the prisoner too insignificant to share with his readers, he cannot conceal the power of an oppressed people to use storytelling as a means of entering, subverting, and even briefly controlling the dominant discourse, if only by leading it astray. While Díaz and other chroniclers failed to acknowledge or record the many such indigenous sources that shape their texts, we *must* assume the influence of such sources on the dominant discourse.

Beatriz Pastor Bodmer, Peter Hulme, and John Chávez are among the scholars who have theorized that storytelling was often used by indigenous Americans as a defense against European colonization. Pastor Bodmer comments that

> repression is never total, silence never absolute. And just as the voices of the marginalized, of the oppressed and the defeated seemed to be lost forever, we listen again to their echoes, in a different way and with a different sound. It is the sound of resistance, and it adopts all of the forms defined by the very vulnerability of the conquerors, while for more than a century, it shaped the discovery, defining objectives, tracing journeys, leading and misleading discoverers and conquerors anxious to materialize their dreams and personal utopias in the unexplored territories of the New World. I am speaking of the lying captives, the false guides and informants, the tireless weavers of fables, myths and lies that appear again and again in the Viceroyal courts and in the expeditions of exploration. ("Silence and Writing" 150)

Although it is now clear that the competing narratives of indigenous peoples and Spanish colonizers created layered myths and histories, it is important to recognize that this narrative structure developed long before the Spanish invasion and predates the superimpositions of Spanish texts. Gillespie argues convincingly that the native authors continued a long tradition of altering history in order to explain the present, a tradition grounded in the Mesoamerican belief that time was cyclical. Current events were thought to be repetitions of earlier ones, and Mesoamerican historians were often faced with the task of scouring the past for an event corresponding to the present, one similar enough that it could be slightly altered or embellished to establish a precedent: "Consequently, the past cannot be considered immutable or irreversible. Instead, it has to be amenable to change as required by later events—it is the past that is altered to conform to, and to be continuous with, the present" (S. Gillespie xxiii–xxiv).

Furthermore, there is evidence to suggest that the codices and the narratives they contain are marked by a strong class bias, as indicated by the work of Enrique Florescano: "Surpassing all of the other attributes that the Mesoamerican communities gave to the past is the utilization of historical memory as an instrument to legitimate power, sanction the order of established things and inculcate in the governed the values that oriented the action of the governors" (*Memoria mexicana* 84; my translation). Florescano emphasizes two important consequences of this tradition. First, the historical discourse that emerges from Mesoamerican texts does not represent a collective voice, but rather that of the governing elite; and, second, scholars trying to comprehend the concept of the Mesoamerican past and its different uses must consider all of its components, not just those texts that Western tradition has certified as historical (84–89). Thus, many of the discrepancies in different Mesoamerican texts relating the same pre-Conquest events may actually be commentaries on the culture shock of the sixteenth century or the ideology of the ruling classes, layered over centuries of similar historical revision and glossed over by Spanish missionaries and colonial authorities, all working to create a complex, multilayered palimpsest.

As Florescano suggests, some historians, when confronted by these traditions of historical revision, have pursued a misguided course and tried to separate "historical truth" from the "distortion" of myth and legend. Gillespie notes that "the idea of an opposition between history and myth is itself an artificial construct of Western culture," an idea that ignores "the reality that both [history and myth] are symbolic narratives" that are equally meaningful (S. Gillespie xxxviii–xxxix). Another disadvantage she sees in such an approach is that the points of contradiction in different versions of the same story are discarded in order to get at "historical truth": "[F]rom the perspective pursued here the contradictions take on greater significance than the consistencies. . . . The mutability of these points is an indication of the complexity of their multiple meanings, and understanding them provides the clues to the cultural categories and relationships that generated the different accounts" (S. Gillespie xxxvii–xxxviii).

There is no need to belabor the point of the impossibility of ever arriving at "historical truth," or of the problems raised by attributing a greater value to accounts that appear more historical than mythical. However, we cannot ignore the important, related point that scholarship has inscribed more layers to this complicated palimpsest, as suggested by Carrasco in the epigraph to this section and by Gillespie in the following passage: "Understanding the latest reworking of this story [Cortés as Quetzalcoatl] should help to illuminate the sixteenth- and seventeenth-century reconstructions of the Aztec past, because archaeologists and ethnohistorians, like Aztecs and Spaniards before them, have manipulated various bits of data to compose a narrative of the past that conforms to their own expectations and organizational principles" (S. Gillespie 201–2).

To conclude this brief discussion of Mesoamerican texts, I want to emphasize that they need to be perceived as a complicated discursive network, a structure that has the advantage of allowing for new considerations of Mesoamerican cultures as ethnohistorians begin to view them as much more complex and diverse than they were previously thought to be. For example, not only has Gillespie contributed greatly to our understanding of the complexity of Mesoamerican history, but her attention to the neglected issue of gender difference suggests that the Aztecs were not as enslaved to ritual as Tzvetan Todorov and others have proposed.[14] Other areas are being reconsidered as well. While both Mexican and Chicano nationalist discourses have had the effect of reinforcing the general perception that the Aztecs were the sole indigenous protagonists in Mesoamerican history, continued work by feminist scholars studying the complex intercultural history of Malintzin promises to undermine such a position.[15] And, as already noted, Florescano's consideration of intracultural class divisions problematizes the Mesoamerican narratives in provocative ways. These are just a few examples of how attention to diversity in the study of Mesoamerican (and Mexican and Chicano) history will increase our understanding of the cultures that produced them. To encourage this new approach, I propose considering the palimpsest as a conceptual tool that offers the following advantages for Mesoamerican historiography and Chicano studies:

1. When understood as a palimpsest, Aztlán ceases to be ahistorical and instead insists on an examination of the Mesoamerican narratives from which it was drawn.
2. Recognizing the multilayered trope underlying these narratives increases our understanding of the complexity of the cultures that produced them and enables us to better apprehend the subversive and contestatory discourse that inhabits most colonial discourse.
3. The palimpsest, because of its network of intricately linked narratives of different types, makes impossible any sort of devaluation of myth vis-à-vis history, nor does it allow one type of narrative to be considered in isolation from others.
4. The palimpsest model forces us to consider the points of divergence in the competing narratives and allows us to trace

cultural categories of thought as they change over time and compete with others for recognition or dominance.

5. Because it is always undergoing revision, the palimpsest can accommodate new information without privileging it.

Finally, this multilayered conceptualization of Mesoamerican history will complicate our understanding of Aztlán in a way that will be valuable for further discussion of Chicano cultural identity, as we will see in the next section.

Chicano Cultural Identity and the Paradoxical Nature of Aztlán

Nonetheless, the appropriation from the elitelore of ancient Mexico of such a seminal emblematic device as Aztlán was the most brilliant political maneuver of the Chicano cultural nationalists. Nothing their critics have done has managed to surpass or equal this feat of organizational strategy. Under no other sign or concept, derived from the left, center, or right, were as many Chicanos mobilized and as much enthusiasm galvanized into political action—except for the concept of Chicanismo itself. For a movement hungry for symbols that could both distinguish it from other movements and unite it under one banner, Aztlán was perfect. So perfect, in fact, that almost two decades after it was unfurled it is still the single most distinguishing metaphor for Chicano activism. The term is ubiquitous: found in the strident political program called the *Plan Espiritual de Aztlán* and in the name of the most sober, scholarly Chicano journal, and it adorns the title of scores of poems, novels, paintings, and organizations, all of which display it both as a sign of their content and as a mark of their political ideology. Why?
—J. Jorge Klor de Alva, "Aztlán, Borinquen and Hispanic Nationalism in the United States"

✿

The concept of Aztlán, as formulated by Chicano nationalism and Chicano scholarship since 1969, presents an overwhelming number of apparent contradictions. Luis Leal maintains that it is both a physical and a spiritual entity, both geographically specific and universal: "As a Chicano symbol, Aztlán has two meanings: first it represents the geographic region known as the Southwestern part of the United States, composed of the territory that Mexico ceded in 1848 with the Treaty of Guadalupe Hidalgo; second and more important, Aztlán symbolized the spiritual union of the Chicanos, something that is carried within the heart, no matter where they may live or where they may find themselves" ("In Search of Aztlán" 8). For Rudolfo Anaya and Francisco Lomelí, the nature of Aztlán is at once "historical, anthropological and symbolic," existing "at the level of symbol and archetype"; it is a legend both "anthropologically sound and historically reliable" (iii). It resides in both historical and mythic narratives, narratives that have continued to evolve and have been continuously revised over centuries (Pina 14–48; Chávez 7–22). Its proponents have claimed that as a symbol of cultural nationalism, Aztlán transcends "all religious, political, class and economic factors or boundaries" and is a "common denominator that all members of La Raza can agree upon," while critics have charged that the symbol ultimately divides more than it unifies.[16] It is said to promote both communal and individual interests, and, as a symbol of cultural nationalism, it is said both to have fostered the maintenance of cultural traditions and to have inadvertently promoted assimilation into the dominant Anglo culture (Barrera 4–5).

But these characteristics of Aztlán are not contradictions, in the sense that to admit the possibility of one is to negate the possibility of the other. Rather, they are paradoxes that have yet to be fully explored as a network with significant implications for Chicanos in terms of both intracultural and intercultural relationships. These paradoxes are most visible in texts written about Aztlán that, when examined closely, contain traces of the issues that Aztlán as a nationalist symbol has been used to elide, namely, those issues outlined in the first part of this chapter. Since it is my thesis that Aztlán is a multilayered textual construct or palimpsest, and since its textual layers include not only historical/mythic narratives but also historiography, scholarship, and political documents, I have selected representative "master texts" from each of those genres for analysis, an analysis that will center on the paradoxical nature of Aztlán. My purpose is not merely to argue that Aztlán is a palimpsest, but also to demonstrate that in examining its competing, interlocking narratives as a discursive network, we are forced to confront important issues surrounding Chicano cultural identity—issues of difference, diversity, privilege, agency, and self-determination. In recognizing Aztlán as a palimpsest, we reconfigure it yet again, self-consciously adding another layer in order to convert it into a structure that will foreground those controversies—and the cultural categories and relationships they encode—as the very objects of study, rather than allow Aztlán to continue to function as a mechanism that disguises or diverts attention from them.

"El Plan Espiritual de Aztlán" and the Paradox of Unity/Diversity

Although Aztlán had been a powerful symbol for both Meso-american and European peoples for centuries, most people today associate the term with the Chicano cultural nationalist movement that began in the mid-1960s and is generally agreed to have fragmented into antagonistic splinter groups by 1975. By the twentieth century the concept of Aztlán had all but disappeared from public discourse: "Few people in the United States were familiar with the concept of Aztlán until Chicano Movement activists of the 1960s revived it and proclaimed it a central symbol of Chicano nationalist ideology. The rediscovery of Aztlán can be traced to a specific event, the Chicano National Liberation Youth Conference that took place in Denver in 1969. There, Colorado political activist Rodolfo 'Corky' Gonzales put forth a brief but influential political document entitled El Plan de Aztlán" (Barrera 3).[17]

Despite Mario Barrera's claim, the precise moment of Aztlán's reentry into contemporary public discourse is subject to debate, Leal attributing it to Alurista in 1968, and Jack D. Forbes claiming that the term was first used to refer to a Chicano homeland in his mimeographed manuscript "The Mexican Heritage of Aztlán (the Southwest) to 1821"—circulated in 1962 by members of the Movimiento Nativo-Americano to Chicanos in the Southwest.[18] However, most scholars agree that the idea of Aztlán as a Chicano homeland was catapulted into the public domain by "El Plan Espiritual de Aztlán," and the plan's main points are worth noting here:

Chicanos staked their claim to the "northern land of Aztlán" by ancestral birthright and as inhabitants and "civilizers" of a territory that had been stolen from them by a "brutal 'gringo' invasion." They refused to recognize the "capricious frontiers" established by European invaders.

Unity was stressed and nationalism was the "key or common denominator" that transcended all internal differences within the Chicano community, uniting all Chicanos in their struggle against the dominant Anglo culture.

The plan committed Chicanos to "social, economic, cultural and political independence" as "the only road to total liberation from oppression, exploitation and racism." Self-determination was a major goal.

Art was to strengthen identity and maintain unity: "We must insure that our writers, poets, musicians, and artists produce literature and art that is appealing to our people and relates to our revolutionary culture."

Aztlán was proclaimed as a nation, a union of free pueblos, and the plan called for the establishment of an independent political party at local, regional, and national levels.

Ironically, Aztlán, in both its uses as an ancient utopic homeland and as a political symbol, has proven to be more durable than the movement that reappropriated and reconstructed it. Closer examination of "El Plan Espiritual" helps clarify this phenomenon and raises several important issues surrounding a Chicano homeland and a unified Chicano community that have been repeatedly ignored or distorted in elaborations of Aztlán.

First, the plan justifies its goals on the basis of European and Anglo American colonization and oppression, yet does not grapple with mestizo colonization and appropriation of Native American lands in the Southwest during the Spanish colonial period. The colonization is instead transformed into a legitimation of Chicano territorial rights based on Chicanos' roles as "civilizers of the Northern land of Aztlán." To date, competing claims to the region by Native Americans, Asian Americans, African Americans, and the *mestizaje* of these different cultures have yet to be addressed in most discussions of Aztlán.

Second, nationalism could not override internal differences for very long, even when those divisions were attenuated by extreme racism on the part of the dominant culture (Saragoza 7). Marxist critics began to charge that the cultural nationalism represented by Aztlán blocked the achievement of the true class consciousness necessary for the workers' revolution. Chicanas began to question whether they should have to set aside internal issues of sexism in the name of unity and the movement.[19]

Finally, even Aztlán's link to a mythic past, thought by many of its proponents to be one of its most galvanizing features, provoked resistance (see Chabram and Fregoso).

Since the authors of "El Plan Espiritual" chose to locate the source of Chicano identity in Mesoamerican history/myth in order to provide a narrative they could reinvent for the movement's political aims, I now turn my attention to the historiography surrounding Aztlán—including one of the earliest versions—in the hope of demonstrating that the reconstruction of the myth of Aztlán for the purposes of cultural nationalism was not a new strategy and that, ironically, previous revisions of the myth had created yet another paradox: they made it appear so free floating that it was easy to appropriate; conversely, in not recognizing its intertextuality and multilayered dimensions (i.e., its palimpsestic structure), the Chicano architects of the movement reconstructed Aztlán as a monolithic narrative that would inevitably force marginalized Chicanos and Chicanas to break away, bringing about the movement's collapse. In other words, just as the attempt to anneal the many different Aztlán stories into a coherent, pristine narrative would ultimately lead many Chicanos to reject it, so too would attempts to pose Chicanos as a monolithic, unified community symbolized by Aztlán fragment under the weight of the diversity of those members who found their individuality, needs, and aspirations lost in Aztlán or not represented. Simply put, the unity offered by nationalism did not overcome intracultural differences, as Gonzales and the other authors of "El Plan Espiritual" claimed it would.[20]

Diego Durán and the Paradox of Mesoamerican Myth/European Myth

One of the earliest written sources to document Aztlán is the *Historia de las Indias de Nueva España e Islas de Tierra Firme* (1581), by the Spanish missionary Diego Durán. Relying on Mesoamerican informants and texts, and motivated by a desire to more effectively convert the Mesoamericans to Catholicism, Durán compiled a history and catalogue of Mesoamerican culture that is surpassed only by the work of Sahagún. Durán mentions Aztlán early in the first chapter of his history: "The only knowledge of their origins that I have obtained from my Indian informants tells of the seven caves where their ancestors dwelt for so long and which they abandoned in order to seek this land, some coming first and others later until these caves were totally deserted. The caves are in Teocolhuacan, which is also called Aztlán, 'Land of Herons,' which we are told is found toward the north and near the region of La Florida" (*The Aztecs* 6). This early reference to Aztlán raises several interesting issues. Rather than locating Aztlán in the Southwest, Durán's informants lead him to believe it is located near La Florida. According to Doris Heyden and Fernando Horcasitas, in Durán's time La Florida referred not only to what is now the peninsula of that name in the United States but also to the region north of Tampico, including northeastern Mexico and southeastern Texas (Durán, *The Aztecs* 330). Even given this large a region, Durán's Aztlán still is not easily placed in the southwestern United States. Also noteworthy is the reference to seven caves, a provocative, specific detail embedded within a description ambiguous enough to provoke a transformative dialogue between Mesoamericans and Europeans. Chávez argues that the Spaniards' interest would have been increased by the mention of the caves, their number coinciding with a European legend about the Seven Cities of Silver, kingdoms rich beyond imagination (7–22). Durán himself provides another example of this cultural synthesis. Puzzled by similarities between Mesoamerican religious rites and beliefs and Catholic ones, he comes to believe that the Aztecs are actually one of the ten lost tribes of Israel, and, as noted earlier, that Topiltzin Quetzalcoatl was Saint Thomas (*The Aztecs* 3–6). These examples demonstrate the pattern of Aztlán's changing history/myth: it would continue to be rewritten in a dialogic fashion, but without the older elements ever quite disappearing.

Chávez's Lost Land and the Paradox of Specificity/Indeterminacy

The transformative dialogic process is difficult to avoid. An examination of John Chávez's *The Lost Land* will demonstrate not only why the palimpsest is a particularly appropriate trope for understanding Aztlán and Chicano identity, but also why even a scholar fully aware of the transformative process that created Aztlán cannot help superimposing yet another layer on the palimpsest. It is a process we must acknowledge if we are to reconfigure Aztlán into a paradigm useful for studying cultural identity and history.

Chávez's focal point is not Aztlán, but rather the southwestern United States, and he provides a fascinating history of the images associated with that region. According to Chávez, the practice of referring to the Southwest as Aztlán developed during the six-teenth century but disappeared in the seventeenth century when the first Spanish settlers in New Mexico sent back reports that caused a "new, much less glamorous image of the northern bor-derlands" to form in the Spanish mind (18–19). We have already noted how a transformative dialogue arose from the cultural clash between Spaniards and Mesoamericans when the two groups were each confronted with startling unknown phenomena. Both sides often turned to myths to explain these phenomena, but there is a misleading tendency to recognize this cultural response only on the part of the Mesoamericans; for example, in the popular but much contested theory that the Aztecs thought Cortés to be Quetzalcoatl. Yet, we have seen that Durán responded by turning to Judeo-Christian myth for his answers. One of the strengths of Chávez's work is that he insists quite convincingly that other Spaniards also frequently relied on myths for explanations:

After taking Tenochtitlan in 1521, the Spanish looked to the north for new lands to conquer and projected their own myths onto the unknown region that was to become the Southwest. They imagined that to the north there was a rich land of warrior women, that in that direction there were silver cities, or that at the very least the unexplored region touched on a waterway that would link Europe to the wealth of the Orient. . . . While this image was the invention of the foreign Spaniards it soon influenced and was influenced by Indians both in the north and in central Mexico. The Indians on the northern frontier, probably to encourage the Spanish to move on to other areas, sometimes agreed with the invaders' conceptions of the region and elaborated on them. In this way the European legend of the Seven Cities of Silver, which led to Spain's exploration of the Southwest, became the native legends of the Seven Cities of Cíbola and the riches of Quivira. (8)

The interwoven narratives that arose from this dialogue soon be-came indistinguishable from each other, causing confusion for both indigenous and Spanish authors:

In central Mexico the Spanish myth of the golden northern land aroused interest in the legend of Aztlán, the Edenic place of origin of the Mexica (the Aztecs). Aztlán, meaning either "land of the herons" or "land of whiteness," was an old name by Cortés's arrival. According to their own histories, the Aztecs had left that homeland, located somewhere in the north, in 1168 and journeyed to the lakes where in 1325 they founded Tenochtitlán. After the Spanish conquest Indian, Mestizo, and Spanish chroniclers, relying on native informants, recorded the legend of Aztlán along with the rest of the history of the Aztecs. However, in their histories the chroniclers, influenced by the myth of the golden north, placed Aztlán in the Southwest; in fact it was probably in Nayarit, only four hundred miles northwest of Mexico City. This error would later lead Chicanos to refer to the Southwest as Aztlán, an application of the name that would, nevertheless, be paradoxically appropriate. (8)

Chávez argues that the myth/history of the Spaniards merged with that of the Mesoamericans, and that "these superimposed images formed the guiding myth of the Spanish exploration of the Southwest" (15) and became a part of the palimpsest of Mesoamerican, Mexican, and Chicano history. But despite his excellent discussion of the layered myth/histories, Chávez believes that Aztlán may very well have been located relatively close to Mexico City, based on reports that, in 1530, Nuño de Guzman encountered a place called "Aztatlan" four hundred miles northwest of Mexico City, "whose name and environment resembled those of the legendary Aztlán. Though the evidence indicated (and still indicates) that Aztatlan and Aztlán were one and the same place, it must have seemed too mundane a location for a land that had been idealized to the point of a paradise on earth" (30).

This apparent discrepancy troubles Chávez, and he goes on to argue that although Aztlán may not have been located in the southwestern United States after all, Chicanos still have an ancient claim to the land by virtue of their Native American ancestors, the ancient Cochise people of what is now southern Arizona.

In a complicated series of maneuvers that draws on the work of Florence Hawley Ellis and James A. Goss, Chávez asserts that the Aztecs are descendants of the Cochise, as are the Ute, the Gabrielino, the Pima, the Pueblo, the Comanche, "and many other southwestern tribes." He concludes, "Thus, while Aztlán, the Aztecs' homeland of 1168 was relatively close to Mexico City, their more distant homeland in both time and space was in the Southwest" (9).

This last statement is revealing of the pervasive, misleading belief among scholars that there is a clear distinction between myth and history. Chávez's odd argument seems to arise out of a belief that the existence of a place called Aztatlan/Aztlán near Mexico City somehow threatens Chicano claims to the Southwest as a homeland that are based on a myth of Aztlán, a myth Chávez believes has been erroneously transposed to the Southwest. Thus he tries to shore up the Chicano claim to that region by rewriting Chicano genealogy and linking it to the ancient Cochise civilization. Here the validity of Chávez's argument does not interest me as much as his strategy, developed to protect Aztlán's borders. Chávez believes that Chicanos have an ancient claim to the Southwest, a claim asserted in 1969 through the myth of Aztlán, but his work appears to dispel that myth by locating Aztlán near Mexico City. Therefore Chávez needs another story to re-create the Chicano borders in the Southwest, and so he rewrites Chicano genealogy in order to legitimate Chicano presence there, in essence creating another myth.

Let me emphasize once again that I am not concerned with the truth of his claim, for, as Bruce Lincoln notes, a myth is just a different kind of authority, not a less convincing one (23–24). Instead, I want to point out that there is a pattern to suggest that whenever histories and genealogies are rewritten, whenever boundaries are redrawn to stake the claim of one group to a particular region, whether geographic or social, there is always another group that is disempowered as a result. Many Mesoamerican scholars, for example, believe that the Aztecs rewrote their

ancestral records in order to erase their nomadic past and legitimate their presence in the Valley of Mexico by claiming direct
descent from the Toltecs.[21] Another Mesoamerican narrative that
would serve Chicanos well as a cautionary tale is the story of the
Aztec emperor Itzcoatl, who allegedly ordered the Aztecs' historical records burned and dictated a new version of history that promoted the interests of the military and ruling classes.[22] Ironically,
the Aztlán that the members of the Chicano movement found
so appealing because it harkened back to a time of freedom and
equality may very well have been a similar construct of the Aztec
elite, created to ensure their power over other social classes and
to legitimate their privileged status, a point Chicanos should keep
in mind when considering the other Aztláns presented to them:

> For all the interest the notion of Aztlán has generated among both
> nonworking-class ethnohistorians in Mexico and primarily working-
> class-origin Chicanos, who identified it with the Southwest of the
> U.S., most Aztecs by the sixteenth century, shortly before and after
> the arrival of the Europeans, seemed generally indifferent to it. It
> seems that whatever orthodoxy existed on the subject was main-
> tained only among those for whom the idea had political utility. In
> effect, Aztlán was a "class"-based symbol useful to the ruling elite
> as a part of their founding myth and charter of legitimacy; the non-
> privileged sectors seemed to have derived little of value from this
> notion. (Klor de Alva, "Aztlán" 148–49)

We should also ask who is being excluded when Chicanos stake a
claim to the Southwest based on Aztlán, whether that claim is legitimated through myth, history, or genealogy. Obviously Native
Americans must be included in these debates, as must the Asian
Americans and African Americans living in the region. Certainly
genealogy can be used to establish a Chicano link to Native
Americans and thus the Southwest, but it could just as easily be
used to claim the region exclusively for Asian Americans, as the
group whose ancestors initially came across the Bering Strait
long ago. We need to move away from such cultural isolationism

and instead think in terms of cultural *mestizaje* and shared claims to different regions. As Saragoza says, "The commonalities in the Chicano experience have waned; historians cannot refashion the past to vindicate political purpose or need. For activists, the diversity among Chicanos—history argues—must be the linchpin of any political strategy or project" (52).

In fairness to Chávez, he does briefly acknowledge a Native American claim to the Southwest: "Both Indians and Chicanos see themselves as indigenous to and dispossessed of their homelands, which in the Southwest means they claim the same territory" (3). He adds, "Since Chicanos are racially 70 to 80 percent Indian, they do indeed have much in common with Native Americans, a fact that must be considered in discussions of claims to the Southwest" (4). While I question Chávez's generalization about Chicano racial makeup, I would also point out that despite this disclaimer, he does not include Native Americans in his discussion about the region, except when he requires their presence to legitimate Chicano claims to the Southwest. Any sort of productive discussion about regional claims requires the attention to diversity that Saragoza speaks of, both intracultural and intercultural, and it has been noticeably absent to date.

What we can take from Chávez is his astute observation that the various versions of the Aztlán story (or the layers of the palimpsest) caused the legendary region to shift as necessary to meet the demands of the dialogues between and within cultures. For example, he notes that the Spaniards' discovery of the Pueblo villages in New Mexico caused them to be identified in the Codex Ramirez as Aztlán because the villages contained houses, which to the Mesoamerican audience signified civilization. As a result, Aztlán came to appear in later versions as a highly civilized place. Paradoxically, this idealized vision would lead explorers who actually saw the Pueblo villages to reject the idea that they were Aztlán, because the reality of the villages did not—could not—match the utopic grandeur of the chronicles that had been inspired by their discovery. Chávez concludes, "Because accurate informa-

tion about California, New Mexico, and Florida was poorly dis-
seminated, the chroniclers and their informants frequently confused those places with one another; with the result that Aztlán,
even after being linked to the Pueblo villages, could be placed
anywhere as long as it was to the north" (17).

This example is emblematic of the paradoxical qualities of
Aztlán, and it helps us to understand why the Aztlán constructed
by the Chicano movement held the coalition together for only a
few years: the palimpsestic qualities of Aztlán make it fluid and
unanchored and thus an easy myth to appropriate and invest with
new meaning; however, the paradoxes embedded within the
myth and its multilayered structure also make political claims
based on the myth vulnerable (witness Chávez's attempt to shore
it up), because its multiple renderings are not easily contained
within the outermost narrative and surface in a chorus of competing voices. In restricting Aztlán to just one version, the leaders
of the Chicano movement created a nationalist myth so narrow
that the nation it offered suffocated many within, and excluded
many without, causing them to reject it. The paradox is that
Aztlán becomes so indeterminate that it can be located anywhere
"to the north," but carries with it layers of competing narratives
that are potentially disruptive. Bruce Lincoln notes that "[a]ny
synthetic entity, having its origin in a prior dialectic confrontation, bears within it the tensions that existed between the thesis
and antithesis involved in its formation, and this residual tension
remains ever capable of undoing the synthesis" (11). This "residual tension" helps us to understand why the image of the Southwest as Aztlán was able to reappear after 350 years, and it explains
why the Aztlán of the Chicano nationalists did not completely
erase the earlier images of the Southwest onto which it was
superimposed:

Needless to say, not all Mexican Americans accepted the image of
Aztlán. Among the masses the images of the Spanish Southwest
and the American Southwest continued to predominate during the
1970s, and into the 1980s, largely because these were still promoted

by the educational system and the mass media. Through bicultural and Chicano studies programs, Chicano intellectuals worked to change this situation. However, a small group of Mexican Americans conversant with the affairs of their ethnic group refused to abandon borrowed images of the Southwest, usually, because their lives had been formed within those images or because those views continued to help them accommodate themselves to the standards of Anglo society. (Chávez 148)

Borrowed indeed.

One last issue remains to be addressed in this discussion, and it is a significant one: the implications of attempting to fix Aztlán firmly in the Southwest while claiming its universality for Chicanos everywhere. Chávez, for example, claims that although "'Aztlán' came to refer in a concrete sense to the Southwest, it also applied to any place north of Mexico where Chicanos hoped to fulfill their collective aspirations" (130). He concludes that while the creation of an independent Chicano state of Aztlán is unlikely, continued migration of Mexicans to the region would allow "Chicanos to entrench themselves until revolutionary changes in the general society of the United States could allow true self-determination" (155).

This argument fails to consider Chicanos living outside the Southwest, or is at best overly optimistic in its assumption that Chicanos living in the Southwest can use political leverage to help Chicanos living elsewhere. As Juan Flores and George Yudice (drawing on the work of Nancy Fraser) point out, how a group's needs are defined and who gets to define them affect the type of remedy that will be applied. For instance, Flores and Yudice document that Latino demands for bilingual education are reinterpreted by the dominant culture as indicative of an obstacle to assimilation, and thus the remedy offered is not bilingual education but intensive English instruction. It seems to me that as long as Chicanos inhabit the Southwest in the mental geography of the dominant culture, it is there that Chicano needs will be addressed, and not in those Chicano communities that exist outside

Aztlán, spiritual universality notwithstanding. Gilberto Cardenas, one of the first scholars to address this issue, points out that "the Southwest regional approach [to Chicano studies] has also failed to incorporate an adequate perspective toward the Chicano experience outside (north of) its boundaries. Thus, apart from the numerous problems associated with the study of the Chicano and Chicano studies in the Southwest, the regional approach as a conceptual category has become a major limitation" (146). Despite the fact that Cardenas's call for a broader approach to Chicano studies was published in 1976 in a special issue of *Aztlán* devoted to Chicanos in the Midwest, the problem has failed to be adequately addressed by scholars. Thus, ten years later Sergio Elizondo would need to echo Cardenas's observations. Referring to the substantial Chicano presence in Chicago, he wrote, "[I]t should prompt us to ask for a new description of our actual physical presence, the extent of our cultural dimension, the atlas of our language use, and the limits of the Borderlands" (209). We begin to see that unless Aztlán is understood in all of its layers, in all of its complexity, it will never be an attractive model to the diverse culture its leaders seek to encompass within its borders, borders that have been and will continue to be fluid.

My final remarks are made in the context of the Chicanos who have rejected Aztlán as the movement leaders conceived of it and are searching for a better vehicle for understanding Chicano history and identity. I have argued that Aztlán is not without value, provided we recognize its multidimensionality as key to understanding a multidimensional people; and that in thinking of Aztlán as a palimpsest we can better understand the wide array of experiences, identities, and allegiances that constitute the complex Chicano culture. In addition to the advantages I have already enumerated, Aztlán as palimpsest would

1. enable us to track the remapping of a cultural territory, and thus political maneuvering, and discuss what is at stake in

each remapping; and have the capacity to accommodate new remappings

2. allow us to understand political and historical rewritings in relationship to each other
3. always acknowledge the *provisional* nature of cultural identity, and
4. force us to acknowledge and examine the exclusionary power of any model of cultural identity.

The last two qualities are especially valuable. Any reconsideration of cultural identity is strategic and provisional; that is, it responds to real and perceived pressures that are in constant flux. Therefore, it is important to realize that even a fluid, shifting model of cultural identity is potentially exclusionary—-and it is this exclusionary power that must be acknowledged and examined if we are to move toward a more sophisticated understanding of how and why identities change. Conceiving of Aztlán as a palimpsest acknowledges both its exclusionary power and its provisional quality, and in that acknowledgment constitutes a major step toward further discussion and understanding of the interwoven and shifting nature of Chicano identity.

Part Two

English-Language Literature and Mexicanness

Chapter Two

✣

Mexico as Infernal Paradise

The scene is Mexico, the meeting place, according to some, of mankind itself, pyre of Bierce and springboard of Hart Crane, the age-old arena of racial and political conflicts of every nature, and where a colorful native people of genius have a religion that we can roughly describe as one of death, so that it is a good place, at least as good as Lancashire or Yorkshire, to set our drama of a man's struggle between the power of darkness and light. Its geographical remoteness from us, as well as the closeness of its problems to our own, will assist the tragedy each in its own way. We can see it as the world itself, or the Garden of Eden, or both at once. Or we can see it as a kind of timeless symbol of the world on which we can place the Garden of Eden, the Tower of Babel and indeed anything else we please. It is paradisal: it is unquestionably infernal. It is, in fact, Mexico.

—Malcolm Lowry, *Selected Letters*

✣

It is, *in fact,* a mythologized Mexico, constructed to suit the author's needs, a culture to be tampered with freely, as Lowry makes clear in his comment "we can see it as a kind of timeless symbol of the world on which we can place . . . anything else we please." I quote from Lowry's celebrated 1946 letter to publisher Jonathan Cape—a chapter-by-chapter defense of *Under the Volcano*—because that novel constitutes an important part of the complex, interdependent Anglo literary tradition constructing Mexicanness. In chapter 1 we saw how Chicano nationalists appropriated and revised a Mexican narrative in order to create a political and symbolic space for Chicanos to inhabit within the United States. One of the unforeseen repercussions of that strategy was the fixture of Chicano cultural identity in monolithic terms that proved inadequate to deal with the fluid, diverse, and evolving nature of Chicano communities. In chapter 3 I will argue that this nationalist discourse has had a similarly limiting effect on Chicano literary representations of Mexicanness. The focus of the present chapter is the production of Mexicanness by Anglo writers—a production that again bears similarities to a palimpsest and has contributed to another Mexican myth that, like Aztlán, has paradisal elements, has developed over a lengthy period, and continues to exert tremendous influence in Mexico and the United States, particularly as it has become a blueprint for a commodified Mexicanness exploited by the tourist industry.

In his letter, Lowry coins the phrase "Infernal Paradise," which Ronald Walker has used to characterize the Mexican works of Lowry, D. H. Lawrence, Aldous Huxley, and Graham Greene.[1] The term is a particularly appropriate one for the Mexican myth that these and other works have promoted in that it vividly suggests the tendency to perceive and represent Mexico as a place of paradoxical extremes. Lowry's comments are also useful in that they encapsulate other key features of the tradition and the complicated myth it has fostered. For example, Mexico is frequently perceived as the "meeting place" of the Old and New Worlds, resulting in "racial and political conflicts of every nature." Another tendency is to portray Mexicans as a "colorful" or exotic people fixated with death. And in suggesting that Mexico is an appropriate site on which to stage the drama of an Englishman's struggle between the powers of darkness and light, Lowry points to the utilization of the Mexican landscape as a symbolic backdrop against which a spiritual quest is played out, a backdrop often represented as "timeless" or ahistorical, its inhabitants frozen in time. Finally, in his references to Ambrose Bierce and Hart Crane, Lowry alludes to perhaps the most curious feature of this tradition: the authors themselves have assumed mythic proportions, their legends interwoven and mirrored in their Mexican works.

Shortly before disappearing in Mexico in 1913, Bierce wrote to his nephew's wife, Lora: "If you should hear of my being stood up against a Mexican stone wall and shot to rags please know that I think it is a pretty good way to depart this life. It beats old age, disease or falling down the cellar stairs. To be a Gringo in Mexico—ah, that is euthanasia" (O'Connor 299). Again we have the linkage of Mexico with death, but, significantly, Bierce implies that the death Mexico offers is attractive, a death to be desired and welcomed. This view of Mexico as a place where merciful death awaits the Anglo American or European is one that we find repeatedly in the Infernal Paradise tradition—for example, in *Under the Volcano* (1947) and Robert Stone's *Children of Light* (1986)—and Lowry's reference to Bierce suggests that he may have had the dying writer in mind as he created his self-destructive ex-consul. In many ways, Bierce's disappearance has come to symbolize Mexico for English readers, fusing the attraction of the country as a place of spiritual or artistic freedom with the threat of physical danger, and fusing the mystique of the writer-adventurer with the mystique of Mexico. The German author B. Traven would later manage a different sort of disappearing act and become an equally mysterious Mexican cipher by constructing false identities so skillfully that even today his biographers cannot identify his birth name with any certainty.[2] But although the Infernal Paradise is primarily a literary construct, it is important to recognize that the concept is supported and maintained by a complicated discursive network comprised not only of literature but also of film, historiography, photography, journalism, and tourism.[3] And despite the long and varied literary tradition at the core of the Infernal Paradise, scholarship examining it has been sporadic and narrow, and has even reinscribed some of the myth's most prominent elements. For example, while Drewey Wayne Gunn comes closest to recognizing the kind of evolving, intertextual discourse I wish to suggest here, he frequently implies that the repetition of certain characteristics within the tradition are due to the timelessness and stasis of Mexican culture (3–4). Ronald Walker, on the other hand, demonstrates a disturbing propensity to see Mexico as "collaborating" with writers in developing the Infernal Paradise myth:

> But imaginative writers, while not uninterested in "accurate" infor-
> mation, have generally been attracted to Mexico because, perhaps
> more than any other country, Mexico assaults the outsider with the
> inscrutable, with bewildering contradictions, with the overwhelm-
> ing sense of a reality beyond the world of Hard Facts. If these writ-
> ers deliberately exploit the "mystique" at the expense of literal
> verisimilitude (as has been charged), then Mexico has repeatedly
> participated as collaborator in the mythopoeic process. (18)

While Walker points unintentionally and provocatively here toward the participation of Mexicans in the discourse supporting
the lucrative tourist industry, I fundamentally disagree with his
allegations of complicity in this context. I will argue that many
Anglo writers arrived in Mexico with preconceptions shaped by
the discursive network already delineated, preconceptions so
strong that they made Mexico appear "inscrutable" or "bewilder-
ing" when personal experience challenged expectation. As Walker
himself notes, Lawrence developed his symbolic ideas about
"America" long before visiting the continent and may even have
postponed the trip for many years out of a fear that what he
would find there would not match his imaginings (29–31). I perhaps belabor this point because I believe it is of paramount importance to recognize that the discourse best equipped to examine and dismantle the Infernal Paradise has instead added its
considerable weight to the myth's power.

It also needs to be borne in mind that although Anglo writers
have been the primary contributors to the Infernal Paradise myth
over the last two centuries, it is not purely an Anglo construct.
Much of the myth is derived from Spanish colonial texts as re-
fashioned and revisioned by the influential nineteenth-century
historians Alexander von Humboldt and W. H. Prescott. For example, Mary Louise Pratt notes that Humboldt's "year in Mexico
was spent mainly in and near the capital with Mexican scholars
and libraries. The *Political Essays* reflect such research, following lines of reportage laid down by [Spanish] colonial bureaucra-
cies" (*Imperial Eyes* 131). (Humboldt was in Spanish America by

special permission of Carlos IV and was expected to report to him.) I point out this connection to Spanish colonial discourse to emphasize the durability of the images and categories that were generated by the first century of contact between Europeans and indigenous Americans. José Rabasa sees these images and categories as constituting "a stock of motifs and conceptual filters prefiguring any possible [later] discovery" (*Inventing America* 194). If one keeps this in mind, it becomes perhaps a bit easier to understand how the Mexican images circulated by non-Mexicans writing in the nineteenth century occasionally bear striking resemblances to the Mexican constructs of Cortés and later Spanish writers. Moreover, as Mary Maples Dunn notes, there is reason to believe that Humboldt's "progressive" recommendations that the living conditions and treatment of the Indians in Mexico be drastically improved were made to shore up white hegemony and Spanish authority there, not to undermine them.[4] Dunn discusses this and other issues at length in her excellent introduction to Humboldt's *Political Essay on the Kingdom of New Spain,* and I will merely point out that another of Humboldt's recommendations—namely, that a "community of interests" binding together Mexicans of all classes was needed to strengthen the colony—bears remarkable similarities to the cultural nationalism advocated by José Vasconcelos after the Mexican Civil War (1911–20). Mexican nationalism, in particular its romanticization and celebration of indigenous pre-Columbian culture, proved to be very seductive to the expatriate Anglo writers in Mexico at the time, as well as quite adaptable to the Infernal Paradise, as the works of Katherine Anne Porter and D. H. Lawrence attest.[5] Moreover, while cultural nationalism may initially have succeeded in reuniting the war-torn country, the Mexicanness it generated and promoted has come to be just as problematic as foreign versions. "Indeed," Peter Wollen notes, "the great works of the Mexican muralists have themselves become [depoliticized] tourist attractions. Post-war Mexican artists, from the generation of the Ruptura onwards, have felt compelled to question the idea of an unproblematic Mexicanidad, itself now seen as mythic and folkloric in a problematic sense" (47). This is, of course, analogous to the problems raised by Chicano nationalism that I examined in chapter 1. For our purposes here, the point to keep in mind is that Anglo writers were not the sole architects of the Infernal Paradise, although they have been its most consistent proponents.

At this point, let me say a bit more about my methodology. I want to make it very clear that my project here is not that of a literary historian, even though I have followed a historical trajectory. Cecil Robinson and Drewey Gunn have already written excellent histories of the tradition, and rather than duplicate their work, I concentrate instead on the recurrent figures, tropes, and representations within the tradition and their evolution in order to consider their wider social implications and to read them as clues to the political agendas they support. To that end I "raid" these texts in order to display the elements of the tradition that seem to me to gather a cumulative emotional and psychic weight, and to help answer the question, what does it mean when so many major literary figures have portrayed a country as an "Infernal Paradise"?

Since this chapter examines the creation and evolution of a complicated Mexican myth—its different elements and its political and social utility as well as its circulation among different groups and generations of writers—I have given myself license to move rapidly through several centuries' worth of English-language representations of Mexicanness, zeroing in on the particular aspects of key texts that allow the Infernal Paradise to emerge rather than providing exhaustive readings of each individual text. These "surgical strikes" alternate with close readings of *exceptional* texts—those that challenge the predominant Mexican myth in important ways (e.g., the recent Mexican novels of Harriet Doerr and Robert Stone). I also offer longer readings of the American works published since 1980, as to date there has been no critical attention given to the Mexicanness they produce.

The Origins of the Myth

The earliest English-language accounts about Mexico, written by ambitious traders and shipwrecked sailors, date back to the sixteenth century and the initial stages of Spain's colonization. They were collected and published by Richard Hakluyt in 1589 (Gunn 4–5). Not surprisingly, considering the political and religious rivalry between Spain and England, many of the reports emphasize the abusiveness of the Spanish colonists and encourage England's intervention in Spanish America. For example, Thomas Gage, the ex–Catholic priest who recorded his fifteen-year fugitive flight through Mexico and Central America in 1648, structured his narrative around military targets and exploitable resources in the hope of ingratiating himself with Cromwell, as evidenced by the title page of his narrative's first edition: "A New and exact Discovery of the Spanish Navigation to those Parts; And of their Dominions, Government, Religion, Forts, Castles, Ports, Havens, Commodities, fashions; behaviour of Spaniards, Priests and Friers, Blackmores, Mulatto's, Mestiso's, Indians; and of their Feasts and Solemnities."[6] A second edition of Gage's text was brought out as a propaganda tactic in 1655 to "increase English interest in the expedition . . . just dispatched to capture Hispaniola" (ed. Thompson xix). Gage's text became so popular in England that it was reprinted five times within a sixty-three-year period and is one of the earliest texts in perhaps the most durable English-language genre contributing to the Infernal Paradise: the travel narrative.[7]

Although Gage's narrative and other early English accounts contributed to the Black Legend propaganda designed to encourage English intervention in Spanish America, they also had the effect of establishing Mexico in the eyes of the English reader as a rich, dangerous, and mysterious country, qualities that the sheer scarcity of English accounts would only intensify. Gunn maintains that until Humboldt's ambitious survey of the country in

1811, Mexico would remain for the English reader a "vague symbol of wealth, error, and high adventure" (12). Incredibly, then, for the entire Spanish colonial rule of Mexico, a period of almost three hundred years, English-language literature about the country was almost nonexistent. Consider that Bernal Díaz's history, long highly regarded as a major source of information about the Conquest, was not translated into English until 1800. Cecil Robinson observes that "the space that might have been occupied by colonial Mexico was a vacuum in North American letters. This lack of a literary record is due to the fact that New Spain was an abstraction in the mind of people in the United States until the early part of the nineteenth century" (*With the Ears of Strangers* 15).[8]

The key to understanding this vacuum is accessibility. The occasional English translations of Spanish colonial histories (some as early as 1578) were limited in circulation and thus did not have the widespread impact that Gage's narrative and Humboldt's Mexican books did. Also, as Eric Thompson points out, the Black Legend constructed about Spain made Spanish-authored accounts unreliable to an English readership (xviii). This situation changed dramatically in the early nineteenth century for a number of reasons, most notably the Mexican revolt against Spain (1810–21) and Anglo American incursions into the northern Mexican borderlands. Both historical actions generated a renewed interest in Mexico and help to explain the popularity of Humboldt's four-volume *Political Essay* (1811).[9] Following these events, the myth of the Infernal Paradise would grow rapidly.

"To Be a Gringo in Mexico—Ah, That Is Euthanasia"

The greatness of the ancient Indians and their happy age was praised, while the living natives were reviled; the idealization of the pre-Columbian, which had been suspended by priests and encomenderos, was continued. . . . [T]he possibilities of the new country were greedily examined; scornful

notes were taken of the successive and simultaneous failures in the attempt to create a republic; the vices and virtues of those who were sud-
denly free were enumerated; a climate favorable to invasions and the ampu-
tation of territories was created; customs were observed with joy or alarm.
      —Carlos Monsiváis, "Travelers in Mexico"

✿

Anglo American literature about Mexico began to appear with increasing regularity in the nineteenth century, typically holding
Mexicans in contempt.[10] Cecil Robinson was the first scholar
to examine the representation of Mexicanness in nineteenth-
century American literature, and his survey reveals that Mexicans were consistently represented as savage, brutal, lazy, backward, and cowardly (31–66). Richard Henry Dana's popular 1840
memoir, *Two Years before the Mast*, represents the Mexicans of
California in typical terms: "The Californians are an idle, thrift-
less people, and can make nothing for themselves" (79). Dana char-
acterizes them as hot-blooded, lazy, vain, promiscuous, and primitive. Notice the corrosive power he attributes to Mexican culture
in the following wistful reflection: "In the hands of an enterpris-
ing people, what a country this might be! we are ready to say. Yet
how long would a people remain so, in such a country?" (181).
     Significantly, Dana views the Mexican land as a future colonial
prospect of the United States, and his rhetoric provides a glimpse
of the political and economic interests that generated and depended on pejorative representations of Mexicanness, particularly in travel narratives such as Dana's and the so-called dime
novels popular during the nineteenth century. Dana wrote after
the Texas rebellion and prior to the Mexican American War, at
the zenith of Manifest Destiny, and his text reflects the nationalist and expansionist ideology of the times. Robinson notes that
Walt Whitman was another advocate of Manifest Destiny whose
words underscore the kind of Mexicanness such a doctrine engendered. In 1846, Whitman wrote in the *Brooklyn Daily Eagle*,
"What has miserable, inefficient Mexico, with her superstition,

her burlesque upon freedom, her actual tyranny by the few over the many—what has she to do with the great mission of peopling the New World with a noble race? Be it ours, to achieve that mission! Be it ours to roll down all of the upstart leaven of old despotism, that comes our way!" (quoted in Robinson 24). In short, many of the Mexican cultural markers that are now so much a part of the Infernal Paradise became ingrained in the Anglo American psyche through a literature supporting U.S. territorial expansion. Antonio Marquez says that

> [t]he Alamo in particular and the Mexican-American War in general helped carve two facets of the American nation's developing identity and nationalism. First, they greatly augmented the myth of the American frontiersman as individualistic, freedom-loving, courageous and a repository of the virtues of American democracy. Second, they strengthened the notion of Anglo American superiority and cemented the image of the Mexican as treacherous, cowardly and barbarous. The notions created by the nationalist fervor of the nineteenth century were widely implanted—until they became axiomatic throughout America. (43)

Following Dana, three writers published works in rapid succession that would have a long-lasting impact on the Infernal Paradise tradition. John Stephens's 1841 travel narrative describing Mayan ruins that were unknown to the non-Mexican world generated tremendous interest and did much to deepen the perception of Mexico as a land of once fabulous and wealthy civilizations, as would Prescott's subsequent history. The following year, the Scottish-born Frances Calderón de la Barca, at Prescott's urging, collected and published *Life in Mexico*, a collection of her letters written during a two-year period as the wife of the Spanish ambassador. In it, Calderón remains throughout the arbiter of high culture and good taste on a Eurocentric scale. Thus, while she is enthusiastic about much of what she finds in Mexico, she carefully ascribes the positive Mexican attributes to European influence.

In examining Calderón's text, I have found it useful to apply Mary Louise Pratt's travel writing paradigm. Pratt identifies two predominant types of travel narratives during the European colonial era: the scientific or informational travel narrative, characterized by an omniscient, self-effacing narrator who views the landscape as a future colonial prospect while describing the natives in homogeneous and ahistorical terms; and the sentimental travel narrative. It is within the latter rubric that I would locate Calderón's text. The sentimental subgenre is characterized by a European narrator who is also the protagonist. The self-insertion of the narrator into the text results in the portrayal of sequences and events that are normally suppressed in the informational account, for example, interaction with the natives. This interaction, including episodes in which the natives comment on the European(s), Pratt likens to moments of parody that fracture the colonial discourse. This is not to say, however, that the narrator relinquishes his or her position of authority or superiority.[11]

Calderón's text bears out Pratt's observation that this particular genre casts colonial discourse in a critical light even as it furthers its goals. Narrator-protagonist Calderón produces a text that reflects contradictory or ambivalent responses to Mexican culture because of the many forces impinging on her sense of cultural identity. A Scottish aristocrat fallen on hard times (which helps us understand her investment in positioning herself as an authority on good taste, art, and etiquette), Calderón regained her aristocratic status through marriage to the Spanish ambassador, the first to Spain's former colony. Thus we see Calderón emphasizing the inferiority of some Mexican customs in order to underscore her European superiority; but at the same time, because she is linked by marriage to a former colony of the Spanish empire, we find her paradoxically defending Mexican culture in order to defend Spain, her husband, and, by association, herself. Her social status as the ambassador's wife has other implications as well. An ambassador is a symbol of one political entity's recognition of another's equal international rights. The fact that the Calderóns are ambassadors from Spain to a former colony means that they certainly cannot view the land and people as future colonial prospects. Rather, they are looking at a lost colony, or, at best, at a prospect of a very different kind. The text thus shifts the cultural arena within which European superiority will be asserted. Instead of political dominance, the emphasis is on the arts, good taste, refinement, intellect, and beauty. Of course, these textual focal points also reflect the limited social arenas within which Frances Calderón, as a woman, was allowed to circulate.

Consider, for example, the costume ball episode. Calderón creates great anxiety among the Spanish and criollo community in Mexico City when she announces her intention of attending the ball dressed in a costume native to the Mexican city of Puebla. A contingent of Spaniards and important Mexicans (including the secretary of state and minister of war!) visit Calderón to advise her that under no circumstance should she wear such a costume because she will link herself with the notoriously promiscuous reputation of the *poblana* women. In addition to showing Spanish superiority in the social arena, this episode demonstrates that the Mexican upper crust continued to derive its status from close association with Spain. Thus Calderón demonstrates the Mexican's dilemma during the nineteenth century: trying to achieve a distinct national culture while at the same time being heavily invested in Spanish culture as an important influence on the Mexican. Let me briefly comment on a few exemplary passages from Calderón that illustrate key features of both the sentimental travel narrative and the Infernal Paradise.

The sentimental narrator's conflicted position. In one of her early letters, Calderón describes herself composing the text that we are reading. This textual production is disrupted by a group of lepers outside her window, a disruption she deals with by writing them into her text while physically ignoring them as she writes. Significantly, Calderón's conflicted position as both narrator and protagonist forces her to insert Mexicans into her text whom she would otherwise ignore (and does ignore in another sense). Also significant is the fact that this rupture in her text is produced by a disruption in its production (75).

The bullfight as archetypal event in the Infernal Paradise tradition. The narration of a bullfight appears in almost every Mexican text by Anglo writers. Calderón's reaction and her rhetoric are representative of this tradition: she is first repulsed by it, then confesses to finding it attractive. "It cannot be good to accustom a people to such bloody sights. . . . [B]ut little by little I grew so much interested in the scene, that I could not take my eyes off it, and I can easily understand the pleasure taken in these barbarous diversions by those accustomed to them since childhood" (91). The oscillation between repulsion and attraction is one of the defining features of the tradition, as the name Infernal Paradise suggests.

Spectator/spectacle. The shifting sense of the narrator's identity as both observer and observed characteristic of the sentimental travel narrative is partly responsible for the oscillation between attraction and repulsion that marks the Infernal Paradise texts. For example, during a trip to the cathedral to observe the "quaint and curious" religious festivities of Holy Week, Calderón and her husband afterward find themselves on the streets long after dark, and Calderón fears they may become of irresistible interest to the merrymaking crowd they must pass through. Although they reach home safely, the very next morning she plans a series of soirées in an attempt to reestablish and reimpose the order, beauty, and culture disrupted by her fear of being an unsanctioned object of desire (147–49).

The ethnographic customs and manners sketch. Although more common in the scientific travel narrative, the ethnographic report can also be found in sentimental narratives like Calderón's. In one letter, she goes on at great length discussing the physical features of Mexicans from different regions and establishes a racist hierarchy of beauty that values the European and admits Mexican beauty only as the product of an interracial relationship with a European: "[O]ccasionally in the lower classes, one sees a face and form so beautiful, that we might suppose such another was the Indian who enchanted Cortés. . . . In these cases it is more than probable that, however Indian in her appearance, there must have been some intermarriages in former days between her progenitors and the descendants of the conquerors" (110).

The colonial gaze into the past. This is a common feature not only of the Infernal Paradise tradition but of colonial discourse in general.[12] The European narrator does not see a scene contemporary with herself, but rather sees into the past. For example, as she gazes on the pyramid at Cholula, Calderón vividly resurrects a horrible and dramatic tableau: "The slaughter was dreadful; the streets were covered with dead bodies, and houses and temples were burnt to the ground. This great temple was afterwards purified by his [Cortes's] orders, and the standard of the cross solemnly planted in the midst" (340).

In addition to producing a text that looms large within the Infernal Paradise tradition, Calderón also served as an important contact for Prescott, who was in the midst of his monumental history of the Conquest. He borrowed freely from her letters in describing the Mexican landscape, but more important, Calderón was able to help him gain access to important Spanish and Mexican documents, and it is his extensive research of these that distinguishes Prescott's 1843 history. He carefully cross-referenced the best available sources in Spanish and in English and to his credit framed his history with an extensive discussion of Mesoamerica prior to Spanish contact. It was by far the best available—for that matter, the only available—comprehensive English history of Mexico before and during the Spanish Conquest. Nevertheless, Prescott's literary bent produced a history narrated as epic drama, its actors superhuman figures.[13] Some of his descriptions are so dazzlingly baroque that one of my students, referring to Prescott's poor eyesight, quipped, "This history could only have been written by a man living his life in a darkened room."[14] Also noteworthy is Prescott's struggle to understand the role human sacrifice played in Aztec society. In a revealing analogy he points to the Spanish Inquisition as a European equivalent, leaving the reader not with a better understanding of the intricacies of Aztec cosmology but rather with a double inscription of Mexican savagery, one derived from the Aztecs, the other from the Spanish.

The impact of Prescott's history and the effect of his tendency to romanticize the Conquest as heroic drama should not be underestimated. The myth of the Infernal Paradise really has its roots in narratives of the Conquest, narratives that, as Inga Clendinnen says, "provided [the] first great paradigm for European encounters with an organized native state; a paradigm that quickly took on the potency and the accommodating flexibility of myth" (65). The "Prescottian fable," as Clendinnen calls it, revitalized the myth for English readers, teaching them that "Europeans will triumph over natives, however formidable the apparent odds, because of cultural superiority, manifesting itself visibly in equipment but residing much more powerfully in mental and moral qualities"—qualities, she argues, that Prescott coded into his oppositional renderings of Cortés and Montezuma: the "ruthless, pragmatic, single-minded" European commander juxtaposed against the "despotic, effete and fatally indecisive" Aztec emperor (65–66). Clendinnen's point, of course, is that in Prescott's history Cortés and Montezuma function as cultural synecdoches, a representation that unfortunately has been reinscribed by many later historians (most notably Tzvetan Todorov).[15] John Ernest, however, argues that such interpretations of Prescott's history do it an injustice by failing to consider the significance of its structure. Noting Prescott's public condemnation of the Texas annexation and the doctrine of Manifest Destiny that supported and evolved from it, Ernest argues provocatively that the textual structure designed by Prescott and the rhetorical strategy he adopted produced a history that functions as a "metahistorical commentary"—a warning against providential interpretations of the past in order to justify political programs (233). Although Prescott believed his subject to be epic and romantic, he also cautioned against confounding historical truth with romance (234–35). Thus, Prescott "self-consciously tried to construct a historical narrative capable of representing . . . a 'dialogical' relation to the past" (235) by creating two parallel narratives: the Conquest story itself, narrated in epic, romantic terms, and his notes and reflections on the historical sources and on the creation of his text. So while Prescott did create a "grand romantic adventure" (the historical narrative), it is qualified by a parallel text, a self-conscious historiography. Ernest summarizes the significance of this design as follows: "If the narrative tells the story of the historical manifestation of Providence, the small-type conclusions of each book, in concert with the reflections and footnotes, remind readers of the all-too-human ability to shape that manifestation according to one's needs and prejudices" (239). In other words, although Prescott would recognize and acknowledge the Spaniards' interpretation of their success (and the Aztecs' interpretation of their defeat, for that matter) in providential terms, he admonishes contemporary readers not to repeat the Spaniards' mistake.[16]

Although I am persuaded by Ernest's reading up to a point, I believe that Prescott's romanticized treatment of the Conquest overshadows as well as permeates his parallel commentary on it. But to some extent, this issue is overshadowed by another: what sort of Mexicanness does Prescott's text authorize, and what might be the political consequences of such an authorization? Here, I must side with Clendinnen. Prescott's indigenous Mexicans are noble savages; his Aztecs are a people *destined* by their cultural beliefs to be conquered, rather than a people whose beliefs enabled them to be conquered or, even more precisely, whose leaders' beliefs and uncertainties in the face of previously unencountered phenomena led to decisions that enabled them to be conquered. Such an attitude is present not only in Prescott's retelling of the Conquest but also in his "philosophical" overview of pre-Columbian Mesoamerica that precedes it. The belief that the Aztecs were a people destined to be conquered was sown by Cortés himself in his *cartas de relación* and has been so influential that it continues to permeate the work of contemporary historians. This is a major flaw in another important assessment of the Conquest, Todorov's *Conquest of America,* in which he credits the Spaniards' victory to their ability to improvise and adapt to new situations, in contrast with the Aztecs' alleged inability to act outside ritual conventions. This kind of argument is undermined by the actions of the indigenous peoples as portrayed in the narratives by the Spaniards themselves. One need only compare the portrait of Montezuma in the letters of Cortés with that in the *Historia verdadera* of Díaz to see that, in the latter, Montezuma was neither incapable of improvising nor taken in by Cortés's claims to godhood.[17] And in both accounts, we are reminded by the constant reference to Cortés as Malinche that a complicated chain of translation was at work, of which the key player was an indigenous woman sold into slavery whose very existence depended on improvisation. In short, I believe that a key problem with most histories of the Conquest is precisely their obsession with explaining Spanish victory, which, of course, encourages viewing one culture as superior to the other and gives most Conquest histories the didactic quality that Clendinnen assigns to Prescott's. Ultimately it is Prescott's romantic epic that makes the greatest impression on the reader, not the metacritical fine print, as Ernest argues.

As for the influence of Prescott's *History of the Conquest of Mexico,* historians were not the only ones who found the Prescottian fable irresistible. In the foreword to his 1893 novel *Montezuma's Daughter,* H. Rider Haggard acknowledges drawing freely from Prescott for details of his own very romantic version of the Conquest, in which a dashing English hero arrives in Mexico just in time to educate Doña Marina and aid "Cuactemoc" in his battle against Cortés. At this point we begin to get a sense of the increasing intertextuality of this literary tradition. Calderón is reading Stephens's first book—given to her by Prescott—on her return from Mexico and publishes her letters at Prescott's urging; Prescott draws on Calderón's letters, Spanish colonial documents,

Humboldt's Mexican writings, and Stephens's travel narratives; H. Rider Haggard draws on Prescott; and, still later, Graham Greene on Haggard. Greene recalls that "surely it must have been *Montezuma's Daughter* and the story of the disastrous night of Cortez' retreat which lured me . . . afterwards to Mexico" (*A Sort of Life* 53). The sense of these works operating in a systematic fashion, in which ideas about Mexicanness are borrowed, reinscribed, and passed on by later authors, begins to impress on us its significance. For example, in assessing the impact of Prescott's work, Drewey Gunn comments, "Our awareness of the savage cruelty of the Aztecs, a characteristic that many later writers (most notably D. H. Lawrence) have insisted continues to permeate Mexican blood, possibly comes from Prescott" (19).

Before I move on to an examination of the next stage of the myth's development, I must mention several other tendencies of the tradition. First, as already alluded to, parallel to the "highbrow" texts I have been discussing ran a tradition of dime novels that relied on formulaic conventions and stock characterizations. These adventure stories, typically set in the West (indeed, they defined the western genre), flourished in a climate of U.S. expansionism and, like Dana's travel narrative, legitimated such expansionism through a racist production of Mexicanness. Cecil Robinson notes that "[i]n the attitudes expressed, this pulp literature reveals more openly than most records of the time the naive and cocky sense of superiority with which young America regarded itself. The 'greaser' provides a most apt foil for the projection of such an inflated self-image, and the dime novels are full of incidents in which Saxon intelligence, strength, and purity of motive, triumph over the guile and treachery of the degenerate 'yellow belly'" (26). One need look no further than the Hollywood western to be reminded that a racist production of Mexicanness is still very much a staple of the genre.[18]

Second, as I suggested at the beginning of this chapter, in the Infernal Paradise tradition the myth of the author occupies a prominent place and, in fact, becomes interwoven with literary constructions of Mexico. Lowry, Bierce, Traven, and Hart Crane all assumed mythic proportions because of their Mexican experiences, as did Katherine Anne Porter. Prescott became a different sort of larger-than-life literary figure; his biographies consistently play up his "competition" with Washington Irving over the histories, as well as his triumph over adversity in the form of his poor vision. But I find the persona constructed by John Stephens in his travel narratives the most interesting example of a highbrow text appropriating a popular formula, as well as of the author as mythic figure. In Stephens's travelogues, he moves through a terrain as exotic and dangerous as any ever produced by Rider Haggard, and the discovery of "lost" cities only adds to the exotic flavor. What Stephens really produces, however, is a "dollar" novel, a highbrow adventure story. Instead of a cowboy as protagonist, we have a learned scientist whose scholarly quest leads him into perilous adventures which he survives as a result of his superior intellect. To summarize, not only did the highbrow and popular genres develop along parallel tracks and produce homologous versions of Mexicanness, they were also produced by authors who became as much a part of the Infernal Paradise myth as the texts themselves.

It's also worth pointing out at this juncture that the road to the Infernal Paradise is paved with good intentions. As noted above, Prescott made a strong effort to understand pre-Columbian Mesoamerica, and the writings of Calderón and Stephens exhibit considerable affection—of a paternalistic sort—toward the Mexicans. But this goodwill did not prohibit them from producing a reductive, racist discourse. A brief discussion of another famous American author will serve both to clarify and to complicate this argument. In 1895, Stephen Crane went to Mexico as a newspaper correspondent, and his reports are distinguished by his disciplined vigilance against passing judgment on another culture. David Spurr argues that Crane was "painfully aware of the compromises inherent in his position" and rejected the idea that one could pass judgment on another culture: "The most worthless literature of the world has been that which has been written by the men of one nation concerning the men of another," wrote Crane. His solution was to concentrate on "form and color," on "objective" description vis-à-vis Mexico, and to save his criticism for fellow outsiders (Spurr 55–56). And as the following passage describing a train ride through Mexico shows, Crane was well aware that there were discursive constructs that filtered any outsider's perception of Mexico:

> Enough light remained to bring clearly into view some square yellow huts from whose rectangular doors there poured masses of crimson rays from the household fires. In these shimmering glows, dark and sinister shadows moved. The archaeologist and the capitalist were quite alone at this time in the sleeping car and there was room for their enthusiasm, their ejaculations. Once they saw a black outline of a man upon one of those red canvasses. His legs were crossed, his arms were folded in his serape, his hat resembled a charlotte russe. He leaned negligently against a door post. This figure justified to them all their preconceptions. He was more than a painting. He was the proving of certain romances, songs, narratives. He renewed their faith. (Quoted in Spurr 56)

Spurr contends that despite this attempt at shedding light on colonial discourse, Crane ultimately fails in his attempt to describe Mexico objectively because "even visual perception carries the burden of aesthetic and ideological value" (56). Crane's retreat into pure description not only produces a more refined version of the myths carried in the songs and romances known to his straw men, but also "opens up a space for domination in the realm of concrete practice" (57). Spurr continues, "When Mexico is removed by interpretation from the actual consequences of political and economic power, the capitalist and the archeologist can more readily go about their business" (57). While I agree with Spurr regarding the problematic impact of aestheticization, I'm less willing to relegate Crane's efforts to this mode of colonial discourse. Rather than removing Mexico from the consequences of power, I see him calling our attention to its plight as a target of foreign scientific and economic interests. I would go so far as to position Crane as a forerunner of the kind of ideal journalism that Spurr advocates in his conclusion, "a kind of writing which takes itself as the object of its own critical examination without giving up the task of describing and representing a world that lies outside of Western subjectivity" (189). Of course, Spurr would rightly point out that Crane is merely being critical, not meta-critical. Still, I would insist that his attempt to link a tradition of mythmaking (the production of romances, songs, and narratives) to economic and social interests (in this case science and capitalism) forces the reader to consider what enables the privileged perspective of the archaeologist, the capitalist, and even Crane himself. And it is here that Crane not only becomes a forerunner of such postmodern texts as Stone's *Children of Light*, but also identifies the quasi-spiritual desire for authenticity that Dean Mac-Cannell argues drives the tourist. In witnessing a tableau that songs, narratives, and romances have made beautiful, nostalgic, and thus authentic, the two Americans experience the spiritual renewal that MacCannell says the modern tourist is seeking. Despite his own blind spots, Crane contributes a crucial insight to projects such as my own that attempt to unmask the connections between cross-cultural representation and exploitative social practices.

By the close of the nineteenth century, then, certain elements of the Infernal Paradise myth were well established and would exert a strong influence on later writers. Among them were the representation of Mexico as a mysterious, dangerous place where death awaited; as a country of exotic but lazy primitives; and as a country once inhabited by powerful and savage ancient races, wealthy beyond imagination, a land of lost and hidden treasure waiting to be discovered and claimed by the superior Anglo American and English explorers. As Robinson says in assessing the impact of early nineteenth-century American literature about Mexico, "It was to take some time before American writers were to make their way into the heart of Mexico, and by the time they did so, a tradition for them of American writing about Mexico had already been established, either to confirm or to confront" (*No Short Journeys* 70). Regrettably, twentieth-century writers have generally chosen to confirm and elaborate on the Infernal Paradise tradition rather than confront it.

Spiritual Trial and Error

From 1910 to 1920 Mexico was ravaged by civil war. During the decade that followed, many American and British writers were drawn to Mexico, some to witness the struggles of the new government, others to be part of an artistic scene fed by the fervor of nationalism, a political and cultural movement perhaps most famous for its muralists, Diego Rivera, Davíd Siquieros, and José Clemente Orozco.[19] At the center of this lively expatriate scene was Katherine Anne Porter, who counted among her satellites (at various points) Hart Crane, Sergei Eisenstein, Lincoln Steffens, José Vasconcelos, Rivera, Siquieros, and many powerful government officials. Like the Anglo writers before her, Porter responded ambivalently to Mexico, as her fiction and essays attest. I find it interesting that the metaphor Thomas Walsh most often applies to her Mexican representations is that of the Garden of Eden. Walsh argues that for Porter, Mexico offered personal renewal in addition to its promise of an innovative, progressive political paradise, although one that seemed destined never to be fulfilled because its ideals had been betrayed by corrupt leaders. Of two of Porter's earliest Mexican portrayals, Walsh says, " 'Xochimilco' is the first and most complete of the Edens that appear in Porter's fiction. It expresses her hope in Mexico as the promised land, but, juxtaposed with 'The Fiesta of Guadalupe,' it reveals the oscillation between hope and despair that characterized her entire life" (35). And: "She fled [Mexico] each time she came, but returned, not just because it promised an elusive Eden, but because, on some opposing unconscious level, it opened old wounds. As a land of death, it held a 'desperate attraction' for her, as it did for D. H. Lawrence" (147).

These quotes obviously suggest that Porter, too, found Mexico to be both infernal and paradisal, yet what is most interesting about her Mexican writing is that she seized on the Infernal Paradise (or was seized by it) and attempted to utilize it in a literature of social protest, particularly on behalf of the Mexican Indian. She holds the distinction of having created some of the most progressive Mexican constructs to date, as well as of being one of the first in this tradition to attempt to examine the ways in which discursive representation could be used for oppressive ends. A discussion of her short story "Hacienda" will demonstrate how she sought to use discursive constructs in a way that would expose their oppressive potential.

"Hacienda" was published in 1932 and again in revised form in 1934; it is a roman à clef drawn from Porter's 1931 visit to the pulque hacienda where Sergei Eisenstein was in the midst of filming *Que Viva Mexico!*[20] In "Hacienda," Porter seeks to critique the failure of the revolution to fulfill its promise to better the lives of the Mexican Indians. To achieve this end, she skillfully creates a world in which image and role playing are crucial and are used to sustain an exploitative political regime. Porter steeps her text in bitter ironies. The Russian filmmakers are trying to re-create on film the feudal system from which the revolution "liberated" the Mexican Indians. They seek to create the quintessential Mexican hacienda worked by quintessential Indians, and have succeeded perhaps too well. The narrator tells us, "They had chosen it carefully. . . . [I]t was really an old-fashioned feudal estate with the right kind of architecture, no modern improvements to speak of, and with the purest type of peons" (142). To which the cameraman responds, "So picturesque, all this, we shall be accused of dressing them up" (142–43). And, of course, they do dress up the Indians to make sure their appearance matches the expectations that have already been established by other Infernal Paradise texts. Moreover, to ensure that the pro-revolutionary message gets across, the Russians are supervised by an "entire staff of professional [Mexican government] propagandists, . . . put at their disposal for the duration of their visit . . . to show them all the most beautiful, significant, and characteristic things in the national life and soul: if by chance anything not beautiful got in the way of the camera, there was a very instructed and sharp-eyed committee of censors whose duty it was to see that the scandal went no further than the cutting room" (146)—scandals like the system of graft that had replaced the feudal land system the film critiques, as Porter makes clear in the story of Don Genaro and Justino. Don Genaro is the now powerless hacendado hosting the film crew, which, ironically, is making a movie about the kind of hacienda Genaro tries to believe he still commands. The change in his political fortune has left him with nothing but a stage on which to pretend. To hide the fact that he is nothing but a government puppet, Genaro arrives and departs from the hacienda in a flurry of pretend activity. Into this web of pretense Porter inserts the story of Justino, one of Genaro's workers selected to portray a quintessential Indian in the film. Justino is jailed for the murder of his sister, and Porter manipulates the incident in several important ways. First, Genaro's façade as powerful hacendado is stripped away when the local judge refuses to release Justino unless Genaro gives him a substantial bribe. Meanwhile, the other characters' responses register not compassion for the dead woman but only concern for how the incident will delay the film, as well as disappointment that the accident was not photographed because a similar scene needs to be reshot: an opportunity was missed to capture life imitating art. And when Doña Julia, the hacendado's wife, complains that "the Indians destroy everything with neglect," the irony is not lost on the reader: it is the Indians who are being destroyed through neglect by the very leaders who rose to power on promises to better their lives. The story ends with the characters in a torpor, living only for the moments when the cameras roll, except for the Indian driver who has the last words in the story: "If you should come back in about ten days, you would see a different place. It is very sad here now. But then the green corn will be ready, and ah, there will be enough to eat again!" (170).

In his excellent analysis of "Hacienda," David T. Peterson argues that Porter deliberately and self-consciously ends the story with this cliché of the innocent peasant in tune with the seasonal cycles of life and death (precisely the kind of cliché the filmmakers want to construct): "Porter uses its banality to make her real point: The revolution has failed to change the conditions of life and living for Mexico's poor. The beliefs and ideologies that spawned a revolution are now masked by the rhetoric circulated by those who fought that revolution. . . . Porter borrows the rhetoric of oppression and failure and turns it against the people who failed Porter's own vision of Mexico."[21] And as Peterson also points out, Porter borrows from the rhetoric of the Infernal Paradise for the same purpose: "Less concerned with the authenticity of a narrative truth, Porter converts the mythologizing misreading of Mexican experience [characteristic of the Infernal Paradise writers] into a critique of the revolution's direction and purpose" (6).

It's important to remember that "Hacienda" was one of Porter's last Mexican stories, and it represents her disillusionment with what initially had seemed a very promising nationalist movement. It stands in stark contrast to her earlier Mexican writing, which displays a tendency to romanticize the Mexican Indians similar to that of the Russians in "Hacienda," and not unlike the Mexican representations advocated by Vasconcelos—chief architect of the cultural arm of the nationalist movement in Mexico—which greatly influenced her. One of the movement's most successful strategies was its emphasis on Mexican folk art, on which she authored a monograph in 1922 entitled *Outline of Mexican Popular Arts and Crafts*, which displays her tendency to view the Indians as noble savages: "The artists are one with a people simple as nature is simple: that is to say, direct and savage, beautiful and terrible, full of harshness and love, divinely gentle, appallingly honest" (33, as cited in Gunn 109).

Porter's best known Mexican story, "Flowering Judas," occupies an important place in the Infernal Paradise literary tradition. The ending of the story depicts a dream in which Laura, the Anglo protagonist, is accused by a messianic Mexican revolutionary of having killed and eaten his flesh, suggesting the beginnings of a new element in the tradition: the idea that immersion in Mexican culture will lead to a spiritual trial that may bring about a new understanding of self, a spiritual cleansing, or a higher consciousness. This was an idea crucial to D. H. Lawrence's *Plumed Serpent* (1926) and one that would occupy many of the writers who followed him and Porter to Mexico. Walker comments: "In *The Plumed Serpent* Lawrence created out of his inner divisions a dualistic image, the infernal paradise, and identified it with Mexico. Such was the potency of that image, and the collaborative magnetism of the land itself, that it would be difficult for the novelists who followed him there (whatever they might think of Lawrence and his work) to escape its influence" (78). But, of course, Lawrence himself could not escape the influence of the myths that had already been firmly established. By 1926 he had read, among others, Calderón, Prescott, and Bernal Díaz (Walker 48). Rather than creating the Infernal Paradise myth, as Walker suggests, Lawrence engineered an important shift in its development. *The Plumed Serpent* marks a new phase in the tradition, one distinguished by a preoccupation with spiritual concerns directly affected by the Mexican setting. More specifically, the epic histories, romantic adventures, and exotic travelogues that dominated the nineteenth century would henceforth be recast as exotic, romantic *metaphysical* adventures.

In the works of Lawrence, Huxley, Greene, and Lowry, as Walker ably shows, Mexico is reduced to a dramatic backdrop that highlights the spiritual quest of a European or North American protagonist.[22] In these works, the Mexican landscape is far more important than the Mexican people or culture(s). Indeed, the terrain of Mexico becomes a kind of spiritual testing ground filled with symbolic import, as in the fertile, sexualized landscape of *The Plumed Serpent*, the Golgotha-like hills of Greene's *The Power and the Glory*, or the infernal barranca of *Under the Volcano*.[23] Furthermore, the Mexicans populating these novels are dehumanized through metonymic association with the landscape, as in the dark, tightly coiled serpents and dormant volcanos poised within the breasts of Lawrence's Mexicans or Lowry's Indian women likened to dark ceramic idols. Mexico becomes a savage land that threatens to release the savage in the European or North American. The rugged isolation of the Sierra Madre drives Traven's Dobbs to attempt the murder of his partner, Curtin, who finds it difficult to maintain his moral ideals when confronted with Dobbs's psychotic behavior. Similarly, in Charles Portis's *Gringos*, published in 1991, the American protagonist travels deep into the dark heart of Yucatán to ancient Mayan ruins where he murders a young American hippie. I deliberately invoke Conrad here because these texts are modeled on the familiar theme he established in *Heart of Darkness*: the destabilizing effect of the "dark" and "primitive" land on the "civilized" European.

The Mexican works produced by these modernist authors are also characterized by reductive ethnic representations, particularly of Mexican Indians, heavily influenced by stereotypes promoted in earlier texts. Willa Cather calls attention to this disturbing phenomenon early in *Death Comes for the Archbishop*. Told that the Indians of the Mexican northwest do not live in wigwams, a Spanish cardinal replies, "No matter, Father. I see your redskins through Fenimore Cooper, and I like them so" (13).[24] Perhaps Cather was addressing Lawrence, who in 1923 invoked the same literary predecessor in describing his disillusioning first encounter with a group of Apache Indians in New Mexico: "And to my heart, born in England and kindled with Fenimore Cooper, it wasn't the wild and woolly West."[25] Lawrence turned to Mexico to search for his ideal primitive humans, and his Mexican writings indicate that the Mexican Indians both repelled and fascinated him. Ironically, however, there is evidence to suggest that, like the cardinal in Cather's novel, Lawrence transposed one distinct Native American culture onto another; more specifically, he superimposed the Pueblo culture he observed in Taos onto the Mexican Indians surrounding Lake Chapala. Frank Waters comments that when we read *The Plumed Serpent* we "almost forget that all the Indian values come directly from New Mexico, from Taos, like everything Lawrence wrote of Mesoamerica" (Walker 75).

Kate Leslie, an Irish expatriate living in Mexico and the protagonist of *The Plumed Serpent,* is clearly presented to us as a racist, and the novel's central dramatic tension centers on her horrified discovery that she is sexually attracted to the Indians she despises. Her story becomes little more than a vehicle for Lawrence's exposition of his belief that through carefully supervised miscegenation between Europeans and Native Americans, a transcendental collective subject could be achieved. Alesia García convincingly argues that Lawrence's philosophy bears striking parallels to that of Vasconcelos, whose 1925 treatise *La Raza Cósmica* would have been accessible to Lawrence while he worked on his novel; and Marianna Torgovnick points out that the ideas expressed in *The Plumed Serpent* bear disturbing similarities to fascism.[26] Moreover, while Lawrence acknowledges regional differences among Mexican Indians, he overrides those differences with a totalizing primitive sexuality that he offers up as the antidote to stagnant Western culture, thereby reducing all Mexican Indians to a sexual fetish.

At this point another basic characteristic of the Infernal Paradise tradition becomes clear: since all Mexicans are perceived as inherently inferior (simpleminded, naive, evil, promiscuous, primitive, and so on), it is possible for the author to note intercultural and intracultural differences among them without ever questioning the implicit superiority of the Anglo characters in the book. Thus Lawrence's Kate gives an incredibly detailed and

racist analysis of Mexicans by region in which she describes
the Indians variously as "wild, degenerate, little, spiders, queer-
looking, half-Chinese, erect, prancing, scaly with dirt, poisonous,
stiff, thin little men, cold and unliving like scorpions and as dangerous, pure brutish evil, insect-like, people not quite created and
reptilian" (81–83). Given this characterization, it is important to
note that Kate never changes her views of racial superiority vis-à-
vis Indians, despite the sexual liberation she feels in their company. Torgovnick's analysis of the novel is particularly helpful
here. She theorizes that Lawrence found himself trapped within a
vicious philosophical circle firmly grounded in a Western tradition emphasizing a Self/Other distinction. In *Plumed Serpent* he
struggles to create a paradigm in which Self and Other fuse into a
collective subject, yet his means to that end doesn't erase the
Self/Other dichotomy, it merely hinges them together by the
solidus between them. It strikes me that this inability to let go of
the dichotomy is borne out most clearly in Lawrence's allowing
Kate to fantasize until the novel's end about simultaneously being a partner in the collective *and* retaining her own identity.
Consider also how Cipriano, the Mexican Indian Kate has married, is described in the final scene: he is a "little fighting male,"
"uncanny," "inhuman," soft, wet, hot, "almost foolish": he remains clearly positioned as a primitive, and his union with Kate
has not changed that. Ultimately, what Lawrence demonstrates
is not a transformation of the Self/Other relationship, but rather
a heightening of it as essential to the survival of the European
self: while it's true that Lawrence seeks to harmonize or balance
those two categories, he also seeks to maintain them. Torgovnick
says that "for Lawrence, as for Conrad, the primitive Other, like
all others, must be processed and reprocessed as a potential sign
and symbol of the self" (171), not as an equal but different subject. So while Lawrence would write before coming to America
that "Americans must take up life where the Red Indian, the
Aztec, the Maya, the Incas left it off. They must pick up the life-
thread where the mysterious Red race let it fall. They must catch

the pulse of the life which Cortés and Columbus murdered," his writing after he visited Mexico demonstrates that such an enterprise was repugnant to him and would be achieved not *with* the "Red race" but at their expense.[27] "[E]ven if there were no such continent as America," Walker says, "Lawrence would have invented one: which, in a sense, is what he did anyway" (104).

Mexico or Greeneland?

In 1938, Graham Greene traveled through southern Mexico in order to ascertain the veracity of claims that religious persecution begun under the Calles regime of the late 1920s still existed. His experiences there resulted in two books: the travelogue *The Lawless Roads* (1939) and one of his most famous novels, *The Power and the Glory* (1940). As students of Greene are well aware, the transformation of physical settings into symbolic, dreamlike locales is a Greene signature, something Greene scholars have come to call Greeneland. His treatment of Mexico, then, comes as no surprise, but it certainly does further the myth of the Infernal Paradise.

In a very perceptive article that examines Greene's Mexican travelogue as the basis of his Mexican novel, Sheryl Pearson illuminates some of the consequences of Mexico as Greeneland. First, although Greene, unlike his predecessors, created his story around a Mexican protagonist, his main character—the unnamed "whisky priest"—betrays a repulsion toward Mexico that is more characteristic of the Anglo literary tradition than the Mexican. Pearson notes that

> evidence of Greene's own outsider's perspective on Mexico sometimes surfaces in disconcerting ways, including cartographical blunders . . . that no one native to the region, as the priest is said to be, would make. . . . [T]he priest also seems to have inherited a faintly hostile, alien, response to the Mexican ambiance which recalls Greene's own. While narratively the priest's multilevel alien-

ation from his environment accounts for much of this estrange-
ment, it does not explain why the particulars of his disaffection reproduce the Anglo-American stereotype of Mexico. Greene exposed
himself to this problem of perspective when he chose to write his
novel around Mexican characters. (279, n. 3)

While Greene's hostility toward Mexico and things Mexican is
muted in the novel, it is full blown in his travel memoir, in
which he admits to an "almost pathological hatred" for the country (*Lawless Roads* 145) that, as Pearson points out, is reminiscent of Lawrence's response to Mexico (284). There is a great deal
of irony in the fact that Greene's revulsion for the people, place,
and culture is frequently located in the country's "underdevelopment," precisely the same quality that he and other Anglo writers who respond similarly to Mexico find attractive. Greene, we
should remember, despite his investigative mission, was a tourist
in Mexico, and I find it interesting that his response to the country perfectly echoes Dean MacCannell's ideas of the motivation
behind tourism: the search for something meaningful and sacred
that has been lost in the profane modern world. Pearson says that
"[Greene] wants to believe that at least in Mexico the subter-
ranean fight for eternal verities goes on. . . . When newly arrived
in Mexico he imagines that the inroads made by the materialism
of the outside world are short and limited. Deep in Chiapas he
is moved by evidence that here are native enclaves almost un-
touched by outside influences, practicing a primitive and powerful Christianity, and as yet impervious to the governments' misguided attempts at modernization" (286). That what Greene seeks
in Mexico should so closely resemble that sought after by the
tourist suggests the presence of important links between the literary tradition of the Infernal Paradise and the tourist industry in
Mexico; this is precisely the argument I make in my final chapter. For our purposes here, it is worth noting that, like the tourist,
Greene wants Mexico to exist in some imagined past, a past prior
to the revolution; yet again, ironies abound. The Catholic Mexico
he longs for is a result of the Spanish Conquest, itself a revolu-

tionary and destructive event. Time and time again, we witness Anglo writers either placing Mexico outside time or suggesting that it would be better off existing outside time, with relatively little thought given to the implications for the inhabitants. In trying to preserve some imagined remnant of the premodern, these writers condemn Mexicans to a past without the benefits and amenities that they take for granted. Like the tourist, they want a nostalgic, backward Mexico to be available to them at all times. Like the tourist, Greene wants to preserve the qualities that make Mexico a nice place to visit, which of course are the same qualities that make it the kind of place "you wouldn't want to live in." The Mexico that Greene validates with the sacrificial death of his reluctant priest is a Mexico deeply rooted in faith and values that have long vanished from his own world, faith and values that have been placed in jeopardy by the changes the revolution brought about. While we may be sympathetic to his condemnation of religious persecution and his warning of extremist political programs, we must also recognize that the Mexico Greene longs for is really one that would exist primarily to serve the needs of Europeans; it is a Mexico that would function primarily, to use Dean MacCannell's phrase, as a "cultural service stop for modern man" (*The Tourist* 178).

Spiritual Trial and Heir

Although Malcolm Lowry would probably have denied it, his protagonist Geoffrey Firmin owes a great deal to Lawrence's Kate Leslie. In turning our attention to the Mexico that Lowry's British ex-consul moves through in *Under the Volcano*, we can elaborate on the range of attitudes regarding Mexican culture commonly found in the Infernal Paradise tradition. The inhabitants of Lowry's Mexico fall easily into well-defined categories. There are Dr. Vigil and Señor Bustamente, the Consul's charming but clownish friends; there is the confident, life-affirming Indian horseman who will die by the side of the road as the Consul watches; there are the benevolent but inscrutable Indian women like Señora Gregoria and Concepta; there is Maria, the dark, sultry prostitute; and finally there are the cartoonish bandidos who threaten the Consul at the Farolito. Curiously, these Mexicans are all characterized by their use of broken English, and here Lowry illustrates another of the racist moves typical of the adventure novel: classifying the Other as inferior through inferior speech. Yet, why should any of these characters be speaking English in the first place? Equally ludicrous is the fact that the Consul, Hugh, and Yvonne all speak excellent Spanish.

As his reference to Bierce and Crane in his letter to Jonathan Cape makes clear, Lowry was well aware of the literary tradition he was working in, and in the final, crucial scene of *Under the Volcano* he satirizes the western adventure novel: at a remote cantina, the drunken Consul gets himself in trouble by refusing to give his correct name to a group of Mexicans who all resemble and speak like Mexican bandits from a Hollywood western. An argument ensues and the Consul is pushed outside. In a drunken rage he frees a horse that he believes was stolen by one of the Mexicans, who, in characteristic dialect, tells him, "I blow you wide open from your knees up, you Jew chingao. I blow you wide open from your knees up, you cabrón, you pelado" (373). To which the Consul responds with equally characteristic movie bravado—"No, I wouldn't do that. That's a Colt .17, isn't it? It throws a lot of steel shavings" (373)—which prompts the Mexican to shoot and kill him.

Michael Cripps, Ronald Walker, and others have pointed out that having the Mexican call the Consul a Jew is meant to paint the Mexican as a fascist, since it was Lowry's plan to have the novel (set in 1939) mirror the crisis in Europe. Cripps also argues that this death is the Consul's deserved punishment for his egocentrism, his selfish quest for higher knowledge, and his refusal to view the Mexicans in anything but the simplest terms. I would ask, however, whether this ending really makes the reader reassess his or her sympathy for the Consul or recognize the consistently stereotypical portrayal of the Mexicans. Nor can Lowry erase the cumulative effects of those stereotypes in one line of satiric dialogue.[28] As he makes clear in his letter to Cape, Lowry (like Lawrence before him) saw nothing wrong with molding Mexico to suit his allegorical needs.

To summarize, we can see that in addition to continuing to represent Mexicans and Mexican culture as inferior, the modernist Anglo writers added a new element: Mexico as a spiritual testing ground, a symbolic landscape through which the outsider could achieve higher consciousness and salvation, even while succumbing to a tragic end.

"It Isn't Anything or Anywhere": The Infernal Paradise since 1980

As far as I have been able to determine, British writers lost interest in Mexico as a literary locale after World War II. Anglo American writers showed sporadic interest (Steinbeck contributed his allegorical *The Pearl* [1945], and Jack Kerouac's *On the Road* [1957] and Bellow's *The Adventures of Augie March* [1953] both have segments set in Mexico), but no works that engage fully with Mexicanness appeared again until the 1980s. I have no explanation for this sudden turning away from Mexico, other than to suggest that other events (the aftermath of World War II, the cold war, Vietnam, and the various civil rights movements) occupied the concerns of Anglo writers.[29] Conversely, Gunn suggests that the political stabilization of Mexico following World War II made it appear less exotic and thus less attractive to foreign writers (196). Whatever the case, there are important Mexican American representations of Mexicanness that bridge this literary gap. For example, Josephina Niggli's *Mexican Village* (1945) and José Antonio Villarreal's *Pocho* (1959) are two sides of the same coin, examining the relationship of Chicano protagonists who return to and emigrate from Mexico. Moreover, as discussed in chapter 1, the Chicano cultural nationalist movement of the late 1960s depended heavily on Mexican representations. As for the Anglo tradition, a renewed interest in Mexico began in the 1980s. Beginning in 1981, five American authors who have each achieved critical and commercial success—Richard Ford, Harriet Doerr, Robert Stone, Charles Portis, and Cormac McCarthy—would publish novels set in Mexico. I will discuss Ford and McCarthy very briefly and Portis not at all, because their works are largely formulaic and add little to the patterns already discussed. Stone and Doerr, on the other hand, create more complicated texts that challenge prevailing tendencies within this tradition, and thus merit closer analysis.

The first to appear was Ford's *The Ultimate Good Luck* (1981). It is, just as the jacket copy describes it, "[s]o hardboiled and tough that it might have been written on the back of a trench-coat." Indeed, it is clearly within the genre of the hardboiled detective story and its plot is simple: the American protagonist, Harry Quinn, has gone to Oaxaca, Mexico, to buy his lover's brother, imprisoned for running drugs, out of jail. As in most novels of the genre, Quinn is cynical and bitter, burned out by his experiences in Vietnam. The world around him is alternately peopled by naive American tourists and sinister Mexicans. There are suggestions of guerrilla activity in the surrounding countryside, and the city is teeming with soldiers who shoot first and ask questions later. Quinn and the other Americans in the novel find Mexico disturbing. One of the tourists proclaims, "It's so boring. Nothing ever happens. I'm sorry I ever came" (5). Quinn shares this view and finds it dangerous: "Mexico was like Vietnam or LA only more disappointing—a great trivial abundance of crap the chief effect of which wasn't variety but sameness. And since you wouldn't remember the particulars from one day to the next, you couldn't remember what to avoid and control" (15). And Quinn's lover, Rae, concludes, "I know what's wrong here. There's just too much here that's uninteresting. It isn't like Europe" (163).

Despite the fact that attitudes like these dominate the narrative, there are brief moments when Ford attempts to consider the Americans from a Mexican point of view. The *only* Mexican character of importance in the book is Bernhardt, the lawyer hired by Quinn to get Sonny out of prison. Bernhardt, once idealistic but now a part of the corrupt legal system, feels pity for the campesinos and *marginales* living in poverty but does not believe anything can be done to help them, and watches them from the safety and comfort of his Mercedes Benz. Despite his cynicism and detachment, he claims to understand things that Quinn cannot, and he criticizes Quinn for not attempting to understand the complexities of Mexican culture: "You see in a tunnel. Outside what you see, things are not one way, but other ways at once. You need to be tolerant" (106).

In another revealing passage that briefly challenges the prevailing attitudes in the book, Quinn reads an American newspaper and wonders what a Mexican reader would think of the happenings in the United States: "There was a story about a grandmother in South Dakota stabbing a lion to death with a button hook inside her travel camper. The story didn't say how the lion had come inside the camper or why there was a lion around at all. Mexicans would understand it. Americans lived in an ocean to ocean freak show, and there was a good reason to be here where things were simple instead of up there where things were bent wrong" (49). Quinn also makes an observation that suggests a new and significant trend in the Infernal Paradise tradition: "The wire mesh Christmas bells were strung all the way round the zócalo, and there were lights in the jacarandas, and a big silver tree stood riotously on top of the band kiosk. Mexicans thought Americans wanted it to be Christmas everyday and they were happy to provide the illusion" (48). For the first time in an Infernal Paradise text we have a suggestion that the Mexicans are turning the exoticism characteristic of the tradition to their own economic advantage. In cultivating the tourist trade, they are deliberately conforming to the expectations of Americans and Europeans, expectations that have been constructed over a lengthy period through the discourses constituting the Infernal Paradise. This response on the part of the Mexicans is what de Certeau would characterize as tactical: they recognize that they are unable to overcome the strategic constructs of institutionalized power, but improvise within institutionalized constraints for some degree of personal gain. This new element does not move Ford's novel out of the Infernal Paradise tradition, of course. The intertextuality that so marks the tradition is again present in *The Ultimate Good Luck*, which contains some striking allusions to *Under the Volcano*, as well as a similar resolution. Like the Consul and Yvonne in Lowry's novel, Quinn and Rae are estranged lovers attempting a reconciliation in a small Mexican city. And as in *Under the Volcano* (and so many of the Infernal Paradise novels), the protagonist is driven to violence by the novel's end. In a scene that inverts the climax of *Volcano*, Quinn shoots and kills two revolutionaries who attempt to steal his money. Moreover, both Quinn and the Consul achieve a moment of self-awareness at these crucial moments, an awareness of their selfishness and destructiveness. Quinn returns from the murders recognizing that he cannot live without Rae, and he is finally able to tell her that he loves her and wants to stay with her. Unlike the Consul and Yvonne, who are both killed, Quinn and Rae survive and are reconciled.

We can see, then, that Ford's novel is firmly within the Infernal Paradise tradition both in terms of its depiction of Mexico and Mexicans and in terms of its invocation of the achievement of new self-knowledge through spiritual and physical hardship brought on by the Mexican setting. What I find most interesting about *The Ultimate Good Luck* are its flashes of recognition that there is a Mexican consciousness, that Mexicans are aware of the way their culture is perceived by outsiders and have begun to turn it to their own advantage. This is a new theme that will be treated with much more skill and depth in Robert Stone's *Children of Light* (1986).[30]

Children of Light alternates between the vicissitudes of two characters: Gordon Walker, an alcoholic screenwriter living in Hollywood, and Lu Anne Bourgeois, a delusional actress who had an affair with Walker years ago. She is in Mexico, or more precisely in Baja California, working on a film production of Kate Chopin's *The Awakening*—scripted by Walker—in which she plays the lead role. We quickly learn that Walker is methodically destroying himself with alcohol and drugs, despite the fact that his career shows signs of improving. As the novel opens, a hungover Walker looks out at a California morning "dappled with promise" and representing "the pursuit of happiness," to which he responds with self-disgust and a premonition that he may die quite soon (3–5). The sense of death increases as the novel progresses. Like Ambrose Bierce, Gordon Walker, convinced that he is dying, will choose to go to Mexico. This sense of impending death also causes him to think obsessively about Lu Anne, who he knows is in Mexico filming his script of *The Awakening*, and he fights unsuccessfully against the pull to go see her. It becomes clear to both Walker and the reader that Mexico is the dangerous, perhaps deadly, terrain he must move through to reach his objective. We see Walker attempting to rationalize the trip to Mexico in various ways. He wants to see how they are handling his script. He tells his agent, "I feel the need to go down to Mexico for a while. When I get back—I'll be refreshed. I'll be able to work." Still later he offers, "I need a trip. Travel is therapy for me" (16–17). Obviously, these rationalizations mask Walker's hope for reconciliation with Lu Anne, but they also point toward the ambivalence so characteristic of the Infernal Paradise. He hopes a trip to Mexico will be therapeutic, that he will return refreshed and able to work, yet at a deeper level he believes he may very well die there. Mexico thus becomes positioned as both a possible place for recovery (both physical and emotional) and a place to die. Significantly, Walker heads for the border immediately after firing his agent, severing his most important professional tie with California. He must sever this tie because California symbolizes the promise of success that he has come to fear. California and Baja California become oppositional symbolic landscapes, and Walker must first reject the land of promise before he can plunge into the land of despair and death that lies *abajo*, underneath.[31]

To this point, approximately the first third of the narrative, Stone's novel appears to be following neatly along the path established by his literary predecessors. As Walker crosses over into Mexico, the description of the landscape is at times reminiscent of Lawrence and Lowry. The light in Baja is repeatedly described as strange and sinister, but also as holy and edged with hope. Even the place-names are overtly symbolic: Walker's first glimpse of the movie locale at Bahía Honda (Deep Bay) comes from atop "Cerro Encantada," the Enchanted Hill. He looks down into a mountain valley described in Lawrentian terms as a "sinister reptilian emerald" (128). Such details are surprisingly few, however, and *Children of Light* has a strange quality that I can only describe as an intense "placelessness." Stone very deliberately erases Mexico and onto this tabula rasa places layer upon layer of artificial constructs. In fact, he appears to want to emphasize the artificiality of the setting in order to comment on the many discursive constructions superimposed on it. In essence, he enables us to recognize the Mexico produced by discourse as a palimpsest, and also the danger in this endless superimposition of fantastic images. Let me clarify this argument.

In the first description of the hotel serving as the movie set in Bahía Honda, we are told: "A sweet expensive tropic darkness had enveloped the Villa . . . ; it was included in the budget and thought to enhance production values. Beyond the tiki torches stood illuminated fences and armed men" (49). In his choice of words, Stone suggests that the exotic tropical atmosphere has been purchased at a high price "to enhance production values." But just on the periphery of this expensive hotel, with rooms themed like *Carmen* and illuminated by the tiki torches that give it some of its exotic flavor, are ominous shadowy soldiers, suggesting that

those who cannot afford the price of admission will be turned
away. In just two brief sentences, Stone conveys the disparity between the haves and have-nots in most Mexican tourist towns,
and also emphasizes the totally constructed nature of the Mexican tourist resort (the "sanitized" nature, as one of the characters describes it [50]). The resorts are, in Bob Shacochis's words,
"Third World theme parks," or, as Stone himself has suggested,
"theaters" for American entertainment.[32]

Stone heightens our awareness of the artificiality by superimposing yet another artificial layer onto it in the form of the movie
sets. Characters joke about the live oaks and moss, which had to
be shipped in from another part of Mexico in order to re-create the
Louisiana of Chopin's novel. And still later, as the novel builds
toward its climax, Lu Anne takes Walker to a place she believes
to be a religious shrine, which Walker recognizes as the abandoned movie set of an old B. Traven remake that the Mexican
government at one time was going to make into a museum, but
now is being used as a corncrib on a pig farm. Stone mocks the
Infernal Paradise tradition as he emphasizes that the multiple
layers of textual constructions superimposed onto Mexico have
reduced it to a place whose meaning can be reshuffled as quickly
as a deck of cards, a place where the fictive constructs mingle
tightly and maddeningly with reality. As Walker puts it, "It isn't
anything or anywhere. It's fake" (233).

The sense of placelessness is further emphasized by the almost
total marginalization of the Mexicans in the novel—a key and deliberate move by Stone. With one important exception they are
nameless hotel or movie employees, chauffeurs, and, of course,
police. Stone grants only one Mexican an identity: Maldonado, an
artist who in a drunken dinner conversation denounces himself
and his work and challenges the Americans to tell the truth about
themselves, to reveal their shameful secrets. Stone renders Maldonado sympathetically, and his speech is meant to emphasize
the hypocrisy of the American artists, to underscore the sense that
they are deluding themselves. Stone gives us a Mexican whose

self-awareness serves to illuminate the lack of same in the American characters. In his excellent critical reading of *Children of Light*, Robert Solotaroff suggests that "since more than three-quarters of the novel deals with the behavior of Americans in Mexico, the scarcity of significant interactions between the visitors and the natives speaks strongly for the essentially nonpolitical character of *Children of Light*" (122). John McClure concurs: "What is missing in such scenes, of course, is any serious attempt to represent Mexico. Stone has ceased to think politically about the implications of the American presence, and one consequence is that Mexico and its people are reduced once again to their traditional roles as colorful figures of futility, suffering and spirituality" (115). Although this does seem to be a logical conclusion, I have an antithetical reaction to Stone's treatment of Mexicanness in *Children of Light*. In its absence or shadowy presence on the novel's margins, the Mexicanness produced by Stone forces us to reconsider the implications of what is located at the novel's center: the displacement of Mexico by artificial constructs, usually of American origin. This emphasis on themed, carefully crafted façades seems to me a *very* political maneuver on Stone's part. Not only does Stone force the reader to examine the consequences of the erasure of Mexicans from the text, he also effectively satirizes the spiritual adventure novels such as *The Plumed Serpent* and *Under the Volcano* that have contributed some of the most durable elements to the Infernal Paradise. For example, as Lu Anne reviews Walker's script for the climactic scene of *The Awakening*, in which Edna Pontellier, her character, commits suicide by walking into the sea, she comes on the following stage directions: "She senses a freedom the scope of which she has never known. She has come beyond despair to a kind of exaltation" (120). Lu Anne's response is mocking:

Of course, that was the spirit of the book and its ending. But exaltation beyond despair? She had never found anything beyond despair except more despair. There were some questions to take up, some

questions for the writer. Did Walker really believe in exaltation beyond despair? Did that mean she had to? Would she be able to play
it? For that she had an answer which was: absolutely, you betcha.
We play them whether they're there or not. And once we've played
them they're there and there they stay, just like Marcel Herrand's
Larcenair, Henry Fonda's Wyatt Earp, Jimmy Dean's Jimmy Dean.
(120)

The metacritical vantage of this passage jars Stone's reader out of
the fictional illusion and prompts her to "take up some questions
with the writers," to question them about this quest for higher
consciousness that underlies so many of the Infernal Paradise novels. Stone's innovative narrative strategies, like those of Porter in
"Hacienda," force us to recognize the durability of such myths,
regardless of their connection to reality: "We play them whether
they're there or not. And once we've played them they're there
and there they stay."

But although Lu Anne has rejected the metaphysical yearnings
of the script, Walker has not, and Lu Anne's satirical comments
are followed by a scene in which Walker, from atop the Enchanted Hill, watches the filming of Edna Pontellier's suicide.
Spellbound by the sight of his script coming to life, Walker feels

> at the point of understanding the process in which his life was
> bound, as though the height on which he stood was the perspective
> he had always lacked. Will I understand it all now he wondered, un-
> derstand it with the eye like a painting? The sense of discovery, of
> imminent insight excited him. He was dizzy; he checked his foot-
> ing on the uneven ground, his closeness to the edge. Her down
> there, himself on a rock miles away—that's poetry, he thought, The
> thing was to get it straight to understand. . . . Tears came to his
> eyes. But perhaps it was not poetry, he thought. Only movies. (129)

Walker's fear of his "poetry" being really something much more
banal appears to be the conclusion eventually reached by Lu
Anne, not only about Walker's revision of The Awakening (another sort of palimpsest) but of the original text itself. Lu Anne's

feelings about the character she plays are extremely ambivalent, a combination of sympathy and resentment. Lu Anne comes to believe that ultimately what drives Edna to kill herself is self-recognition, an awakening not so much from passivity to action as an awakening to true self, the recognition of which is too much to bear. Consider the evolution of Lu Anne's attitude toward Edna in the following passages: "Edna was independent and courageous. Whereas, Lu Anne thought, I'm just chickenshit and crazy. Edna would die for her children but never let them possess her. Lu Anne was a lousy mother, certified and certifiable. Who the hell did she think she was, Edna? Too good for her own kids? But then she thought: It comes to the same thing, her way and mine. You want more, you want to be Queen, you want to be Rosalind" (98).

In the preceding we see the characteristic ambivalence. Lu Anne doesn't measure up in her comparison with Edna; there is a sudden flash of anger and resentment at Edna's decision, and then a just as sudden conciliatory identification with her. A few moments later, the conciliatory note that ends the preceding passage continues with an added bit of envy as Lu Anne further contemplates the character: "Edna knew what living was worth to her and the terms on which she would accept it. She knew the difference between living and not living and what happiness was. It occurred to Lu Anne that she knew none of these things. Too bad, she thought, because I'm the one that's real, not her. It's me out here" (99–100). Significantly, this passage signals a shift in Lu Anne's attitude toward the novel/screenplay/movie, as she becomes increasingly critical of its romantic resolution and, as pointed out above, its metaphysical yearnings. There is also a shift in her attitude toward Edna. If earlier Lu Anne acknowledged that her way and Edna's amount "to the same thing" (self-destruction?), she now is careful to distance herself from the character. Acknowledging that it is dangerous to confront one's "inward places" because self-recognition can destroy a person as it does Edna, like Medusa looking on her own reflection (Lu Anne's simile), Lu Anne nevertheless carefully ascribes to herself a stronger constitution: "If I, who see everything in mirrors, who cannot approach the glass without some apprehension, were to see my inward self there, I would not die. But Edna might" (135). As she repeatedly enacts the suicide for the cameras, it is difficult not to interpret Lu Anne's thoughts about Edna as satirical, even mocking: "Poor old Edna, little Dixie honey, sees her own self on the shield of hot blue sky and dies. Sees all that freedom, that great black immensity of righteous freedom and swoons, Oh My. And dies" (135). This irreverence culminates in a throwaway line following the suicide scene's final take. Asked by the assistant director what she calls her most recent interpretation of Edna's death, Lu Anne responds, "Lupe Velez Takes a Dunk" (137). The actress playing Chopin's strong-willed protagonist claims to base her interpretation of the character's suicide not on the novel or her ex-lover's stage directions, but on the film actress better known as the Mexican Spitfire, the archetypal Mexican seductress. The implications of the satirical barb are hard to miss: there is no textual integrity, just endless erasures and absurd superimpositions. As the film's director points out, the novel's ending has become a worn-out chestnut, a cliché he must reinvent at the risk of producing another "walk-into-the-ocean movie" (180–81).

Given these attitudes, what are we to make of Stone's decision to end *his* novel with another walk into the ocean? What are we to make of Lu Anne's fatal walk into the sea just days after she dismissed Edna's suicide as a poor solution to the character's existential dilemma, or at least as a solution that is not right for her? As always with Stone, the scene is difficult to interpret. Following the harrowing scene at the pigsty during which Lu Anne's psychosis is at full power, she appears moments before her death to be calmer and happier, playfully trying to coax Walker into the water. As Solotaroff points out, it's difficult to know whether she intends to commit suicide or is "swept away by a tall wave that has little interest in such subtleties of motivation" (135). Regardless, Lu Anne's death by drowning heightens the novel's irony in a way that places responsibility for the tragedy squarely on Walker's shoulders. Walker, a writer inclined toward the romantic tendencies of Chopin, who exoticizes the South in a way not so dissimilar to the ways in which Stone's predecessors have depicted Mexico, has his wish come true: his script does become reality and there is nothing poetic about it.[33] But for the reader, Lu Anne's death appears as out of character as Edna's did to Lu Anne when she performed it for the cameras (and as it has for some critics of *The Awakening*).[34] The denouement of Stone's novel is equally problematic. We learn that Walker has returned to the States, has given up drinking, is working again, and has reconciled with his ex-wife; yet we are not left with any sense that he has learned from his experience. What does one make of so much good fortune arising from such tragedy? Mexico appears to have performed both its infernal and paradisal functions. Destroying Lu Anne and healing Walker, it has been both deadly and therapeutic, yet once again the reader is left with a feeling of disbelief at the absurdity of the events. And perhaps that is Stone's point: perhaps in order to complete his parody of the Infernal Paradise he has Walker survive but learn nothing: there are no enchanted hills, no transcendent moments, no higher consciousness as longed for by Lawrence and Lowry.

Other readers may reject my notion that Lu Anne's death is meant as an ironic commentary on the Infernal Paradise tradition, based on the evidence that she is delusional and that her mental illness, coupled with the role playing demanded by her work, cause a fatal slip into Edna's character. Though plausible, such an argument needs to take into account the textual production and superimposition that Stone emphasizes throughout the novel: a hotel in Baja California (itself an exotic, themed construct) becomes the base for a movie set of a reconstructed Louisiana; *The Awakening* is rewritten by a screenwriter and then re-visioned again by filmmakers who consider it not so much a classic text as another in a genre of films that end in drowning; Lu Anne interprets Edna's death and then literally enacts it in a way that replicates not only Chopin's novel but its problematic ending. And all of this is superimposed on a Mexican landscape that has been largely erased of all Mexican markers; it isn't anything or anywhere. When everything is taken into account, we may glimpse a more important idea. It may be that Stone intends Lu Anne's death to represent the dangers of participating in a kind of postmodern play, of a self-aware and deliberate shifting from construct to construct—channel surfing in the Infernal Paradise.[35] To participate in this kind of movement is to become like Lu Anne, playing an unending series of scripted roles that serve mostly as a narcotic buffer: If you don't like being on a pig farm, transform it into a religious shrine. With irony and bitter insight, Stone warns us that to willingly participate in such play is to consign oneself to a textual labyrinth that merely opens on others without end: the only way Lu Anne can escape the Infernal Paradise is to enter a different discursive construct: the Louisiana of *The Awakening.* Moreover, in situating his movie set "atop" a Mexican tourist resort, Stone reminds us that while the Americans can choose to play roles as a way to distance themselves from reality, the Mexicans' economic reality leaves them little choice but to play roles scripted for them by the tourist industry and by the Infernal Paradise myth, which the industry uses as a stockpile of familiar images to attract visitors. For these reasons, I value Stone's novel highly; it is a landmark work, one of a handful to challenge an influential and damaging literary tradition.

Harriet Doerr

Harriet Doerr is another exceptional author who has challenged the Infernal Paradise. Both of Doerr's Mexican novels—*Stones for Ibarra* and *Consider This, Señora*—deal sensitively with different strands of neocolonialism (i.e., foreign investment, tourism, and expatriate arts communities), and both seek to interrogate cultural assumptions. Like Porter and Crane before her, Doerr seems determined to force the reader to think about the representations she authors and authorizes. How well she succeeds is open to debate. Her first Mexican book, *Stones for Ibarra*, was published in 1984 and thus antedates *Children of Light* by two years. It is a novel that revolves around Richard and Sara Everton, U.S. citizens who move to the small Mexican town of Ibarra in order to reopen a copper mine that was owned and operated by Richard's grandfather before the Mexican Civil War. They have come to live out an aristocratic fantasy and set up shop as benevolent patrons, kindly hacendados. Doerr skillfully examines the consequences of this action on both the Evertons and the Mexicans living in Ibarra, consequences that are as often tragic as they are beneficial. While the reopening of the copper mine brings a certain amount of prosperity to the community, it also triggers competitive rivalries that result in senseless deaths. Doerr knows that to become a patron is also to run the risk of becoming patronizing, and in one of the novel's most effective sequences she shows one of the townspeople deftly exploiting Richard Everton's guilt over the accidental death of one of his workers.

Further distinguishing Doerr's text from others in the tradition (Lowry's, for example) is her emphasis on cultural interaction and her repeated views of the Anglo characters through Mexican eyes. In fact, early in the novel Doerr inverts the standard practice of making the Mexicans the object of the colonial gaze and instead portrays the Evertons as a spectacle for the villagers, who peer through the windows and look into the lighted house at night. Doerr makes the different cultural vantage points important narrative structures, building her novel's dramatic tension around her characters' (Mexicans' *and* Americans') cultural assumptions, preconceptions, and perceptions; and she tracks the changes in those perceptions and beliefs as the events in the novel transpire. For example, Sara's initial perception of the Mexicans is that they are "specters," "silhouettes," and "strangers." "They will never speak to me, she thinks. I will never know their names" (11). The Ibarrans, too, draw quick conclusions from their initial observations: Remedios Acosta considers the Evertons' way of living extravagant and impractical, and the Ibarrans conclude that they are *mediodesorientado* (half disoriented; 24). These perceptions, of course, change as the characters get to know one another over a period of years. Nevertheless, the novel is open to charges that it is comprised of an inordinate number of violent tragedies and that the Mexican characters are all creatures of passion ruled by their emotions. Doerr seems to have anticipated this critique and addresses it in an important passage near the end of the novel, when Sara Everton composes a letter to another foreigner thinking of moving to the Mexican state within which Ibarra is located:

> Dear Helga Ronslager, you didn't tell me in your letter whether you intend to live in Concepción, which is the capital of this state and has parks, banks, Woolworth's and a cathedral, or here in Ibarra, a less cosmopolitan town, a village actually, where several incidents have become known to me. In one of these, José Reyes killed two men in the cantina and soon after was stoned into submission on the hill of the Santa Cruz. In another, a helpless boy, an idiot, drowned in the tailings dump of the Malagueña mine. An intern of the government clinic committed suicide one Christmas day. Basilio García, who had enrolled his brother in the state university, shot him to death by mistake. Paz Acosta, the most beautiful girl in Ibarra, is a prostitute. Dear Helga, *you must understand that these things happen everywhere.* (200; emphasis added)

Sara's assertion that these things happen everywhere glosses over the impact of the Evertons' neocolonial venture, which was the catalyst for many of the tragedies she lists. But though Sara overlooks her complicity in these events, Doerr does not, and instead consistently calls our attention to the Evertons' influence on the Ibarrans' lives. For example, she makes a basic point quite well when she draws an analogy between the stray dogs and cats Sara takes it upon herself to feed and the Mexican workers employed by her husband. As one of the Mexicans comments, "Will those animals remember how to hunt mice and hares if they are fed on plates at the door? The señor and señora are preparing them to starve" (16).

Doerr continues to explore these issues in her subsequent novel, *Consider This, Señora* (1993), which bears many similarities to *Stones for Ibarra*. It concerns the development of an expatriate artists' colony in another Mexican pueblo. This time, though, it is the foreigners who are creatures of passion, unable to control their emotions. And the fact that they are artists gives Doerr the opportunity to explore the kinds of Mexicanness they construct. For Sue Ames, a painter, the Mexicanness she produces can never mirror reality since it is inherently transformative: "Realist though she was, Sue saw Mexico through a painter's eye, converting what was actually there to her private way of seeing" (99). In an interesting maneuver, Doerr contrasts Sue's acts of transformation with those of Fran Bowles, who has written a guidebook called *Your Mexico*, which, rather than being a guidebook to Mexico, is a guide to the author's ideas about how Mexico should be. Despite the fact that both artists remake Mexico through their own personal vision, Sue finds Fran's construction somehow less honest than her own. The hypocrisy in Sue's position is brought out by the Mexican characters, who act as important counterpoints to the aesthetic views expressed by the Anglo artists. In Sue's case, she is warned that she is "transforming Amapolas into something more beautiful than it is" (4), an aestheticization that has long been a prominent strand of colonial discourse, as David Spurr demonstrates in *The Rhetoric of Empire* (43–60). Fran's depiction of Mexico is challenged by an expert in constructing Mexican fantasies: her lover, Paco, who works as a resort analyst for the Mexican Department of Tourism. Ironically, he tells Fran that she shouldn't invent or exaggerate what she sees: "When writing of Mexico, the truth is exciting enough" (110).

Ultimately, taking stock of Doerr's two novels is not an easy task. To her credit, she repeatedly and self-consciously directs our attention to the impact of neocolonialism on Mexico, including outsiders' attempts to reconstruct Mexico artistically, all of which points toward her own vision of Mexico. And it is here that I am left with some reservations. Like her characters Sara Everton and Sue Ames, Doerr tends to romanticize and aestheticize Mexico. Despite the self-reflexive nature of her work, the Mexico that emerges is a very beautiful one populated by Mexicans who at times resemble noble primitives in a way that recalls some of Porter's Mexican work. Still, perhaps this is making too fine a point; my critique, after all, owes a great deal to Doerr herself, who anticipated many of my concerns and self-consciously points the reader toward them in a direct fashion. For this, she should be commended and considered as another innovator within a tradition too often lacking innovation. Perhaps she evaluates her work best when she says of one of her characters, "And though, perhaps, . . . none of her imaginings were entirely true, on the other hand perhaps none were entirely false" (78). And therein lies the crux of the problem with cross-cultural writing in general and the Infernal Paradise in particular.

All the Pretty Horses

We have seen that Doerr and Stone have brought welcome complications to the myth of the Infernal Paradise, but the same cannot be said of all of their contemporaries. I conclude this chapter with a discussion of a highly visible and celebrated novel, Cormac McCarthy's *All the Pretty Horses* (1992). Despite winning both the National Book Award and the National Book Critics Circle Award, McCarthy's novel does little to challenge the conventions of the Infernal Paradise tradition.

Set in 1949, the novel relates the story of sixteen-year-old John Grady Cole, who, along with two teenaged companions, crosses from Texas into Mexico. Their journey closely parallels Joseph Campbell's paradigm of the hero's quest.[36] As Campbell notes, the hero is often reluctant to begin the journey and requires some

traumatic event to set him in motion. True to this model, Mc-
Carthy systematically severs all of his protagonist's links to west
Texas in the novel's first forty-five pages. The narrative opens
with the death of John Grady's maternal grandfather, patriarch
of a sizable west Texas cattle ranch. The ranch passes to John
Grady's mother, who intends to sell it, and when John Grady
pleads with her to lease the ranch to him, she refuses. After learning from the family lawyer that his parents are divorced (not sep-
arated, as he had thought), John Grady hitchhikes to San Antonio, where he watches his mother perform in a play in which he
can find no value or meaning. He sees his mother in the company
of a strange man and ascertains that she is no longer using her
married name. Finally, he goes for a last ride with his father and
says good-bye to his ex-girlfriend. Thus, with all his links to west
Texas systematically broken, John Grady sets out for Mexico
with his best friend, Rawlins. They are soon joined by a young
runaway named Jimmy Blevins.

Once in Mexico, it doesn't take the boys long to get themselves
into trouble. Drunk and deathly afraid of lightning, Blevins loses
his horse and his clothes in a thunderstorm. When they come
upon the horse in the next town, Blevins takes it back, setting the
town in an uproar and a posse on the boys' trail. After parting
company with Blevins, John Grady and Rawlins reach an hacienda where they find work. Their arrival at the hacienda coincides with an important shift in the book's tone, formalized
structurally by McCarthy with the beginning of the book's second part. Part 2 of *All the Pretty Horses* is the novel's *paradiso.*
McCarthy isn't subtle: the hacienda is named Nuestra Señora de
la Purísima Concepción (Our Lady of the Immaculate Conception). Here run wild horses that have never before seen a man on
foot. Here John Grady proves himself to be a supercowboy, not
only through such physical heroics as breaking sixteen wild horses
in four days, but also through his knowledge of horses and their
bloodlines. His exploits are rewarded by the hacendado, Señor
Rocha, who puts John Grady in charge of the selection of horses

and the breeding of his prize stallion. While Rawlins continues the unglamorous life of the vaquero, eating and sleeping in the bunkhouse with the other cowboys, John Grady is given his own room and, more important, free access to the horses. Oh, yes—he also falls in love with the hacendado's beautiful young daughter, Alejandra. Here is everything that John Grady dreams of: the perfect woman, the perfect cattle ranch, and the perfect horses, not necessarily in that order. Rawlins is quick to point out that it's not only the daughter that John Grady has eyes for, but the hacienda as well (138)—a chance to reclaim the inheritance denied him by his mother.

But Paradise quickly gives way to Inferno, again indicated formally by the beginning of the book's third part. Mexican Rangers arrive and take Rawlins and John Grady into custody, and the hacendado does nothing to intervene. They are reunited with Blevins, who, they learn, killed one man and wounded two others in an unsuccessful attempt to retrieve his lost pistol. The three of them are accused of being horse thieves, are interrogated and beaten, and then are shipped off to the prison at Saltillo. Along the way, Blevins is executed. Rawlins and John Grady are dumped into a hellish prison where the inmates fight with one another from dawn to dusk. Rawlins is stabbed in the belly and sent out of the prison for medical treatment. A few days later, John Grady kills an attacker in the prison mess hall after being himself severely wounded. He awakes to find that he has received medical treatment and is released along with Rawlins.

As Campbell tells us, if the hero can survive the descent into hell, he will return reborn and even more powerful. After parting company with Rawlins, John Grady sets out to settle his grievances. This involves confronting Alejandra's great aunt, Doña Alfonsa, and then Alejandra herself. John Grady learns that Alfonsa bought him and Rawlins out of prison after exacting a promise from her niece never to see him again. He asks Alejandra to marry him, but she refuses. The remainder of the novel recounts John Grady's struggle to retrieve his horses and to return to Texas with them. He is successful, but his experiences have changed him so much that he is unable to reintegrate himself into the community of San Angelo. The novel ends with him literally riding off into the sunset.

The most interesting Mexican character in the book is Alfonsa, great-aunt and godmother to Alejandra. In perhaps the novel's most astonishing passage, Alfonsa speaks for ten pages, recounting her family's history and that of the revolution, as well as her ideas about fate and free will. Thus, not only does she serve an important function in terms of the story's dramatic action (as an obstacle to John Grady and Alejandra's love affair and as a mechanism to free him from prison), she is also one of several characters who return to the novel's only persistent theme: the question of fate. Rawlins is the first character to raise this issue. He tells John Grady, "Ever dumb thing I ever done in my life there was a decision I made before that got me into it. It was never the dumb thing. It was always some choice I'd made before it. You understand what I'm sayin?" (79). This belief in free will and the individual's ability to control his or her destiny is juxtaposed with the Mexican captain's beliefs and those of Doña Alfonsa. In explaining to John Grady and Rawlins why he killed Blevins, the captain tells them, "A man cannot go out to do some thing and then he go back. Why he go back? Because he change his mind? A man does not change his mind" (181). If for Rawlins a person makes his or her own destiny, the captain maintains that a man's actions are governed by his words, no matter how misguided those words may be. Alfonsa, on the other hand, tells John Grady that the world is a puppet show: "But when one looks behind the curtain and traces the strings upward he finds they terminate in the hands of yet other puppets, themselves with their own strings which trace upward in turn, and so on" (231). Despite the capriciousness of the forces governing the world, she concludes that the individual cannot help but name responsibility, place blame, and seek to control even chaos: "It's in our nature" (241). These philosophical threads are drawn together when John Grady returns to Texas and narrates his adventures to a county judge and confesses to him the murder of the man who assaulted him in prison (288–93). Like Rawlins, he recognizes that his actions had consequences; like Alfonsa, the judge suggests to him that certain things, like Blevins's execution, were beyond his power to alter; and like the captain, John Grady responds that he was still bound by a code of honor to try to alter them.

Extremely entertaining, wonderfully romantic, and beautifully poetic, *All the Pretty Horses* nevertheless remains firmly grounded in the Infernal Paradise tradition. It should be clear from my summary that Mexico again functions as a symbolic backdrop, juxtaposing the paradise of the hacienda with the hell of the prison at Saltillo. The Mexican characters, although fleshed out more than in most novels of the tradition, also are fairly standard. The campesinos are innocent and generous; the hacendado cultured, proud, even a little haughty. About Alejandra we learn very little, other than that she is very beautiful, a characteristic McCarthy emphasizes repeatedly. In the captain, McCarthy walks a fine line between character and caricature, coming very close to the stereotypical sinister Mexican villain. As for Alfonsa, as riveting as her speeches are, one cannot help but feel that she is brought on stage merely to deliver her lines. In sum, I see little that would move this popular and highly acclaimed novel out of the Infernal Paradise tradition.

Concluding Remarks

In assessing the discourse producing an Eastern Other for the West, Edward Said says that, "at most, the 'real' Orient provoked a writer to his vision; it very rarely guided it" (22). We have seen that, in general, the same can be said about the Mexicanness produced by Anglo writers. To even attempt to write about Mexico is to locate oneself within a complicated discursive network that can best be described as a palimpsest. The Mexican images produced in the service of various political interests at different historical moments have become a filter through which we view Mexico and have, through repetition, become so ingrained in our conception of what Mexico is that our imaginings of Mexico—our own Mexican constructs—are strands of truth and falsehood, reality and fantasy, fact and fiction, all so tightly interwoven that they make such distinctions appear meaningless.

Nevertheless, I hope I have shown in this overview of Anglo production of Mexicanness that the tendency to mythologize, exoticize, and primitivize Mexico is not limited to the works of Lawrence, Greene, and Lowry, as much existing scholarship emphasizes. Rather, the myth of the Infernal Paradise began developing with the first English-language accounts, evolving from one of mystery, to one of savagery, to one of spiritual adventure, and finally to a sort of self-fulfilling prophecy for Mexican economic gain. The trajectory I have sketched, however, is by no means compartmentalized, with one element falling away as a new one is added; instead it is a palimpsest onto which more and more layers have been superimposed, until, as Robert Stone demonstrates so effectively in *Children of Light*, it becomes possible to occupy many Mexicos at the same time and never occupy Mexico at all, depending on the number of stories one wants to admit. The value of Stone's approach is that he produces a text that forces us to recognize the Infernal Paradise's most nefarious quality: its interchangeability. What we have is a composition that, no matter the variations or the different registers in which it is performed, remains the same. And at its base, it has served the political and economic interests of Europe and the United States while asserting its self-serving images of Mexicanness as authentic.

The Infernal Paradise is not the product of any one discourse. It comprises literary works, scholarship, historiography, journalism, cinema, photography, and tourism—to name the most obvious. Given this wide-ranging discursive network, we should consider the implications of the myth it promotes for the people it imposes the myth on. The relatively recent phenomenon of the Mexican people themselves appropriating and reworking the myth to their economic advantage, largely through the discourse of tourism, strikes me as a problematic move, one as disempowering in other arenas as it appears empowering in the economic. From my own contact with Mexico, I have sensed a firm belief on the part of many Mexicans that they can separate a nationalist pride from the stereotypical debasements (usually in the form of subservience and exoticism) encouraged by tourism. Yet I wonder if this separation can long be sustained before it takes its toll, if even in subtle ways. It has now been more than forty years since the Mexican tourist industry was reorganized under the close supervision of the Mexican government, and the portrayal of Mexicans in the complex discursive network I have outlined above does not appear to be moving very rapidly in a positive direction. I do not believe that the participation of the Mexican tourist industry in perpetuating a myth of the Infernal Paradise is likely to improve the perception of Mexicans and Mexican culture abroad. To elaborate on this hypothesis, in this book's final chapter I consider the impact of tourism on Mexicanness by focusing on a particular tourist destination as well as a text that sees itself at odds with touristic discourse. But I conclude this chapter with the special hope that scholars will be in the forefront of disengaging from the tenets of the myth of Mexico as Infernal Paradise and that they will begin to recognize Mexicans as complicated human beings with rich cultures, as much a part of the world and the present as those writers who have argued otherwise.

Chapter Three

✿

"Where Do You Get Your Ideas
about Mexico?"

"Where do you get your ideas about Mexico? From Graham Greene?"
—Curator of the National Anthropology Museum of Mexico to Richard
Rodriguez, *Days of Obligation*

✿

At this juncture I want to turn my attention to the kinds of Mexicanness produced by Chicano and Chicana writers. Before I do
that, however, I think it necessary to make some remarks about
Mexican American literature in general.[1] Let me begin by correcting a common misconception: literature about Mexican American identity is *not* equivalent to Mexican American literature in
its broadest sense. This used to be a much more contentious
point among literary historians than it is now, thanks mostly to
the tireless efforts of Juan Bruce-Novoa, who argues convincingly
that to formulate Mexican American literature in such narrow
terms is to exclude Mexican American writers who choose to
emphasize other issues in their work.[2] With that important distinction in mind, it is nevertheless indisputable that the bulk of
literature produced by Mexican Americans to date has centered
on issues of cultural and, particularly, ethnic identity. This is true,
for instance, of the many coming-of-age narratives in the literary
tradition, which typically pivot on generational differences regarding cultural beliefs. In the Mexican American case, the narratives frequently describe a rejection of or break from some more
traditional form of Mexicanness. For example, in Luis Valdez's

Zoot Suit (1978), we see that although the protagonist, Henry Reyna, respects his parents' traditional Mexican ways, he seeks to participate in a more hybrid youth culture, that of the pachuco, a blending of Mexican and American popular forms. Similarly, Esperanza of Sandra Cisneros's *The House on Mango Street* (1984) determines never to "sit her sadness on an elbow," the way her Mexican great-grandmother did, simply because she is a woman of Mexican descent (10–11). Again, such conflicts are not limited to Chicano coming-of-age novels; they are characteristic of the genre—which is not surprising, really, when one considers that the most visible fault lines of cultural identity are usually generational. I am well aware, therefore, that it may appear overly simplistic to say that much of Chicano literature deals with a generational transformation of a traditional Mexicanness into a more hybrid form, yet I believe this significant fact is too often taken for granted. The transformation of Mexican culture and cultural identity has also been catalyzed by specific historical circumstances. Early Mexican settlers to the regions that now constitute the southwestern United States formed insular communities in which distinct regional cultural forms developed and functioned to define and bind the community together—as Américo Paredes has documented of the south Texas corrido, for example.[3] We also need to keep in mind that because of the contiguous border between the two nations, Mexican emigration to the United States has been relatively uninterrupted, unlike emigration from other nations. Thus, in the Mexican American case, the tendency to romanticize the "homeland" even as the immigrant acculturates to his/her new surroundings is offset by the ongoing arrival of *recien llegados,* who serve the important function of bringing with them—and practicing—Mexican customs and belief systems, even as the children of immigrants and Mexican Americans abandon, supplement, or transform those systems. In other words, continued Mexican emigration to the United States contributes important forms of Mexicanness that circulate as cultural currency and influence Mexican American cultural identity. To put it in terms more relevant to this discussion, such varied forces as continued emigration to the United States, cultural interaction, and—paradoxically—cultural isolation have all contributed to conditions in which different ideas of Mexicanness compete and circulate among the Mexican American population; and that competition helps to define the various communities within the population. There are other defining vectors, of course, but the point is that what it means to be or not to be Mexican continues to be an issue of relevance and vital concern for Mexican Americans, and one reflected in their literary production.

Despite this prominent position within the literary tradition, the Mexicanness produced by Chicano writers remains much more difficult to categorize than the Anglo constructs, and, surprisingly, it has been neglected by most critical studies. To date, scholarship has mostly concerned itself with identifying particular Mexican symbols that have been appropriated or revised by Chicanos—as, for example, the triad of the Virgen de Guadalupe, la Malinche, and la Llorona—but the question of how Mexico and Mexicans are represented in Chicano literature and what interests those representations might serve remains a neglected area of inquiry, a lack that I seek to remedy here. Bruce-Novoa's pioneering work in this area provides a useful starting point. In his essay "Mexico in Chicano Literature," he identifies five predominant types of Mexicanness produced by Chicano writers: (1) pre-Columbian, (2) mestizo, (3), Mexican emigrant, (4) nostalgic (the Paradise Lost), and (5) disillusioned reencounter. To his credit, Bruce-Novoa never claims that these five categories are exhaustive, and he correctly observes that several of these forms of Mexicanness are exclusionary in problematic ways. Specifically, he points out that the first two tendencies vehemently repudiate or hold in contempt ties to European cultures, whether Spanish or Anglo, an observation supporting my argument advanced in chapter 1 that past attempts at explaining Mexican American identity have been hampered by an ideological rigidity that prevents the inclusion of contradictory political visions. Despite the reasonableness of Bruce-Novoa's categories, however, some of the subtly nuanced and complex variations of Mexicanness appearing in at least some Chicano writers' work is not easily placed within his framework. (This is not to say that all Chicano images of Mexico are nuanced and complex or devoid of stereotypes, as will soon become clear.) Nor is it possible to posit all Chicano productions of Mexicanness as simply a reversal of the Infernal Paradise formula, despite the temptation to suggest that in place of the economically privileged Anglo protagonist searching for spiritual renewal in Mexico we have economically disadvantaged Mexicans entering the United States in search of a land of plenty, only to find their spiritual and cultural beliefs threatened. Regardless of the irresistible symmetry of this paradigm, it is too limited by its emphasis on the Mexican emigrant. Moreover, the Chicano literary relationship with Mexico differs from the Anglo in that relatively few Chicano authors actually use Mexico as a literary locale.

I would like to propose that while the Anglo literary tradition of the Infernal Paradise operates centripetally—that is, it thrives by adhering to established patterns and building consensus about a Mexican myth—a small but significant number of the Chicano constructs act centrifugally, resisting central consolidation of or consensus about Mexicanness. And to the extent that the production of Mexicanness is deeply implicated in debates about what it means to be Mexican American or Chicano, such centrifugal constructs should strengthen the argument put forward in chapter 1 that a more expansive and flexible model of cultural identity is needed. In what follows, I examine the kinds of Mexicanness produced in prose narratives by five prominent and influential Chicano writers: José Antonio Villarreal, Rudolfo Anaya, Gary Soto, Richard Rodriguez, and Sandra Cisneros. The works of these authors exemplify an important range of responses to Mexico and Mexican culture, responses that both contribute to and challenge the myth of the Infernal Paradise. What follows is neither comprehensive nor conclusive; rather, it is a modest attempt to demonstrate that particular works of Villarreal, Anaya, Soto, and Rodriguez can be said to essentialize Mexicanness in ways not so different from their Anglo counterparts, while Cisneros's work, with its attention to the complexity of cultural difference, becomes a crucial theoretical ground for challenging such reductive visions.

Pocho

As the article-less title indicates ("pocho" refers, somewhat pejoratively, to an Americanized Mexican), Richard represents the often clumsy attempts of second-generation Mexican Americans at assimilation. His near obsession to win acceptance by the dominant culture is ultimately expressed in his decision to join the Navy at the beginning of World War II: what better proof, after all, of one's loyalty to a country than the demonstration of one's willingness to die for it? *Richard's tragedy is that* Pocho *very conspicuously presents no evidence that his gesture will be regarded generously by the Anglo community.*
  —Raymund Paredes, "Mexican-American Literature: An Overview" (emphasis added)

∗

José Antonio Villarreal's novel *Pocho* (1959) has always suffered an uneasy relationship with Chicano literary critics. Published on the cusp of the civil rights movement and a few years prior to the Chicano movement, the novel's lack of an overt nationalist message and its apparent celebration of individualism over communal activism did not endear it to the generation of Chicanos who would go on to form the first Chicano studies programs at universities. The novel has been tagged "assimilationist" by Paredes and others, even though it clearly is not, perhaps because the historical scope of the narrative (1921–41) coincides with a period of history during which Mexican American issues were voiced within the existing political system and a policy of accommodation with the dominant culture was not uncommon.[4]

But I will argue in the following pages that, in fact, Villarreal offers an insistent and perceptive critique of melting pot ideology, and I will speak to what I perceive to be a troubling tendency to label the novel assimilationist solely because it examines the issue of assimilation. A more legitimate critique of the novel can be made on feminist grounds: despite the fact that Villarreal pointedly raises the issue of the subordination of Mexicana immigrants and Mexican American women by men, the narrative advocates that women accept male control over their lives, no matter how unjust, in order to preserve the integrity of the Mexican American family.[5] Finally, I suspect that the dismissive manner with which some critics discuss the novel has much to do with Villarreal's own dismissal of much of Chicano literature as mediocre.[6]

Yet, however embarrassing or infuriating *Pocho* may be for some Chicanos, it is hard to deny its significant position in the literary tradition; it has long occupied a prominent space within the Chicano literary canon (prior to recent archival work by literary historians it was often referred to as the first Chicano novel). Whatever its flaws, the sweeping scope of the book and its vivid portrayal of the difficulties encountered by first-generation immigrants from Mexico and the subsequent generational rift between them and their children born in the United States (the pochos of the title) have cemented its place within the Chicano canon. In the context of the present work, the book also seems to me an important touchstone, for not only are Richard Rubio, the novel's protagonist, and his parents from very different countries, they seem to descend from very different literary lineages as well. Paredes argues that "*Pocho* is an assimilationist book not only in theme but in style and technique. Its language, so important a cultural indicator in Mexican-American writing, is, with scattered exceptions, standard English. Furthermore, . . . nothing about *Pocho*'s structure or sensibility as a novel suggests a significant link to any literary tradition other than Anglo American" (41). Although this is the prevailing view about the novel's genealogy, such a position overlooks important textual evidence that links *Pocho* to earlier Mexican American literary forms. For example, Villarreal incorporates distinctive Mexican American oral narrative traditions into the novel: Juan Rubio often tells Richard stories about his life (including the popular folk anecdote about the Mexican immigrant whose English vocabulary, and consequently whose diet, consists solely of "hahm an' ecks" [133]). In addition to recounting his own history, Juan also teaches Richard about the history of Mexico (96–102). There are narrative eddies, too, such as the story of Mario, the Mexican American sharecropper dispossessed of his earnings by a corrupt Anglo landowner and sheriff (19–21), that clearly draw on and invert the tradition of heroic border corridos such as those documented by Américo Paredes and José Limón.[7] In addition to incorporating older forms of Mexican American narrative in his novel, Villarreal also foreshadows the themes and icons of much subsequent Chicano prose. Ironically, Juan Rubio's denigration of the Spaniard and his celebration of indigenous Mesoamerican cultures (8) foreshadow the cultural nationalism of the Chicano movement; the fruit pickers' rebellion in *Pocho*—one of the most impressively crafted episodes in the novel (45–60)—would be tackled full blown by Raymond Barrio in *The Plum Plum Pickers* (1969); and the pachucos of Valdez's *Zoot Suit* (1978) seem to owe more to the pachucos of *Pocho* (149–57) than to the earlier, mocking portrayal of the pachuco in Mario Suarez's short story "Kid Zopilote" (1947). I suppose the reluctance to acknowledge the role that *Pocho* plays in linking contemporary Chicano literature to older Mexican American narrative forms may have something to do with the critical insistence that *Pocho* mirrors Joyce's *Portrait of the Artist as a Young Man.* Given the textual evidence just cited, however, we might consider whether the novel is formally assimilationist, as Paredes suggests, or whether it is a more interesting hybrid sort of narrative, one that contains a multiplicity of narrative acts within its existential, modernist trajectory. Whatever the case may be, it seems to me important to recognize the influence of the Mexican American literary tradition in *Pocho*, as well as that of the Anglo American.

Pocho is also an important work as far as the production of Mexicanness is concerned, particularly in the relationship between Juan Rubio, whose problems seem to stem from his unwillingness to adapt his Mexicanness to his new circumstances, and his son, whose problems seem to stem in part from his readiness to get rid of his Mexicanness. As a way of examining this relationship, let us first consider Villarreal and Juan Rubio as historians of resistance. As many critics have noted, *Pocho* is bracketed by two wars: the Mexican Revolution of 1910–20 (encompassing World War I) and World War II. The symbolic import of the wars increases when we consider that the novel begins with Juan Rubio's reluctant farewell to arms and ends with Richard Rubio's reluctant enlistment in the navy as the United States prepares to enter World War II. Between these two poles, Villarreal historically grounds his novel to a degree that I find remarkable, given the book's central theme of Richard's struggle for individuality. A few examples: Richard's family hosts uprooted Okies during the Depression; he and his father participate in the formation of an embryonic labor union and witness a fruit pickers' strike; and he becomes involved with the pachuco counterculture movement of the early 1940s. As mentioned earlier, Villarreal also uses narrative eddies to ground the novel historically. In relating the death of Mario, the man shot for cheating at cards in chapter 1, Villarreal digresses to tell us the story of his exploitation by a corrupt Anglo rancher and Anglo sheriff. Such narrative digressions function, first, to complement the Rubio family's struggle with stories about the struggles of other Mexican Americans, suggesting that the obstacles the Rubios face are not anomalies but rather are part of a larger social environment; second, they allow the reader to become aware of the multiple forms of economic and racial discrimination faced by the immigrants. In other words, through the course of the novel, Villarreal displays a panorama of discriminatory methods directed at nonwhites, so that while the omniscient narrator may claim that Mario's story does not matter because "there were thousands like him at this time" (19), Villarreal's narration of his story demonstrates that this man's experience does matter, precisely because it was one common to thousands and is one commonly left out of dominant histories.

Much of the history in the book is given through the oral lectures of Juan Rubio and the reminiscences of Juan and Consuelo. Although their remembrance is nostalgic at times (97–101), neither has forgotten the hard times they faced in Mexico, and as they speak we get a glimpse of their awareness of Mexican history and Juan Rubio's cynical view of the oppression practiced by the refugees themselves. He argues that oppressed emigrés to the United States quickly forget their own oppression and, in forgetting this history of abuse, enable racial oppression to continue:

> They are people who were stepped on, much the same as we were in our country. That is the wonder of this country of yours, my son. All the people who are pushed around in the rest of the world come here, because here they can maybe push someone else around. There is something in people, put there only to make them forget what was done to them in other times, so that they can turn around and do the same thing to other people. That is why they teach their children to call you a cholo and a dirty Mexican. It is not in retribution because they remember they were once mistreated my son; it is because they forget. (99–100)

Significantly, we see Juan Rubio the historian arguing that it is the attempt to erase, forget, or ignore history that enables the cycles of oppression to continue. The cynical spin that Juan gives to the idea of the United States as melting pot seems especially important, given the tremendous anxiety that Chicano literary historians and critics demonstrate in regard to the novel's stance toward assimilation. This anxiety seems to stem from the fact that Richard appears to break away not only from Mexican cultural values but also from nascent Chicano values, as represented by the pachucos. Both of these observations are easily documented within the text. From an early age, Richard comes to perceive traditional Mexican values as obstacles to his education (see, e.g., the conversation with his mother on pp. 61–62). The quest for knowledge is the driving force in Richard's life, and his belief that traditional Mexican expectations threaten this quest intensifies as the novel progresses. Also, throughout the course of the novel, Richard repeatedly self-identifies as an American, particularly when he is referred to as Mexican by Anglo Americans. Two passages reveal the extent to which Richard is, to use Paredes's term, Americanized:

> Until now, Richard believed that someday they would live in Mexico, and he fancied himself in that faraway unknown. He realized that it would be difficult for him in that strange place, for although he was a product of two cultures, he was an American and felt a deep love for his home town and its surroundings. So when he was certain the family would remain, he was both elated and sad. Glad that he would be raised in America, and sad for the loss of what to him would be a release from a life that was now dull routine. (129)

Regarding his loss of Mexican cultural values and practices (such as language use), we are told:

> As the months went by, Richard was quieter, sadder, and, at times, even morose. He was aware that the family was undergoing a strange metamorphosis. The heretofore gradual assimilation of this new culture was becoming more pronounced. Along with a new prosperity, the Rubio family was taking on the mores of the middle class, and he did not like it. It saddened him to see the Mexican tradition begin to disappear. And because human nature is such, he, too, succumbed, and unconsciously became an active leader in the change. (132)

As for the pachucos, in a passage that could have been lifted almost word for word from the first chapter of *The Labyrinth of Solitude,* the omniscient narrator tells us that their contempt for both Anglos and Mexican immigrants is born of an inferiority complex: "The result was that they attempted to segregate themselves from both their cultures, and became truly a lost race" (149). And: "[I]n spite of their behavior, which was sensational at times and violent at others, they were simply a portion of a confused humanity, employing their self-segregation as a means of expression" (150). Richard (and, one suspects, Villarreal as well) writes off the pachuco culture as a fad, a vicissitude of society (150). Also revealing is Richard's attitude toward the pachucos. He is fascinated by them, but fascinated as one would be by an exotic curiosity; his association with them has nothing whatever to do with rebelling against traditional Mexican values or those of the dominant culture. Rather, he infiltrates a group of pachucos in much the same manner as an anthropologist of old, hoping to gain access to the group in order to study its members as specimens. His partial acceptance by them as well as his reserve are used by Villarreal to reveal Richard's characteristic naiveté about life. He exults, "I can be a part of everything . . . because I am the only one capable of controlling my destiny. . . . Never—no, never—will I allow myself to become a part of a group to become classified, to lose my individuality. . . . I will not become a follower, nor will I allow myself to become a leader because I must be myself and accept for myself only that which I value, and not what is being valued by everyone else these days" (152–53). All of which the narrator dismisses with, "He thought this and other things because the young are like that and for them nothing is impossible" (153). Richard's idealistic proclamation echoes earlier ones in the novel. In one of the book's more significant passages, he reflects,

Codes of honor were really stupid. It amazed him that he had just learned this and what people thought was honorable was not important, because he was the important guy. No matter what he did and who was affected by his actions, in the end it came back to him and his feelings. He was himself, and everything else was there because he was himself, and it wouldn't be there if he were not himself and then of course it wouldn't matter to him. He had the feeling that being was important, and he was—so he knew that he would never succumb to foolish social pressures again. (108)

Such idealistic belief in individuality and a refusal to recognize any social constraint on the individual are at the core of Richard's young personality, and it is this belief that the events in the novel challenge and ultimately shatter. I want to be clear on this point: Richard's assimilation into the dominant culture is never in question, nor is the naiveté of his belief that he can live his life unlimited by social constraints. But what needs to be said and said loudly is that *Pocho* does not advocate assimilation. What it demonstrates with deliberate and stark clarity is that in the racist United States of 1921–41, individuals are not judged solely on their own merits and there are no rewards for assimilation. Raymund Paredes is correct when he says that "Richard's tragedy is that *Pocho* very conspicuously presents no evidence that his gesture [enlisting in the Navy] will be regarded generously by the Anglo community" (41), but he is wrong to conclude that the novel's examination of the issue of assimilation is "ideologically naive" (41). On the contrary, Villarreal's systematic and conspicuous portrayal of the lack of any benefit from assimilation is the book's greatest virtue and major point. The novel is hardly "achingly innocent about the coercive powers of American institutions" (R. Paredes 42). To make such a statement one must not only overlook the events and motivation that drive Richard to enlist, but also the fate of the other characters in the book. Once we begin to look carefully at these people and events and destinies, we must conclude that *Pocho* is not only a novel aware of the coercive powers of American institutions, but also one that forces such awareness on the reader.

I find it interesting that few critics have commented on the decidedly multicultural group of friends with whom Villarreal equips Richard. Such diversity is not coincidental. Richard's neighborhood "gang" is in effect a microcosm of the melting pot, and the fates of the individual members contribute to Villarreal's critique of assimilation. Of the group, Ronnie and Mary Madison—Anglo Protestants—are shown to have the most social mobility. Their father is able to get another job during the Depression and they move away to Chicago. During their time in Santa Clara, however, their Protestant religion puts them at odds with the Catholic children. Villarreal also portrays Ronnie and his mother as racist snobs. In a parting confrontation with Richard, Ronnie exclaims, "My mother's right about this lousy town. No decent people at all—just a bunch of Mexicans and Japs and I don't know what kind of crud!" (139). While Mary dreams of someday marrying Richard, it is clear that her mother and brother would never allow such a union. Ricky Malatesta, an Italian American and perhaps Richard's closest friend, is the group member who most strongly desires to assimilate. He tells Richard that he plans to Anglicize his name when he is legally of age because he believes it will be good for business ("'cause Malatesta's too Dago-sounding" [111]), a move that strikes Richard as ridiculous. A few years later, after the police beating, Ricky distances himself from Richard, presumably because of Richard's Mexicanness: "Something had happened to their relationship, particularly to his relationship with Ricky. More than ever he knew they could never be friends again, because somehow he represented an obstacle to the attainment of certain goals Ricky had imposed upon his life" (164). Still later, Ricky's distrust of pachucos and homosexuals will be contrasted with Richard's open acceptance of them. Such intolerance reflects that of the larger society as a whole and Ricky's internalization of that society's values. By the end of the novel, Ricky plans to apply to Officer Candidate School in order to avoid combat, and his plan appears likely to succeed. But Ricky's apparent acceptance by the dominant culture is offset by the fate of another of Richard's friends, Thomas Nakano. In the days following the bombing of Pearl Harbor, Thomas loses his girlfriend, who no longer wants to be seen with a Japanese American, and suffers a beating at the hands of a rival gang. Even his own friends are reluctant to be seen with him. Ultimately, Thomas and his family are ordered to report to an internment camp and the bank forecloses on their ranch. But perhaps the saddest fate of all awaits Zelda, the Anglo American tomboy who once ruled the neighborhood gang. As the boys enter puberty, they force Zelda to become their sexual plaything; eventually Richard comes to dominate her completely, with no regard for her feelings. In sum, Villarreal skillfully dramatizes the failure of the melting pot through its representation in Richard's circle of childhood friends. For the Madison children and their WASP parents, social mobility is never in question. Nor does it appear out of reach for those like Ricky, whose racial difference is not visible enough to preclude assimilation, provided he take certain steps such as changing his name. But for those with dark skin, like Richard, or Asian features, like Thomas, and for young women, like Zelda, U.S. society strictly regulates their place and what they can achieve, regardless of the degree of their desire to assimilate.

As already noted, Richard insists on an American identity when members of Anglo society refer to him as Mexican. Two of these instances are so similar that they invite closer examination. In the first instance, Richard is encouraged by a boxing promoter to take up fighting. He tells Richard, "I'm giving ya the chance of your life. It's the only way people of your nationality can get ahead." When Richard replies that he is an American, the promoter responds, "All right, you know what I mean. Mexicans don't get too much chance to amount to much. You wanna pick prunes the rest of your life?" (106–7). In this case, twelve-year-old Richard shrugs off the promoter's remarks, not only with righteous indignation but also secure in the belief that the man is wrong and that his ambitions will never be limited by his ethnicity. But this exchange is echoed by a later one that produces a very different response in Richard. When Richard is sixteen, he and his friends are beaten and arrested by police, who try to force the boys to confess to various unsolved crimes, including the rape of a white girl from Willow Glen. When the detective interrogating Richard tells him the girl was raped by three Mexicans, Richard asks how he knows they were Mexicans: "[D]id she see their birth certificates? Maybe they were Americans?" To which the detective responds, "You know what I mean when I say Mexican, so don't get so Goddamn smart. She said they were Mexican, that's how we know. Maybe it was your gang" (160–61). This is a very important moment in Richard's coming of age and in the novel's attack on the melting pot. For the first time, Richard's previously unshakable belief that he can achieve whatever he wants regardless of his ethnicity is severely challenged and he begins to doubt himself. It dawns on him that institutionalized prejudice and racism may be more of an obstacle to his dreams and goals than he had thought:

> He was amazed at his naiveté. Hearing about Mexican kids being picked up by the police for having done something had never affected him in any way before. . . . One evening had changed all that for him, and now he knew that he would never forget what had happened tonight, and the impression would make him distrust and, in fact, almost hate policemen all his life. Now for the first time in his life, he felt discriminated against. The horrible thing that he had experienced suddenly was clear, and he cried silently in his bed. (163)

Significantly, this epiphany marks a turning point in the novel as Richard's sense of being trapped by racism, on the one hand, and tradition, on the other, increases. But more important, both episodes clearly illustrate the fact that American citizenship does not confer the same privileges on all its members. The statements made by the boxing promoter and the police detective complicate a reading of *Pocho*: Richard's assimilation is clearly located within a racist environment that will continue to view him as Mexican and thus inferior. Thus the ironic pathos of Juan Rubio's plea that Richard never forget that he is a Mexican: from the perspective of the dominant culture it doesn't matter whether or not Richard remembers that he is a Mexican, for from the point of view of white society there are no Americans of Mexican descent, only Mexicans. Assimilation will bring Richard no rewards, and that is the critique of U.S. society that this novel repeatedly drives home.

As for Richard's decision to go to war, despite those who would like to see his enlistment as the "ultimate expression" of his desire to win acceptance by the dominant culture, Villarreal repeatedly emphasizes that Richard sees enlistment as the only way to escape the deadening restrictions of familial responsibility: "There was nothing to be done now except run away from the insidious tragedy of such an existence. And it came to him that it was all very wrong, somehow, that he should think of himself at this time. All very wrong that he should use the war, a thing he could not believe in, to serve his personal problem" (186). Rosaura Sánchez perceptively comments that

> Richard Rubio rejects his family's patriarchal prescriptions for male sons and joins the navy, not for any patriotic reason, but simply to get away from his family, to escape and thus avoid a restrictive situation that suffocates him with expectations of domestic and filial obligations and forces his transformation into what to him is a nonentity, that is, into a steel mill worker, a family man. Much like his father, who in his youth had set his political and personal allegiance to Pancho Villa above the needs of the family to the point of neglect, the protagonist Richard too felt that his personal goals should take priority. (115)

This self-centeredness and Richard's complete disinterest in any sort of politics are other reasons that the novel has not been more warmly received by Chicano critics.

In sum, *Pocho*'s position vis-à-vis the American myth of the individual and Horatio Alger success stories (which Richard reads as a young boy) is precisely the opposite of what Raymund Paredes claims for it. Villarreal systematically demonstrates that in America, individuals are judged by and treated on the basis of their color, their ethnicity, their gender, the language they speak, and so on. In no way is *Pocho* an assimilationist novel; rather it is a powerful condemnation of melting pot ideology. But *Pocho* is also a critique of the restrictions imposed by traditional Mexican values and expectations. Thus, Richard's decision to join the navy is hardly the action of a young Mexican American who wants to assimilate or serve his country; it is the desperate act of a man trying to escape the strictures of familial and cultural expectations. From the very beginning Richard has opposed and rejected all institutions that he felt stood in the way of his quest for knowledge and individuality, whether it be the church, schools, or his family. The book's final irony is that the price he chooses to pay to continue on his quest is to give up—at least temporarily—his individuality.

I conclude my discussion of *Pocho* with a few more observations about the kinds of Mexicanness it produces. I have already commented on the use of Mexicanness by Villarreal as a set of cultural values that restrict Richard's search for knowledge. But Mexico also appears as a physical presence in the novel's first chapter. With its opening actually set in Mexico, as well as its focus on a Mexican family in the United States, *Pocho* is a good place to start a consideration of the kinds of Mexicanness produced by Mexican American authors and the social pressures inducing that production.

Few of the numerous critical studies of *Pocho* comment on the extremely anomalous nature of the book's first chapter, which describes the circumstances that force Juan Rubio to leave Mexico for California.[8] In every regard—stylistically, plot, dialogue, and narrative structure—the first chapter stands apart from the rest of the novel; it reads like a bad pulp western. Consider the novel's opening pages: Juan Rubio arrives in Juarez, wonders "carelessly" how many men he had killed there, and enters a cantina: "It was still early in the day, but the cantina was full and lively. A mariachi was playing sentimental ballads of unrequited love, and on a table across the large room a young girl was dancing a jarabe tapatío to the olés of a group of men, an occasional glint of brown thigh visible as she nimbly moved her small feet around the brim of the sombrero" (2).

It would be difficult to fit more Mexican stereotypes into a single paragraph: a dangerous Mexican revolutionary, a cantina, mariachi music and olés, while the sexualized Mexican Spitfire dances

the Mexican hat dance. Not two pages into the novel and Villarreal has given us a virtual catalogue of Mexican stereotypes. A
moment later, after a meal washed down with mescal, Juan Rubio tells the unnamed dancer that she "pleases" him and orders
her to sit with him. When the woman's lover objects, Juan Rubio
kills him and forcibly takes the dancer to a hotel, where he orders
her to make love to him (and where we learn that she is fifteen
years old). A few pages later, his machismo fully established, Rubio's military prowess is extolled for several pages. He is a hero of
the revolution who feels that the ideals he fought for have been
betrayed. Finally, Juan Rubio gives us a treatise on the treachery
of the Spaniards, the glories of pre-Columbian Americans, the
beauty of Indian women, and the size of Pancho Villa's balls.
Villarreal's motives are completely transparent here, of course.
He is establishing Juan Rubio as a Man—and, more important, as
a Man of Honor. But he does so in such a ham-fisted fashion that
by the time Juan Rubio exclaims, "There must be a sense of honor
or a man will have no dignity and without dignity a man is incomplete," the reader finds it almost comical. Significantly, this
characterization of Juan Rubio determines the portrayal of the
Mexican setting: to underscore the honor of his character, Villarreal creates a chaotic postwar setting where there is no honor
and everyone except his protagonist is an opportunist. But in order to emphasize the heroic stature of the honorable man strug-
gling to maintain his code in an amoral world, Villarreal produces
a Mexico that is more infernal than most of those created by his
Anglo counterparts.

We can verify this proposition by noting that as soon as Juan
Rubio crosses the border, the function, and thus the representation, of Mexico changes dramatically. It is transformed from
a hellish land where life is cheap into a nostalgic but lost land,
a depiction typical of many Chicano-authored texts, as Bruce-
Novoa has noted. In fact, *Pocho* is the paradigmatic narrative of
the Mexican emigré who flees a dangerous and impoverished
Mexico in search of safety and economic prosperity (as Villarreal's

narrator comments, it was the quest for El Dorado all over again [16]). Once across the border, the immigrants are treated with resentment by Anglo Americans who nevertheless recognize the necessity for cheap labor. And while moving from job to job, Juan Rubio continues to dream of returning to Mexico even though "deep within he knew he was one of the lost ones" (31). In addition to such nostalgic forms of Mexicanness, the novel also demonstrates that continued immigration temporarily renews traditional Mexican customs and values and slows the process of assimilation:

> In the summer also now, it became the custom for his father to allow two or three families to pitch their tents in the large back yard, or to use a portion of the barn to live in until the prune season was over and they would return to their own part of the state. And so Richard had Mexican friends and learned more about them from living with them. They held small Mexican fiestas and sang Mexican songs, and danced typical dances, so that there, in the center of Santa Clara, a small piece of Mexico was contained within the fences of the lot on which Juan Rubio kept his family. (43)

Finally, Mexicanness also functions in *Pocho* as an important marker of gender relationships. The novel clearly links the breakup of the Rubio family to Consuelo's refusal to remain within the traditional Mexican woman's role. Her rebellion begins midway through the novel, and the first time she challenges Juan Rubio's authority, everyone, including Richard, feels she is in the wrong because she has transgressed Mexican social custom. Consuelo's defense reveals how her attitude is changing: "We [women] have certain rights in this country. It is not the primitive way here that it is in Mexico" (93). The episode seems to end with Richard condemning and rejecting the Mexican traditions and social expectations that trap women. The narrator remarks that Richard "knew that he could never again be wholly Mexican"; he rejects the Mexican males' privileges over women (95). This declaration will prove short-lived however, as Richard's relationship with Zelda duplicates in alarming fashion his father's authoritarian attitudes toward his mother. Moreover, the novel proposes that Zelda's submission to Richard is the beginning of her happiness and the beginning of her life as a woman, while Consuelo's rebellion is linked to the jealousy that arises from her first experience of sexual pleasure. The not-so-coded message here, of course, is that Mexican American men must continue to carefully control women, and women's sexuality in particular, or the Mexican American family will disintegrate.

In conclusion, Mexico functions in *Pocho* in four distinct and important ways. First, as a physical locale, it is decidedly within the narrative tradition of the Infernal Paradise: it is a violent, dangerous, licentious place, a representation that serves almost exclusively to emphasize the masculinity, sexual virility, and honor of Juan Rubio. Second, Mexico also functions in abstract terms as a nostalgic homeland for the Mexican emigrant, becoming decidedly more paradisal as more and more temporal distance separates the homeland from the emigrant (occasionally attenuated by the relatively uninterrupted nature of Mexican emigration to the United States, as seen in the description of the Mexican migrant workers hosted by the Rubios). Third, Mexico becomes a marker of patriarchal authority, on the one hand, and patriarchal oppression, on the other. It is significant that Consuelo identifies her oppression as a woman with Mexico ("that primitive place") just as Juan Rubio believes his "right" to command Consuelo is justified by his identity as a Mexican male. But as noted above, despite acknowledging Consuelo's position, it is Juan Rubio's that Villarreal validates. It is this third function of Mexico in texts such as *Pocho* that has prompted a counterstrategy by later writers, especially Chicanas, who appropriate and revise Mexican icons such as la Llorona, la Malinche, and la Virgen that have traditionally been used to instill submission in Mexican American women. Finally, Mexicanness appears in *Pocho* as a set of cultural values and traditions that inhibit Richard's search for knowledge and meaning. In the following section we shall see that Mexicanness operates in almost the opposite fashion in the work of Rudolfo Anaya—as a force that propels rather than inhibits Mexican Americans, but one that, ironically, produces an essentialized Mexicanness not so different from that created by Villarreal.

Rudolfo Anaya and (Infernal) Paradise Regained

Rudolfo Anaya is a Chicano writer who regularly makes use of Mesoamerican, Native American, Mexican, and Chicano folklore in his work.[9] Proponents of Chicano cultural nationalism have praised those elements of his work, and Anaya himself has actively promoted the symbolic and political utility of Mesoamerican culture for Mexican Americans. In particular, Anaya has advocated the idea that Aztlán, the legendary, paradisal birthplace of the Aztec people, is also the spiritual and political homeland of the Chicano people. This ideology is dramatized in his novels *Bless Me, Ultima, Heart of Aztlán,* and *Tortuga,* in which Aztlán and contact with ancient Mesoamerican culture are crucial for the Chicano protagonists' well-being and success, because they provide the spiritual strength necessary for survival. For example, in *Heart of Aztlán,* Clemente Chávez and his family move from a rural New Mexican village to Albuquerque, where the new urban environment gradually pulls the family apart. Driven to drink by this disintegration and his inability to find work, Clemente undergoes a mystical journey to Aztlán, the origin point (according to the narrative) of his ancient forebears. Not coincidentally, this journey is accomplished with the aid of two objects linked to Mesoamerican myth: Crispín's blue guitar, an instrument created in ancient times as a "subterfuge," a place within which to store the history and sacred knowledge of its creators; and a magical rock created by the god Quetzalcoatl.[10] As a result of the journey made possible by these two Mesoamerican artifacts, Clemente is transformed into a messianic figure who galvanizes the barrio residents into political action, a political mobilization that is successful only because it is rooted in a spirituality that has indigenous elements. Thus *Heart of Aztlán* clearly demonstrates the idea of political activism enabled by immersion in a Mesoamerican past. Anaya's continued interest in Aztlán is further evidenced by his collection of essays on the subject coedited with Francisco Lomelí, in which he argues passionately in support of the relevance of Aztlán to the Chicano people.[11]

Since the Anaya text I will examine is the story of a Chicano writer who goes to Mexico in search of literary inspiration, I would like to frame my discussion with some of Anaya's remarks about Aztlán. As recently as 1989, Anaya argued that the myth of Aztlán has been and continues to be a crucial unifying force for Chicanos, linking them with their ancient Mesoamerican ancestors and creating a collective Chicano identity:

> I believe the essence of the Chicano Movement was the naming ceremony [christening the Chicano homeland as Aztlán] I have described, and the creation of a cultural nationalist consciousness which brought together our community. This coming together in the naming ceremony duplicated the earlier time in the history of our ancestors. Yes, there was a real Aztlán, but there was also the spiritual Aztlán, the place of the covenant with the gods, the psychological center of our Indian history. During the period of awareness, the collective soul of the group renewed itself through myth; it is what the tribes of humankind have done throughout history. ("A Homeland without Boundaries" 236)

In the same essay, Anaya also writes, "Those of us who saw the potential of myth as truth, or myth as self-knowledge, argued that it was indigenous America that held the tap root of our history; its mythology was the mirror by which to know ourselves. Chicanos had to experience a new awareness of self, just as our Native American ancestors had come to that new plane of consciousness eight centuries before in Aztlán, and coming to this knowledge of our historical continuity was a means toward community action" (238). In the introduction to the anthology, Anaya also makes what I consider to be a key statement in light of the kinds of Mexicanness he has produced in his fiction: "It should be kept in mind that by reappropriating Aztlán the Chicano did not choose to live in the past; rather, the community chose to find its tap root of identity in its history so that it could more confidently create the future" (ii).

But in order to sustain this image of a Chicano people propelled confidently by the Mexican past into the future, Anaya and other Chicano nationalists must preserve and reinscribe the image of Mexico as Aztlán. It is crucial to recognize that by helping to sustain the myth of Aztlán, which he argues empowers the Chicano to move forward in time, Anaya condemns the Mexican to the ancient past. As an advocate of a myth that is grounded in ancient Mexican cultures, Anaya must portray Mexico as the ancient source of Chicano identity, and also must portray contemporary Mexico in Mesoamerican terms. The twentieth-century Mexico that Anaya depicts in his short story "B. Traven Is Alive and Well in Cuernavaca," for example, is merely a contemporary veneer covering a much older civilization that is "alive and well." The palimpsest is a useful tool for analyzing the configurations of Mexicanness present in the text, in which a Mesoamerican Mexico is visible beneath the supposedly contemporary Mexico that Anaya's protagonist moves through. The way Anaya depicts Mexico, Mexicans, and Mexican culture in his fiction is strongly influenced by his ongoing commitment to the maintenance and promotion of the myth of Aztlán. However, Anaya's treatment of Mexico in this story also bears many of the characteristics of the Infernal Paradise tradition articulated in chapter 2, and I believe there is an important connection between the myth of Aztlán and the myth of the Infernal Paradise. If we stop to consider that, for Chicano nationalists, Aztlán is a mythic narrative about a *paradisal* Mesoamerican homeland lost to its Native American people as a result of the rupture caused by Spanish and Anglo American imperialism and the repudiation of Chicanos by Mexicans (the infernal elements), we begin to understand why Anaya romanticizes the Indian elements of Mexican culture while criticizing its Europeanized components in a manner completely in line with Bruce-Novoa's paradigm described early in this chapter.

Finally, I will argue that, while on one level Anaya's story is about the search for literary authenticity, it can also be read as an allegory about cultural authenticity and imposture. That is, read allegorically, Anaya's story reveals an obsession with asserting an authentic Chicano identity, which the Chicano can accomplish only by allying himself/herself with the Mexican Indian, the personification of Aztlán. For Anaya this assertion of identity also involves the devaluation of nonindigenous cultures. Thus my reading of Anaya's text provides an example of the argument advanced in chapter 1; namely, that in turning to the Mesoamerican past to authenticate and legitimate their cultural identity, Chicano nationalists alienated many Chicanos whose issues of cultural difference could not be addressed by merely embracing the idea of a collective identity formed in the Mesoamerican past, or who, because of their cultural differences, felt far removed from Mesoamerican culture. I will elaborate on each of these points in the close reading that follows.

"B. Traven Is Alive and Well in Cuernavaca"

The narrator, a male Chicano writer, begins his story about writing stories by invoking B. Traven, the pseudonym of a popular German author of Mexican-based novels whose identity is still debated.[12] Traven, you will recall, not only created popular fiction, he also *became* a popular fiction by virtue of the secrecy surrounding his "true" identity and his reputed desire for privacy. This paradox is suggested to us by Anaya's narrator early in the story when he identifies Traven as a Mexican institution and the subject of folklore among the Mexican working class (1).[13] This is the first step in Anaya's systematic development of Traven into the primary symbol of his major theme: the idea that the quest for literary fame is a threat to the "serious" writer. On one level, Traven would seem to be the perfect symbol of the committed artist who avoids notoriety in order to let his work speak for itself. The irony, of course, is that in shunning all public contact and in adopting a new identity, Traven became a cipher that fascinated the public, shifting attention away from his work to himself. This irony challenges the superficial reading of Traven as an uncomplicated symbol of art uncompromised by fame. After all, we can theorize fairly plausibly that Traven's mysterious identity may have been a deliberate way of constructing a literary persona of mythic proportions, and thus evidence of a writer very concerned with his public stature. My initial reaction was to credit Anaya with an intentional irony that would undercut the banal cliché of the writer striving against worldly temptation; however, I will go on to show that this is not a reading of Traven that Anaya seems willing to admit into the story. Regardless, the invocation of Traven cannot help but force us to consider the ways an author often very deliberately cultivates a mythic persona, as well as what literary persona Anaya's narrator may be cultivating for himself in this text.

The storytelling motif is reemphasized when the narrator tells us that this story began while he was sitting in a train station at Juarez, waiting for the train to Cuernavaca, "which would be an exciting title for this story except that there is no train to Cuernavaca" (1). Although a good deal of the remainder of this story is indeed set in Cuernavaca, this throwaway line challenges us to keep in mind that everything that follows is a narrative within a narrative. The scene is also remarkable because the narrator's musings clearly situate him as a writer who views Mexico much like the writers of the Infernal Paradise tradition do. Note the high degree of romanticization and exoticization of Mexican people and culture in the following passage:

I was drinking beer to kill time, the erotic and sensitive Mexican time which is so different from the clean-packaged, well-kept time of the Americanos. Time in Mexico can be cruel and punishing, but it is never indifferent. It permeates everything, it changes reality. Einstein would have loved Mexico because there time and space are one. I stare more often into empty space when I'm in Mexico. The past seems to infuse the present, and in the brown, wrinkled faces of the old people one sees the presence of the past. In Mexico I like to walk the narrow streets of the cities and the smaller pueblos, wandering aimlessly, feeling the sunlight which is so distinctively Mexican, listening to the voices which call in the streets, peering into the dark eyes which are so secretive and proud. The Mexican people guard a secret. But in the end, one is never really lost in Mexico. All streets lead to a good cantina. All good stories start in a cantina. (1–2)

By now we can easily recognize characteristic elements of the Infernal Paradise tradition, including the ideas that time functions differently in Mexico, that Mexicans are a people living in and reliving the past, and that they are secretive and inscrutable. The Mexico Anaya's narrator describes is paradoxically cruel and pleasurable, and this infernal/paradisal ambivalence is, of course, another key feature of the tradition. Significantly, this desire to view the "Mexican past infusing the present" and Mexicans as representatives and guardians of secret, ancient knowledge is a central tenet of Anaya's conception of Aztlán. Therefore, although we may be tempted to read this passage ironically, I believe Anaya is deadly serious; when he describes his narrator peering into the dark, secretive Mexican eyes, it is because the narrator (and Anaya through him) longs for the Mexican past he sees there, longs to know its secrets, longs to be accepted by people who to him represent his Mesoamerican ancestors. I would suggest at this point that the passage quoted above demonstrates the relationship between the myth of Aztlán and the myth of the Infernal Paradise: in order to maintain the idea of Mexico as Aztlán—a paradise lost that existed in the Mesoamerican past—and Mexicans as guardians of its secrets, Anaya must represent Mexico in terms that further the myth of the Infernal Paradise, that is, a paradisal but mysterious land inhabited by an inscrutable people with access to the past. Put more succinctly, the myth of the Infernal Paradise provides the imagined space that Aztlán inhabits in Anaya's fiction, as well as the terminology with which to apprehend it; thus, each time Aztlán is invoked, it must to some degree further the myth of the Infernal Paradise. We now begin to see how these two mythic palimpsests exist in a state of symbiosis.

At this point the narrator discovers a B. Traven novel on the seat next to him, prompting another revealing series of thoughts:

> What's so strange about finding a B. Traven novel in that dingy little corner of a bar in the Juarez train station? Nothing, unless you know that in Mexico one never finds anything. It is a country that doesn't waste anything, everything is recycled. Chevrolets run with patched up Ford engines and Chrysler transmissions, busses are kept together, and kept running, with baling wire and home-made parts, yesterday's Traven novel is the pulp on which tomorrow's Fuentes story will appear. Time recycles in Mexico. Time returns to the past, and the Christian finds himself dreaming of ancient Aztec rituals. He who does not believe that Quetzalcoatl will return to save Mexico has little faith. (2)

Significantly, Anaya draws attention not only to the recycling of time but also to the recycling of a literary tradition, a way of writing about Mexico. We could easily substitute "Anaya" for "Fuentes" in the passage in order to underscore the highly intertextual literary tradition that Anaya is a part of, as his story perpetuates the elements of the Infernal Paradise just cited. Note that once again we have the reinscription of the idea that Mexico is a place where the past repeats itself. Again, there is a connection here between the rhetoric of the Infernal Paradise and the rhetoric of Aztlán: the myth of the Infernal Paradise is invoked because of Anaya's Chicano nationalist sensibilities. If "time returns to the past," not only can Quetzalcoatl return to save Mexico, but paradise lost can be regained: Aztlán can exist again and Chicanos can have a homeland.

At this point the story shifts abruptly to Cuernavaca, where the narrator has been invited by a friend to share a villa and write, and where he meets an Indian gardener named Justino, who becomes a sort of guide and mentor to him in the pursuit of pleasure. In Justino, Anaya reworks an idea popularized by D. H. Lawrence and addressed in my second chapter: the idea of the Mexican Indian and the Mexican campesino as primitive, uninhibited sexual beings with whom contact can bring sexual liberation for the American or European. Justino is the stereotypical Lawrentian Mexican Indian: in touch with the earth, simpleminded, devoting his energies to pleasure, and working only when necessary.[14] In one of the story's most ironic moments, Anaya's writer, savoring the privilege of a villa and the pleasures of a brothel, muses very seriously about the economic disparity in Mexico that could explode into revolution at any time (3). The story becomes even more disturbing as it repeatedly invokes the stereotype of the promiscuous Mexican woman. One passage will suffice as a representative example:

> The following night when I awakened and heard the soft sound of the music from the radio and heard the splashing of water, I had only to look from my window to see Justino and his friends in the pool, swimming nude in the moonlight. They were joking and laughing softly as they splashed each other, being quiet so as not to awaken my friend, the patrón who slept so soundly. The women were beautiful. Brown skinned and glistening with water in the moonlight they reminded me of ancient Aztec maidens, swimming around Chac, their god of rain. They teased Justino, and he smiled as he floated on a rubber mattress in the middle of the pool, smoking his cigar, happy because they were happy. (4)

In addition to the sexual stereotypes contained here, the passage clearly illustrates how the depiction of Mexican culture in romanticized Mesoamerican terms characteristic of Chicano nation-

alism produces a Mexicanness that furthers the myth of the Infernal Paradise (e.g., Mexicans are hedonistic and primitive sexual beings in the Lawrentian sense). Anaya wishes to contrast the
creative impotence of his male writer (who tells us repeatedly
that he has been unable to write since coming to Mexico) with
the masculine virility of Justino, a Mexican Indian clearly linked
in the passage to Mesoamerican culture. This linkage of virile
male energy (even down to the phallic cigar), Indianness, and the
Mesoamerican past is significant because it is the first of several
associations that allow us to read this story about an artistic crisis as an allegory for a crisis of cultural identity. Just as we will
see Anaya's writer eventually renew his creative spirit by tapping
into Mexico's indigenous culture, so too did Chicano nationalists
attempt to renew their cultural identities by tapping into indigenous Mexican culture and promoting the myth of Aztlán.

After watching him frolicking with the women in the swimming pool, the writer tells us, "I liked Justino. He was a rogue
with class." This perhaps unintentional pun reminds us that class
is an important element of the story: Mexicans of Justino's class
are more likely to clean swimming pools than frolic in them. The
pun also makes increasingly ironic the narrator's musings about
the economic disparity in Mexico without any self-awareness
of his own very privileged position. By this point, we have also
learned that, like Traven, Justino has multiple identities (4).
When Justino asks about the Traven novel, Anaya's writer tells
him it is an adventure story, prompting Justino to tell the writer
a Travenesque story about a wealthy patrón who killed all of his
enemies, stole their money and possessions, and buried the treasure in a well. As punishment for his crimes, the patrón could not
retrieve the stolen goods—every time he reached for it, the treasure vanished. Swearing that the story is true, Justino attempts to
convince the writer to help him get the treasure (6–7). Although
the writer does not believe the story is true, he is intrigued by it
and wants to use it as the "seed" for a story of his own (6). At this
point, Traven appears to him in a dream and encourages him to

write the story of the buried treasure. The next day the writer witnesses an old friend, traveling with Mayan Indians, who tells him the following story:

> "I only want you to know for purposes of your story, that I was in a Lacandonian village last month, and a Hollywood film crew descended from the sky. They came in helicopters. They set up tents near the village, and big-bosomed, bikined actresses emerged from them, tossed themselves on the cut trees which are the atrocity of the giant American lumber companies, and they cried while the director shot his film. Then they produced a grey-haired old man from one of the tents and took shots of him posing with the Indians. Herr Traven, the director called him."
>
> "B. Traven?" I asked.
>
> "No, an imposter, an actor. Be careful for impostors. Remember, even Traven used many disguises, many names!"
>
> "Then he's alive and well?" I shouted. People around me turned to stare.
>
> "His spirit is with us," were the last words I heard as they moved across the zócalo, a strange troop of near naked Lacandon Mayans and my friend the Guatemalan Jew, returning to the rain forest, returning to the primal, innocent land. I slumped in my chair and looked at my empty cup. What did it mean? As their trees fall the Lacandones die. Betrayed as B. Traven was betrayed. (9–10)

Although the writer goes on to conclude that his vision is an environmental parable, I would like to suggest that we can read it in several other ways. First, Anaya's narrator views and treats women no differently from the film company he describes and wants us to criticize.[15] Also ironic is the narrator's condemnation of American economic exploitation of Mexican natural resources while he mines Mexican culture for literary resources. Second, the messianic figure leading the Indians back to their "primal, innocent" homeland echoes Lawrence's Mexican character Ramón, leader of the Mesoamerican cult in *The Plumed Serpent*, and points toward the Infernal Paradise; and the reference to the primal, innocent homeland suggests the myth of Aztlán, again supporting a palimpsestic linkage between these two evolving myths about Mexico. Third, the messiah's warning to beware of impostors seems to be an ironic commentary on the narrator, whom we are beginning to view as a literary imposter obsessed with living out the myth of the great American writer. The irony is compounded by the line "Betrayed as B. Traven was betrayed," which suggests not only that Traven's social protest literature has been betrayed, as Yucatán and Chiapas have been economically plundered and its people impoverished, but also the pun "B. Tray-ed as B. Tray-ven was B. Tray-ed," a commentary on the duplicity that is synonymous with Traven's mystique. As the narrator's friend reminds us, even Traven used many disguises and names. Thus, when we are told that Traven's spirit lives on, it is not only the spirit of social protest in support of the poor Mexican and Indian workers, but also the spirit of duplicity and deception. The narrator's weak attempts to ally himself with the Indians and the working man reinforce the idea that he is more an ally of Traven's in the sense of a writer concerned with cultivating a mystique about himself. We can go a step farther and read the anecdote as suggestive of the deceptive nature of the entire Infernal Paradise tradition, a tradition that has propelled itself on the familiar images contained in the short parable: the noble Indian savage, the spiritually questing stranger, and the heroic, suffering writer.

The admonition to beware of impostors strikes the first chord of what I think Anaya intends to be this story's moral, and it has to do with being able to distinguish "real" people and stories from fake or imitation—and thus unworthy—people and stories. As the story reaches its conclusion, the writer passes up a chance to go with Justino to seek the treasure in order to attend a party of the "literati of Cuernavaca," a decision that leaves him feeling as though he has missed a rare opportunity. Anaya wants us to see that in choosing the artificial world of the wealthy literati over the down-to-earth world of Justino, the writer has made a great error. This mistake is driven home, of course, by none other than B. Traven himself, whom the writer finally encounters at the party. In the following speech, Traven serves as the mouthpiece for Anaya's message:

> People like Justino are the writer's source. We met interesting people and saw fabulous places, enough to last me a lifetime. . . . You see, I wasn't interested in the pots of gold he kept saying were just over the next hill, I went because there was a story to write. . . . A writer has to follow a story if it leads him to hell itself. That's our curse. Ay, and each one of us knows our own private hell. . . . Yes, a writer's job is to find and follow people like Justino. They're the source of life. The ones you have to keep away from are the dilettantes like the ones in there. I stay with people like Justino. They may be illiterate but they understand our descent into the pozo [well] of hell, and they understand us because they're willing to share the adventure with us. You seek fame and notoriety and you're dead as a writer. (12)

There is more than just a little comic irony here. As already noted, Traven's notoriety arose precisely from his reclusiveness. Moreover, Traven's speech recalls the notion of Mexico as Infernal Paradise (i.e., the foreign writer who comes to Mexico, descends into hell, and suffers in order to produce great art), a mystique invoked by writers with cocktails in their hands. Furthermore, the myth of the Infernal Paradise is fused once again to the myth of Aztlán. Immediately before Traven issues his writer's mandate, he asks Anaya's writer about Aztlán: "He wanted to know about me, about the Chicanos of Aztlán, about our work. It was the workers, he said, who would change society. The artist learned from the worker" (11–12). Here we have perhaps the most direct example of how the maintenance of the myth of Aztlán requires the rhetoric of and furthers the myth of the Infernal Paradise. The passage linking Aztlán to the Chicano working class as the source of artistic inspiration is followed by Traven's account of the hellish Mexican landscape that the narrator must move through if he wishes to accomplish an alliance with Mexican campesinos and workers. Or to take the metaphor a step further, for the writer to reach paradise (Aztlán), he must first descend into hell with the Mexican worker, campesino, and Mexican Indian. Thus we see once again how the myth of the Infernal Paradise opens up the imagined space that Aztlán inhabits, as well as the terms through which it may be apprehended.

The story concludes with the writer glimpsing Justino leading an army of women and children toward the hidden treasure and disappearing into the distance. Traven also disappears, and the writer rushes to his quiet room because the story is overflowing: "I needed to get to my quiet room and write the story about B. Traven being alive and well in Cuernavaca" (13). Once again punning is important in this last line. The treasure Justino searches for is hidden in a well. The impotent creative writer is searching for something to fill his writer's well, and this is accomplished by the ghostly writer-mentor B. Traven, who is alive and well—in other words, the living embodiment of the well of sacred artistic knowledge that is passed on from the mentor to the apprentice writer. So the story, on its most obvious level, is the familiar one of the artist who abuses his/her talent until corrected by a mentor more in tune with what makes worthy material and how an artist must live his/her life. Mexico becomes a land where the writer can be renewed. But the story of the outsider seeking higher knowledge through spiritual trial brought about by contact with Mexico is not only a story of renewal, it is also a renewable story, much like the recycled literature Anaya notes in his reference to Traven and Fuentes. Like Traven and the other authors of the Infernal Paradise tradition, Anaya and his writer perpetuate negative stereotypes about Mexicans, and Mexican women in particular: Mexico is infernal, the writer's hell, as well as the source of masculine pleasure. And by portraying Justino as a happy worker in touch with what matters, Anaya does a disservice to the workers who are exploited by the tourist trade.

My allegorical reading of the story is this: Just as Anaya's writer is threatened by his contact with the literati and intellectuals, and just as he renews his creative self by contact with the indigenous culture of Mexico, so too did Chicano nationalists view assimilation into the dominant Anglo American culture as a threat and attempt to renew themselves by promoting a concept of Aztlán drawn from indigenous Mesoamerican myth. That Anaya's story appears fixated on questions of authenticity and imposture should not surprise us: when it is read as an allegory of cultural identity it forces us to consider that Chicanos are often viewed as cultural impostors by Anglo Americans, Mexicans, and even Chicanos themselves, as they internalize the messages of the dominant groups with whom they struggle in defining themselves. An anxiety arises for many Chicanos out of this sense of cultural masquerade, an anxiety that helps us to understand the powerful attraction of Aztlán. Its connection to ancient Mesoamerican culture offers Chicanos a means to authenticate their cultural identity, just as the narrator's contact with the Indian Justino allows him both to regain his confidence as a writer and to confidently regain an authentic Chicano identity, validated by his contact with the Mexican Indian, the representative of Aztlán. The irony is that he needs to be shown the way to authentic identity by a master imposter of presumably European origin.

If there is a virtue to the story, it is in its metafictional self-reflexivity, continually foregrounding the artificiality of art in various ways (the nonexistent train, the constant references to writing, the allusions to movie making). One could argue, I suppose, that this has the advantage of heightening our awareness of the constructed nature of the Mexicanness in the story, thus making us more critical of the stereotypical images. I, however, am not willing to let Anaya off the hook so easily. As a Chicano, he has an investment in challenging negative stereotypes of Mexicans and Chicanos, and it seems to me that if that had been his intent, he would have done more than merely call our attention to the constructed nature of the world he presents to us. Rather, in his zeal to assert a Chicano identity through an Aztlán that relies on a romanticized idea of Mesoamerica, Anaya condemns Mexicans to the myth of the Infernal Paradise. In short, his metafictional techniques do not lift the story out of the Infernal Paradise tradition, nor does all the praise for the hardworking campesinos as the stuff of worthy fiction change the fact that this is not the story of a campesino, but rather of the travails of a very privileged writer. Thus, I disagree with the late Cecil Robinson, who saw Anaya's fiction about Mexico as an important bridge between cultures: "But it is certain that in extending his range, not only in terms of literary technique but also geographically, from the American Southwest into Mexico, [Anaya] has become an American writer in the hemispheric sense and has provided us with an example of a new and important role which Chicano literature is assuming, that of literary bridge between the two main cultures of the New World" (*No Short Journeys* 121). As my analysis has shown, far from building a bridge between cultures, Anaya is helping to maintain the route down which so many American and British writers have traveled before him. His story promotes no new understanding of Mexican culture; rather, it reinscribes many of the old stereotypes found in the Anglo tradition. What is most valuable about his story is that it allows us to understand the complex, palimpsestic relationship between the Infernal Paradise myth and the myth of Aztlán, a myth some Chicanos have used to deal with their anxiety over cultural identity. This anxiety is evident in the work of Gary Soto, and in my examination of his work in the next section, I will demonstrate that he, like Anaya, reacts to Mexico in ways that reveal much about how he attempts to define himself. Whereas for Anaya Chicano authenticity is legitimated and maintained by asserting a link to the Mexican Indian cultures, for Gary Soto such a link is much more vexed.

Gary Soto's *Living up the Street*

Living up the Street (1985) is a collection of autobiographical vignettes that chronologically follow Soto from childhood to adulthood in episodic fashion. The stories are remarkable in terms of the honesty of Soto's self-examination as he struggles to come to terms with his complicated cultural identity. In the critique that follows, I focus on what I think *Mexican* comes to mean for Soto during the course of that struggle and his ambivalent reaction to Mexicanness. In particular, I discuss the economic and class connotations that Mexicanness seems to acquire for him.

Like the Chicano writers noted in the third category of Bruce-Novoa's paradigm of Mexicanness in Chicano literature, Soto views the Mexican Revolution of 1910 as a key reference point because it marks the emigration of his grandmother from Mexico to the United States, where she picked fruit for a living. Her legacy and the work in the orchards is something that Soto clearly demarcates as Mexican and tries to distance himself from. After spending a summer picking grapes he swears never to do it again ("It's for Mexicans, not me"), but economic necessity forces him to resume the labor the next year (101–9). The theme of economic need is an important one in this book. For Soto it becomes an essential characteristic of Mexicanness: to be Mexican is to be poor. Several of the vignettes detail his efforts to make money and distance himself from the state of being Mexican: "In fact, as a kid I imagined a dark fate: To marry Mexican poor, work Mexican hours, and in the end die a Mexican death, broke and in despair" (119–20).

As an adult, Soto appears to put some distance between himself and his childhood fear of Mexican poverty when he is awarded a Guggenheim Fellowship, which he uses to finance a visit to Mexico (there is no indication in the text that he sees any irony in the visit). In Mexico City, he and his wife and young daughter stay with Soto's friend Ernesto, and Soto spends some of his time helping Ernesto translate speeches by President Lopez Portillo of Mexico to be presented to the United Nations. Offended by what Soto calls "pretentious quips about how the noble Mexican poor are the promise of the future," he and Ernesto begin to rewrite the speeches and manipulate the text (150). Their action suggests two things: first, that Soto sees himself as not poor, and therefore not Mexican (his assessment of the speeches suggests he views himself as distinct from both the president and the poor, in order to be able to pass judgment on them), and, second, that he continues to be gripped by an intense fear of poverty.

Both of these observations are demonstrated in a scene described shortly afterward in which Soto sees an impoverished Mexican woman and young girl walking down the street, dressed in old clothes that were in fashion years ago. Their appearance suggests to Soto a fall from economic stability that frightens him. In a letter to his wife, he admits that even his recent economic success has not alleviated his fear that he might slip into poverty and become like these two Mexicans:

> The truth is, I am unsure about where we will be in a year and what life we will wake up to; we've had close calls in the past when our passbook read close to zero. Anything is possible. Just a few days ago, while I was walking Banjo, I saw a mother and daughter who were absolutely filthy and in rags not even the dead would wear. They were walking up the street, with mother carrying a sack of things and the daughter with a soiled blanket across her shoulder. They were not your typical Mexican poor because their clothes were, from what I could tell, once fashionable, once in style. . . . When they passed me again, the girl's face met mine and I saw a fear so great that it made me step back. I was shaken because they seemed so average, in both looks and dress (if their clothes had been clean and less tattered) and in most ways aren't we average? If poverty could happen to them, then are we far behind from that day when we'll carry all our belongings in a sack and call a blanket in a doorway our bed? When we look up, we'll have the power to make people step back. (153)

Poverty, of course, is not something inherently Mexican, but Soto reveals that in his desire to be free of it he has turned poverty into a marker of Otherness (if one does not wish to be poor, one must assert that he or she is other than poor), and since he has come to associate poverty in particular with Mexicanness, he must deny his own Mexicanness in order to deny that he is poor. Notice, too, that what is especially frightening to Soto about these poor women is that they do not conform to his expectations about "typical Mexican poor." He sees something of himself in them and it frightens him. This recognition and subsequent denial of "Mexicanness" register in Soto's prose as a keen ambivalence, a desire both to be accepted by Mexicans and to distance himself from them. This is revealed in Soto's discomfort around Mexicans regardless of how he is treated by them. Ernesto's friends, for example, treat him with great respect, and this embarrasses him. When he walks in the park with his daughter (who is part Chinese), however, he is bothered by the fact that a policeman regards them as a curiosity, as Other.

The ambivalent attitudes toward cultural difference are highlighted in a key scene in which Soto is stopped and interrogated by two Mexican policemen. Seeing his California driver's license, one of the police officers abruptly becomes abusive. He accuses Soto of being a "jipi" and of "eating cocaine" and smoking marijuana. Soto attempts to invoke a familiarity with the policeman in order to resolve the incident: "I tried to be jolly as a good friend of his, and I told him that he was mistaken, that we had had a few beers but most certainly not cocaine." This only angers the policeman, who pulls out a gun and orders Soto into his car, where the other police officer tells him ominously, "Cabron, we're going to do what American cops do to our people." The policemen search Soto and steal his money and credit cards. By this time the car is moving through traffic, and Soto's description of what he sees is particularly revealing: "By then we were driving up Reforma where we stopped for a few minutes at a corner that was so gaudy with neons and Christmas lights it was like a poor man's fair. And the poor were there, along with children and the crippled selling lottery tickets, flowers, cough drops, peanuts and balloons" (154–55). Significantly, as Soto is being robbed of his money, he interprets what he sees outside the car in terms of poverty. Told to disrobe, Soto believes he is going to be shot, "a routine bang in the head." But after taking Soto's new leather jacket, one that he bought with the Guggenheim money, the policemen let him go (153–55). The scene emphasizes the complete otherness with which Soto and the policemen view each other. Both are quick to lapse into preconceived ideas about Californians, Mexican policemen, and American policemen (the Mexican police officers use the alleged racism of American cops to justify their racist abuse of Soto). Soto has perhaps succeeded too well in marking himself off as not Mexican and not poor. When he attempts to invoke a shared Mexicanness, a camaraderie with the first policeman, he fails. Furthermore, his new jacket, which he admits symbolizes his successful economic rise and has become a marker of his nonpoverty, seems to be one of the items that fuels the policemen's abuse. As he is stripped of the accoutrements that distance him from poverty (money, credit cards, expensive jacket), Soto interprets the Mexican scene outside the car window in terms of poverty, intimating that he sees the gap between himself and the poor Mexicans closing dramatically (and perhaps, just for an instant, Soto wishes he could be a member of that community). Significantly, the event does nothing except reinforce Soto's fear of poverty/Mexicanness. He returns to Ernesto's apartment and sits alone, turning "over ideas about making money" (155).

Given these issues of cultural difference and economics, it seems fitting that the book ends with a story of ambiguous import. Soto, his wife, and their friends go as tourists to Cuernavaca for the day. There they consume as tourists, buying beer, trinkets, jewelry, the culture on display at a museum. The narration of the seemingly banal tourist events is interwoven with an interesting emphasis on getting good value for their purchases; Soto emphasizes the bartering that takes place with the Mexican merchants. Outside the city, beside a river, Soto and his friends photograph boys who dive into the river for a few pesos. Soon after, they meet a blind harpist who tells them the history of his instrument, how it was discovered stringless by some Indians who were baffled by it and traded it to the blind man in exchange for a frying pan and a pocket knife. In the book's final scene, the blind harpist plays a song for Soto and his group; when Ernesto offers him money, the blind man tells him, "It's nothing, young man. Be a Mexican and go on" (159).

As I said, this scene does not lend itself easily to interpretation. Soto, who has revealed himself to be terrorized by poverty and obsessed with getting his money's worth, is contrasted with the blind harpist who refuses money for his musicianship. The old man's mandate, "Be a Mexican and go on," when considered as a remark to Ernesto appears to be a comment about graciously receiving a gift when one is offered. Yet if considered in relationship to Soto, the remark becomes ironic. As his experiences in Mexico have shown, Soto can never just be a Mexican. His interracial marriage, his U.S. citizenship, and his economic status should not preclude his Mexicanness, but those around him, and Soto himself, have allowed them to become markers of his non-Mexicanness, of his difference. And he, too, operates on similar unreliable markers of difference: just as the policemen reacted to his leather jacket and citizenship, so, too, did Soto react to the dated, worn clothes of the "poor" Mexican woman and girl whom he saw in the street.

Finally, if we remember the old man's story about the harp's discovery by a group of Indians, his mandate becomes doubly ironic. Whereas Rudolfo Anaya's narrator wishes very much to ally himself with Mexican Indians, the Mexican harpist in Soto's story clearly maintains a distinct non-Indian identity, just as Soto finds it important to sustain a distinction between himself and Mexicans. The story of the harp implies that Mexican and Indian are clearly viewed as separate groups, yet the Mexican is, of course, a product of a complicated *mestizaje* of different groups, including various Indian peoples. The old man's distinction between himself and the Indians points to the very complicated nature of Mexicanness and the social hierarchy that has been built around supposedly uncomplicated divisions between Indian, mestizo, and European. Furthermore, the terms of the trade (a frying pan and a pocket knife) underscore the economic need of the Indians and undercut the cavalier generosity of the blind harpist. Ultimately, the anecdote reveals more than anything else the unreliability of cultural markers and the need for a fluid concept of cultural identity.

I'm aware that my reading of Soto may appear unduly harsh, given the fact that the text would not even be available were it not for his desire to lay bare some of his deepest fears in honest terms. On the contrary, I'm very sympathetic to his project. The ambivalent response to Mexicanness that I trace in his memoir is clearly linked to his own childhood experience with poverty and is completely understandable. What I hope I have accomplished in my critique of his ambivalence is to point out how Soto is governed by a fixed concept of what it means to be Mexican or Mexican American. Were he to consider that cultural identities (whether they be Mexican, Mexican American, or Chicano) are constantly in flux and open to change, he might have less at stake in projecting a particular fear onto Mexico.

An Argument with Richard Rodriguez

> I used to stare at the Indian in the mirror. The wide nostrils, the thick lips. Starring Paul Muni as Benito Juárez. Such a long face—such a long nose—sculpted by indifferent, blunt thumbs, and of such common clay. No one in my family had a face as dark or as Indian as mine. My face could not portray the ambition I brought to it. What could the United States of America say to me? I remember reading the ponderous conclusion of the Kerner Report in the sixties: two Americas, one white, one black—the prophecy of an eclipse too simple to account for the complexity of my face.
> —Richard Rodriguez, *Days of Obligation*

*

In this passage, taken from the second essay in Richard Rodriguez's provocative collection, *Days of Obligation: An Argument with My Mexican Father* (1992), Rodriguez decries the reductive, official vision of America, a vision predicated on a binary opposition that leaves no room for his complicated self. How ironic, then, that Rodriguez's own visions of the United States and Mexico are just as reductive as the Kerner Report's conclusions. In *Days of Obligation,* the relationship of the United States and Mexico is reduced to a series of binary oppositions: Protestant/Catholic, rich/poor, optimistic/fatalistic, new/old, future/past, public/private, male/female, and comic/tragic. Mexico operates in the book as Rodriguez believes it operates in regard to the United States: as alter ego, as antithesis, as Other. All the more maddening as there is ample evidence in the essays that Rodriguez recognizes the complexity of cultural identity:

> Groomed for leadership by an Ivy League college and by Democratic Party officials, [Henry] Cisneros was then unveiled to the constituency he was supposed already to represent. He must henceforward use the plural voice on committees and boards and at conferences. We want. We need. The problem, in this case, is not with the candidate; it is with the constituency. Who are we? We who have been to Harvard? Or we who could not read English? Or we who could not read? Or we who have yet to take our last regard of the lemon tree in our mother's Mexican garden? (69)

This last sentence illuminates an important point: Rodriguez formulates Mexicanness in monolithic terms (despite the fact that he criticizes Mexican generalizations about Chicanos that overlook intracultural differences). For Rodriguez, Mexico is maternal (Mother Mexico); it is obsessed with the past and with tradition; it is prideful (and considers emigration an act of betrayal); it is arrogant and condescending toward Mexican Americans (whom it calls pochos). In perhaps the most revealing moment in the entire collection, Rodriguez's ideas about Mexicanness are challenged by the curator of Mexico's National Museum of Anthropology (Rodriguez is in Mexico to produce a television documentary on Mexico for the BBC): "Where do you get your ideas about Mexico?" she asks him. "From Graham Greene? You have the opportunity to say something in public, and you go on and on about old churches and old mothers. You do a disservice with your reactionary dream of Mexico. Here, we are trying to progress" (74). The confrontation "demoralizes" Rodriguez, whose shift into defensive resentment can't hide the doubt that the curator's comment has momentarily raised in him, even as it makes abundantly clear his desire to perceive Mexico in fixed terms: "They don't even seem like Mexicans. They are more like Americans of my generation. I would have avoided a dinner like this one, in a restaurant like this one, in California. Do I have it all wrong? Was the Mexico I had imagined—the country of memory and faith—long past? Its curator a woman who reviles the past? I lower my eyes. I say to Mexico, I say to my ice cubes: I cannot understand you. Do not pretend to understand me. I am but a figure of speech to you—a Mexican American" (75).

The essays are also intended to track Rodriguez's views about different topics, including Mexico, over time. He tells the reader that he has arranged the essays in reverse chronological order, beginning with the ideas of the middle-aged adult and moving backward toward those of the boy. The boy's perception of Mexico is understandably shaded by distance, family stories, and the Catholic schools he has attended:

> Mexico was the old country. In the basement of my Aunt Luna's house, I'd seen the fifty-gallon drums destined for Mexico, drums filled with blankets, flannel shirts, wrinkled dresses, faded curtains. When things got old enough they went to Mexico, where the earth shook and buildings fell down and old people waited patiently amid the rubble for their new old clothes. I was repelled by Mexico's association with the old. On the map in Sister Mary Regis's classroom, Mexico was designated OLD MEXICO. In my imagination, Mexico was a bewhiskered hag huddled upon an expanse of rumpled canvas that bore her legend; Old Mexico. (209)

One would expect his views about Mexicanness to become more complex over time, yet they frequently are mere echoes of conventional platitudes about Mexico (the curator would have been closer to the mark by suggesting Octavio Paz as Rodriguez's Mexican source, despite Rodriguez's disdain for Paz's remarks about the pachuco in *The Labyrinth of Solitude*). Equally problematic are Rodriguez's ideas about Native Americans. Although he cogently criticizes the common rhetorical device of placing the Indian outside time, and the practice of romanticizing the Indian while ignoring contemporary Indian issues, he also reimagines the Conquest as a struggle that the Indians ultimately won by virtue of their ability to adapt to ideas, people, and institutions foreign to them: "The Indian stands in the same relationship to modernity as she did to Spain—willing to marry, to breed, to disappear in order to ensure her inclusion in time; refusing to absent herself from the future. The Indian has chosen to survive, to consort with the living, to live in the city, to crawl on her hands and knees, if need be, to Mexico City or L.A." (24). He elaborated on this idea in a recent interview:

The issue of the Indian, which very few people have remarked on, is a public issue. My rewriting of the Indian adventure [into a story in which the conquistadors' culture was in effect conquered, absorbed, and transformed by Indians through conversion and miscegenation] was not only to move the Indian away from the role of victim but to see myself in relationship to Pocahontas, to see myself as interested in the blond on his horse coming over the horizon. It occurred to me there was something aggressive about the Indian interest in the Other, and that you were at risk in the fact that I was watching you, that I wanted you, that I was interested in your religion, that I was prepared to swallow it and to swallow you in the process. Maybe what is happening in the Americas right now is that the Indian is very much alive. I represent someone who has swallowed English, and now I claim it as *my language,* your books as *my books,* your religion as *my religion*—maybe this is the most subversive element of the colonial adventure. That I may be truest to my Indian identity by wanting to become American is really quite extraordinary. (N. Gillespie and Postrel 79)

This position is not as novel as Rodriguez apparently thinks it is. Many scholars have noted the inventive strategies devised by colonized peoples, including those in New Spain, in order to survive under oppressive conditions. Moreover, there are troubling elements in Rodriguez's version of this theory: his vision of the Conquest is gendered (Europe/male, America/female) and highly sexualized; his argument that the miscegenation of the sixteenth century resulted in something positive ("the renewal of the old, the known world" [25]) obscures the fact that it was forced on the indigenous Americans of Mexico. Indeed, his comments to the interviewer suggest that he perceives this mingling of the races as something the Indians anticipated, participated in willingly, and even invited, in a way that parallels sexist arguments that rape victims instigate their own rape. Furthermore, while his project appears to be that of challenging conventional interpretations of the Conquest, he nevertheless accepts at face value key elements of the Conquest myth that have been called into question by contemporary critics. For example, Rodriguez says that la Malinche's role in the Conquest challenges the Eurocentric myth that Europe overwhelmed Mesoamerica, but his argument rests on the most conventional nationalist formulation of la Malinche: traitor and seductress ("Marina was the seducer of Spain" and a "curious Indian whore" [22, 24]). From what we know of her life, Malintzin was sold into slavery by her parents, then given as tribute to the Spaniards. Her multilingualism made her useful to Cortés as a translator and perhaps spared her the fate of other indigenous women, but she was still a slave. The term *seductress* implies an agency and power that she never had and a moral judgment that again blames the victim.

The essay is a genre that does not thrive on timidity, and Rodriguez is anything but timid. For much of the book he speaks with great authority on Mexico, yet for the most part he uses sweeping generalizations. Better, I think, to trust the exceptions, those Mexican moments that baffle Rodriguez because they don't follow conventional wisdom, those times when he tells us he doesn't understand Mexico. Or the visceral reactions to it like the one that opens the book: "I am on my knees, my mouth over the mouth of the toilet, waiting to heave. It comes up with a bark. All the badly pronounced Spanish words I have forced myself to sound during the day, bits and pieces of Mexico spew from my mouth, warm, half-understood, nostalgic reds and greens dangle from long strands of saliva" (xv). Despite his call for a more complex understanding of indigenous Americans and Mexican Americans, his vision of Mexico is ultimately reductive and simplistic.

The "Mericans" of Sandra Cisneros

In *Woman Hollering Creek* (1991), Sandra Cisneros both returns to familiar ground and ventures into new territory. Like her earlier prose work, *The House on Mango Street* (1984), many of the stories in this collection document ways in which women, and Mexican American women in particular, are subordinated to men. The stories also feature many strong women, ranging from the hollering woman of the title story—who helps an abused Mexicana escape back to Mexico—to the predatory protagonist of "Never Marry a Mexican," who seduces the son of a former lover. As the latter example suggests, these stories are not tidy celebrations of feminist empowerment, but richly problematic; Cisneros is both sympathetic to and critical of her heroines. Also valuable is her exploration of the continuing impact on Chicano communities of Mexican immigration and the powerful discursive network that transmits stereotyped images of Mexicans (including the *telenovela,* one of her favorite targets). But what interests me most about her work is the way she challenges readers' ideas about cultural identity, and Mexican identity in particular. Although we have seen that Anaya, Soto, and Rodriguez clearly view and represent Mexicans as Other, we have also seen them respond to Mexicanness in ways that minimize the possibilities of cultural differences *among* Mexicans. With his emphasis on a romanticized pre-Columbian Mexico, Anaya relegates Mexico to the mythic past, a move resulting in exoticized forms of Mexicanness. Soto struggles to move beyond a conception of Mexican as impoverished. For Rodriguez, Mexico operates as the antithesis to the United States. In contrast, Cisneros deliberately foregrounds issues of culture difference in her work in ways that complicate our understanding of both Mexican and Chicano identity and resist the consolidation of Mexicanness into monolithic terms. This is what I mean when I say that her work operates centrifugally in regard to cultural identity. However, Cisneros does occasionally produce a Mesoamerican Mexico not so different from Anaya's. Like other Chicana writers, perhaps most notably Gloria Anzaldúa, Cisneros sometimes locates the source of Chicana empowerment in indigenous American cultures. The story in which she comes closest to Anaya's problematic Mexicanness is "Little Miracles, Kept Promises." Using a creative narrative structure that draws on the tradition of *ofrendas*, offerings accompanied by thanks for or requests for divine intervention, Cisneros gives the reader twenty-three vignettes that catalogue a variety of problems both within and outside Chicano communities, including sexual and racial discrimination, domestic violence, and homophobia. But the focal point of the story is the last *ofrenda*, a longish testimony by Rosario De Leon, a young woman declaring her independence. Cisneros makes clear that this young woman's empowerment is tied to a recognition of indigenous religious and cultural beliefs: "I don't know how it all fell in place. How I finally understood who you are. No longer Mary the mild, but our mother Tonantzín. Your church at Tepeyac built on the site of her temple. Sacred ground no matter whose goddess claims it" (128). This recognition enables Rosario both to come to terms with certain aspects of Mexican Catholicism, like the Virgin of Guadalupe, without rejecting them wholesale, and to recognize the strength in her mother and other Mexican American women who accept traditional women's roles in their family and community. In other words, we might say that by retrieving that which the Spanish colonial mission suppressed, or by returning to a syncretic spirituality not uncommon in the first century of Spanish colonial rule in New Spain, Rosario is brought into a state of harmony that allows her to empower herself while accepting and understanding the women who have chosen a different path. As we have already seen, such syncretic philosophies led Lawrence and Anaya to reductive Mexican representations, and it is in this story that Cisneros comes closest to producing a pre-Columbian Mexicanness not so different from Anaya's. But what ultimately redeems the collection as a whole is Cisneros's ability to criticize such appropriation of and overemphasis on indigenous Mexican cultures.

Her most successful critique of this tendency is contained in the collection's final story, "*Bien* Pretty," which details how a Mexican American artist named Lupita falls in love with Flavio Munguía, a recent Mexican immigrant. Lupita has a passion for anything indigenous to the American continents, especially Mexican and Mexican American folklore and folk art. She is attracted by Flavio's Indianness—or perhaps I should say his Mesoamericanness—and wants him to model for a painting, "an updated version of the Prince Popocatépetl/Princess Ixtaccíhuatl volcano myth. . . . And you might be just the Prince Popo I've been waiting for with that face of a sleeping Olmec, the heavy Oriental eyes, the thick lips and wide nose, that profile carved from onyx. The more I think about it, the more I like the idea" (144). Although he poses for her painting, Flavio's cultural identity does not conform to the narrow terms within which Lupita wants to contain it. For example, Flavio loves the tango, but Lupita wants him to dance indigenous dances like the Tarascan *baile de los viejitos.* He also wears American-style clothing, and this bothers her as well: "I said, 'What *you* are, sweetheart, is a product of American imperialism,' and plucked at the alligator on his shirt," to which Flavio retorts, "I don't have to dress in a sarape and sombrero to be Mexican. I *know* who I am" (151). With this rejoinder, Flavio forces Lupita to realize that in her celebration of and immersion in folk and pre-Columbian forms of Mexicanness, she has reduced her vision of Flavio to a stereotype. She herself practices a form of cultural imperialism that is every bit as proprietary as that of the collector of Mexican iconography whose home she sublets, and whose collection includes Oaxacan black pottery, a Diego Rivera monotype, a piñata, a replica of the goddess Coatlicue, a Linares papier-mâché skeleton, and a shrine to Frida Kahlo (139–40). "I wanted to leap across the table, throw the Oaxacan black pottery pieces across the room, swing from the punched tin chandelier, fire a pistol at his Reeboks and force him to dance. I wanted to *be* Mexican at that moment, but it was true. I was not Mexican" (151–52).

Cisneros offers a similar critique of reductive Mexicanness in the story "One Holy Night," in which a teenage girl falls in love with a Mexican emigré who calls himself Chaq Uxmal Paloquín and claims to be descended from Mayan kings. From the tiny storeroom of an auto repair shop, Chaq plots a revolution of sorts. He makes the girl his queen, Ixchel, and tells her that he is destined to sire a son who will "bring back the grandeur of my people" from their conquerors and fulfill a promise Chaq made to his father to bring back the ancient ways (29–30). All of this Cisneros undercuts in a wicked parody. After impregnating his "queen," Chaq disappears. To hide her pregnancy, the girl is sent to a Mexican village to live with relatives until she gives birth, just as her mother was sent to the States when she conceived her. The girl subsequently learns that Chaq isn't Chaq at all, but Chato (Fat Face), a man literally born into misery (the town of Miseria, Mexico) to poor parents. "There is no Mayan blood" (33). When she receives newspaper clippings from Chato's sister suggesting that Chato has been murdering women over the last seven years and hiding their bodies in caves (34), the girl's loss of innocence is complete.

In addition to criticizing faddish obsessions with pre-Columbian Mexicanness, as she does in "*Bien* Pretty" and "One Holy Night," Cisneros also effectively forces on the reader a more

complicated notion of Mexicanness. In "Mericans," three Chicano children visit the shrine of the Virgin of Guadalupe in Mexico City with their Mexican grandmother. While she enters the
shrine to pray, the grandchildren are left outside with instruc-
tions to behave themselves. Because Micaela, the granddaughter,
is a girl, her brothers refuse to play with her, and she wanders
into the church to seek out her grandmother, who is knitting
"the names of the dead and the living into one long prayer fringed
with the grandchildren born in that barbaric country with its barbarian ways" (19). When she refuses to sit quietly in church, Micaela is sent back outside, where she finds an Anglo American
woman—obviously a tourist—offering her brother chewing gum.
In Spanish, the woman asks the boy if he will pose for a photograph. He responds by calling to Micaela and his brother in English. The American tourist is taken aback: "'But you speak English!' she exclaims. 'Yeah,' my brother says, 'We're Mericans.'
We're Mericans, we're Mericans, and inside the awful grandmother prays" (20). This, the story's ending, reinforces its title
and clearly suggests the fusion of Mexican and American cultures that has produced individuals who may pass among the two
cultures yet are culturally distinct. This cultural fusion is highlighted in several ways in the story: the children speak both Spanish and English and enjoy the popular cultures of both countries:
the Lone Ranger is a favorite, but so is *La Familia Burrón.* More
significant, however, are the revealing ways in which the grandmother and the tourist regard the children. In juxtaposing the
Mexican grandmother who prays for her Chicano grandchildren,
"born in that barbaric country with its barbarian ways," against
the Anglo tourist who is startled that the children speak English,
Cisneros emphasizes that neither Mexican nor Anglo American
society easily recognizes or accepts the fusion of cultures that influences and shapes Chicano identity and culture, nor does either
accept the fluidity of cultural identity. Not surprising, really,
since the function of fixed conceptions of cultural identity is always to maintain privilege: Micaela is excluded from her broth-

ers' games simply because she is a girl; she is a "barbarian" simply because she is from the United States.

Cisneros further develops these issues in the story "Never Marry a Mexican," which begins with a paragraph that immediately challenges the reader to consider that "Mexican" is neither a static term nor a homogeneous culture: "Never marry a Mexican, my ma said once and always. She said this because of my father. She said this though she was Mexican too. But she was born here in the U.S., and he was born there, and it's *not* the same, you know" (68). The story moves on to explore the many intracultural differences within the group of people who think of themselves as Mexicans. The narrator-protagonist, a Chicana living in San Antonio, reflects on her mother's history, and it is through this recollection that the complexity of Mexican identity begins to emerge:

> Having married a Mexican man at seventeen. Having had to put up with all the grief a Mexican family can put on a girl because she was from *el otro lado,* the other side, and my father had married down by marrying her. If he had married a white woman from *el otro lado,* that would've been different. That would've been marrying up, even if the white girl was poor. But what could be more ridiculous than a Mexican girl who couldn't even speak Spanish, who didn't know enough to set a separate plate for each course at dinner, nor how to fold cloth napkins, nor how to set the silverware. (69)

Here, Cisneros succinctly dismisses common beliefs about Mexicanness that are based on assumptions of language, political borders, class, and race. Most obviously, she dismisses the common assumption that all Mexicans speak Spanish. She also points out the social divisions that are based on notions of race and class. It is clear that in eyes of the father's family, to be white is even more important than to be wealthy. The use of table etiquette as a gauge of Mexicanness and womanhood is also interesting because it reveals the notions of class and gender that govern the father's family. For them, poverty is not as fixed a marker of Mexicanness as it is for Gary Soto. Instead, Mexicanness is attenuated by class and racial divisions that set out different kinds of Mexicanness in a hierarchical fashion. Furthermore, we see that the geopolitical border separating the political entities Mexico and the United States paradoxically has very little and everything to do with Mexicanness: very little from the point of view of the Mexicans who have emigrated to the United States or were born there of Mexican parents, and everything from the point of view of the Mexicans who define and legitimate their Mexican identities vis-à-vis those *del otro lado*. In other words, by asserting that the Mexicans living in the United States are not as Mexican as themselves, Mexicans living in Mexico affirm their own cultural identities as more legitimate and genuine, and therefore superior.

Moreover, Cisneros underscores the bizarre notions of race, class, and gender that operate not only in Mexico but in the United States as well. The narrator's father came to the United States and "sat on the back of a bus in Little Rock and had the bus driver shout, You—sit up here, and my father had shrugged sheepishly and said, No speak English" (70). We can infer from this that her father was "white" enough to sit at the front of the racially segregated bus—destabilizing the notion that race is always a fixed and visible marker—while his response foreshadows the use of language as another means of discrimination. The narrator continues:

> But he was no economic refugee, no immigrant fleeing a war. My father ran away from home because he was afraid of facing his father after his first-year grades at the university proved he'd spent more time fooling around than studying. He left behind a house in Mexico City that was neither poor nor rich, but thought itself better than both. A boy who would get off a bus when he saw a girl he knew board if he didn't have the money to pay her fare. That was the world my father left behind. . . . My father must've found the U.S. Mexicans very strange, so foreign from what he knew at home in Mexico City where the servant served watermelon on a plate with silverware and a cloth napkin, or mangos with their own special

prongs. Not like this, eating with your legs wide open in the yard, or in the kitchen hunkered over newspapers. *Come, come and eat.* No never like this. (70–71)

These passages are loaded with implications about difference. Cisneros reminds us that not all Mexicans come to the United States out of economic necessity, while the story of the bus fare suggests the code of male chivalry that is instilled in the middle and upper classes of Mexican society and functions to keep the Mexican woman in a passive and dependent role. There is also the economic disparity between the classes and the social status that depends on it. One does not have to be rich to be superior, but one does need the trappings of the rich: servants, silverware, cloth napkins, special prongs for fruit, and so on. Unlike Anaya or Soto, Cisneros is forcing us to admit the factors of region, class, and gender into any discussion of privilege and cultural identity, and into any discussion of Mexicanness. She is stressing that ideas about what exactly "Mexican" is shift as these intracultural differences are factored in, and that different forms of privilege (e.g., economic, social, and political) frequently depend on asserting the differences of another person or group as static and inferior.

Conclusions

We have seen that sharing in a Mexican cultural heritage does not inherently bestow an enlightened view of its Mexican elements. In this chapter I have suggested that José Antonio Villarreal, Rudolfo Anaya, Gary Soto, and Richard Rodriguez all, in their own ways, offer reductive representations of Mexicanness in order to serve their particular agendas. For Villarreal, Mexico as narrative setting functions to establish the heroism and masculinity of Juan Rubio. Once the narrative shifts to the United States, Mexicanness clearly demarcates the roles of men and women and indelibly marks Richard in ways that preclude the achievement of his dreams within a racist society. The emphasis on Mesoamerica in Anaya's work can be traced to his commitment to Chicano nationalism: Mexicanness is perceived and portrayed in Mesoamerican terms in order to reinscribe and reaffirm the myth of Aztlán, resulting in an exoticized Mexicanness not so different from the constructs of the Infernal Paradise, and that of D. H. Lawrence in particular. For Soto, Mexicanness is fixed as a marker of poverty, and thus his response is to distance himself from it as much as possible, an endeavor that, because of his Mexican-American heritage, is never completely successful and results in an ambivalence toward Mexicanness. Furthermore, Soto's memoirs show how fixed ideas about Mexicanness have largely proven inadequate for understanding the complex web of factors that shape and impinge on Chicanos and Mexicans. Were Soto to allow the possibility of a more fluid model of cultural identity, he might have less at stake in maintaining the image of the Mexican as an inferior Other. Rodriguez, on the other hand, recognizes the complexity of cultural identity yet insists on viewing the relationship of Mexico to the United States as oppositional, resulting in the assignation to Mexico of stereotypical attributes (tragic, impoverished, fatalistic, passive, maternal, etc.). Finally, I have offered the fiction of Sandra Cisneros as an example of work that both constructs Mexicanness in a complex and provocative manner and challenges homogeneous and static models of cultural identity. And she, too, although in a more productive way than Soto, shows us how people can become trapped within the fixed social categories that support groups occupying privileged social positions. It is my hope that more Chicano writers will follow her lead and engage more frequently with these difficult issues of cultural identity, and that literary critics will more consistently consider what Anglo, Mexican, and Chicano writers have at stake as they position these ethnic groups against each other, and what they have at stake in maintaining and asserting difference or otherness.

Part Three

Tourism and Mexicanness

Chapter Four

✿

If a Tree Falls ...
Tourism and Mexicanness

For a little more than twenty years, international tourism has been growing rapidly in a large number of developing countries. Its economic, social
and cultural effects are beginning to be better known. Far from being a
panacea, it requires considerable precautions if it is to be economically
advantageous. Its socio-cultural effects may be fraught with consequences
for local societies. When it goes beyond certain limits, it is likely to plunge
developing countries even more deeply into an international system of
dependency.
  —François Ascher, *Tourism: Transnational Corporations and Cultural
  Identities*

I'm talking about Otherly fantasylands erected up the mountains and down
the coasts of what we call the Third World or the developing world or the
post-colonial world—the hot, dark-skinned nations that still bear the shape
of Empire's boots across their sweaty backsides. Now, where the Kiplings
and Conrads once poked around, hundreds of millions of white people
spend billions of dollars each year for the exotic tickle of the five-day, four-
night excursion into the mythological but much diluted, faraway but perfectly scrubbed heart of darkness.
  —Bob Shacochis, "In Deepest Gringolandia"

What is an expeditionary force without guns? Tourists.
  —Dean MacCannell, *The Tourist*

✿

We are poised, finally, to consider the complicated relationship of
tourism to the production of Mexicanness. At the risk of stating
the obvious, let me begin by saying that tourism has become
extremely important to the Mexican economy. It successfully
competes with the oil industry as the country's primary source of

external revenue. In 1988 the country's tourist revenues were tenth in the world and first in all of Latin America, and tourism is Mexico's second-largest source of employment (after small farming operations).[1] Thus, as a powerful economic force that brings great numbers of foreigners into the country, tourism's influence extends deep into the social and political fabric of the nation. As one would expect, such influence also extends to discursive constructions of Mexicanness and the perception of Mexicans both at home and abroad. But that is an understatement. It is my contention that tourism in Mexico *relies on* the controlled production and manipulation of Mexicanness. Nor is Mexico unique in its increasingly intricate bond with tourism; Third World countries across the globe are embracing tourism as an economic panacea, despite warnings such as Ascher's. Consider Linda Richter's mind-boggling estimate that one in every sixteen people in the world works in the tourist industry and you have some sense of its massive scope (36). Given the global reach of tourism and Third World nations' increasing reliance on it, I also seek in this chapter to articulate a warning of the consequences of tourism on the Third World if it continues unchecked along the same channels it has carved for itself to date. That I am not the first to raise some of these warnings is no reason not to raise them again, especially since I put them forward in the context of new problems that current theories are only beginning to recognize. I begin by briefly considering the development of tourism as a social phenomenon and reviewing some of the more significant theoretical work on the subject, then move on to an examination of its relationship to the Mexican myth I have thus far articulated, and conclude with a discussion about tourism and the Third World in general.

The Rise of Mass Tourism and the Tourist Gaze

Although tourism may seem so commonplace as to require little explanation, an attempt to define it proves more difficult than one might expect. Valene Smith defines tourism as a voluntary leisure activity, usually involving a visit to someplace outside the tourist's community, that is facilitated by discretionary income (1–2). While tourism is not limited to industrial societies, Denison Nash adds, it is only in industrial societies that it becomes a "pervasive social phenomenon" (39). But John Urry notes that the frequent characterization of tourism as a leisure activity is no longer so easily taken for granted as the boundaries between what constitutes work, education, and leisure begin to blur (as, e.g., in the increasing popularity of ecotours, which involve the tourist in research or environmental cleanup activities) (153–54).[2] Less problematic and more useful, I think, is Nelson Graburn's juxtaposition of tourism with the quotidian: tourism as extraordinary.[3] We might also consider at this point Nash's argument that inasmuch as contemporary tourism is generated in metropolitan, industrialized centers and radiates outward, it is a form of imperialism, regardless of the degree of participation of the host nation or community (37–52). Those who find such an argument too sweeping for their taste might want to look again at MacCannell's dark riddle that begins this chapter and consider how closely tourist industry rhetoric about fostering goodwill and understanding between cultures parallels colonial discourse emphasizing the "civilizing nature" of empire. However, I do not subscribe to the idea that tourism as an imperial force is immutable, and therein lies a certain degree of hope that its negative and oppressive effects can be mitigated, about which more later.

While most studies to date agree that tourism is an ancient phenomenon (Feifer begins her history of tourism with imperial Rome, and Nash with ancient Greece—starting points that should heighten our suspicion of a relationship between tourism and empire), there is little question that 1841—the year Thomas Cook organized his first tour in England—marks a turning point in its practice. Taking advantage of new technology permitting rapid mass transit, Cook ushered in an era of mass tourism that would also—forgive the pun—see tourism transformed into an increasingly visual activity. Judith Adler, John Urry, and Susan Sontag have each made significant contributions to our understanding of the increasing importance of the visual to tourism. In her essay "Origins of Sightseeing," Adler notes that the dominance of the visual in tourism is a relatively recent phenomenon. Prior to the nineteenth century, travel was a privilege of the elite, a social ritual marking status. Its ultimate purpose was to educate the traveler so that he returned home a more civilized person. Travel was also frequently a masculine rite of passage: In the eighteenth century the "Grand Tour" was mandatory for every English gentleman (Feifer 99). Things changed dramatically in the nineteenth century, due not only to the development of mass transportation technologies such as railroads, but also to the invention of photography and the rapid circulation of photographic images. Now people of different classes and both genders traveled to see sights, and how they responded to particular sights was to some extent predetermined by photographs of the attractions that circulated on postcards and in newspapers and magazines. Moreover, as the reach of the mass media increased, so did the power of visual images to shape the tourist experience before any travel was even undertaken. (Indeed, I think an argument can be made that one can now tour without physically traveling.) Sightseeing has become perhaps the most frequently practiced tourist activity, and photography perhaps the most important type of sightseeing. Sontag's remarks are especially useful here:

> As photographs give people an imaginary possession of a past that is unreal, they also help people to take possession of space in which they are insecure. Thus, photography develops in tandem with one of the most characteristic of modern activities: tourism. For the first time in history, large numbers of people regularly travel out of their habitual environments for short periods of time. It seems positively unnatural to travel for pleasure without taking a camera along. Photographs will offer indisputable evidence that the trip was made, that the program was carried out, that fun was had. . . . A way of certifying experience, taking photographs is also a way of refusing it—by limiting experience to a search for the photogenic, by

converting experience into an image, a souvenir. Travel becomes a strategy for accumulating photographs. The very activity of taking pictures is soothing and assuages general feelings of disorientation that are likely to be exacerbated by travel. Most tourists feel compelled to put the camera between themselves and whatever is remarkable that they encounter. Unsure of other responses, they take a picture. This gives shape to experience: stop, take a photograph, and move on. This method especially appeals to people handicapped by a ruthless work ethic—Germans, Japanese and Americans. Using a camera appeases the anxiety which the work-driven feel about not working when they are on vacation and supposed to be having fun. They have something to do that is like a friendly imitation of work: they can take pictures. (9–10)

Sontag's closing remarks are especially interesting in relation to Urry's argument that, until very recently, in most industrial nations tourism was defined in relation to its perceived opposite—work—and was facilitated by the institutionalization of the paid vacation.[4] He maintains that while the motivation to tour is thus a social expectation (if one works, one must travel at least one week out of the year), the travel—the tour itself—is completely structured around the visual. When one travels, one gazes, almost exclusively; and as Sontag points out, the gazing can be transformed into a kind of work.[5] But is tourism sustained by a deeper motivation than the social expectations supported and institutionalized by capitalism?

The perspective . . . of the tourist ethnographer, focuses on a complex of countertendencies for traditional folks to dramatize their backwardness as a way of fitting themselves in the total design of modern society as attractions. . . . This process is accompanied by the social production of highly fictionalized versions of everyday life of traditional peoples, a museumization of their quaintness. It is here . . . that some new and unstudied problems are appearing: the moderns' nervous concern for the authenticity of their touristic experience; the traditional folks' difficulty in attempting to live someone else's version of their life; the replacement of the special perspectives of the ethnologist, the art historian, the urban planner and the critic, for the general point of view of the tourist in the organization of modern towns, museums, displays and drama. The common goal of both ethnography and tourism is to determine the point at which forced traditionalism ceases to base itself on the truths of day to day existence and begins to crystallize as a survival strategy, a cultural service stop for modern man. (MacCannell, *The Tourist* 178)

Dean MacCannell and the Crisis of Modernity

One of the first important meditations on tourism was Daniel Boorstin's *The Image: A Guide to Pseudo-Events in America* (1961), in which, like Baudrillard after him, the author proposes that tourism is reducing reality in America to a series of completely fabricated "events." But it wasn't until 1976 that Dean MacCannell offered the first comprehensive theoretical analysis of tourism. MacCannell was the first to consider tourism as a semiotic practice; that is, each tourist site is more accurately a tourist sight, a visual sign whose meaning is inherently malleable and context-dependent. Also central to MacCannell's theory is the idea that tourism is a response to a pervasive fear that modern life is increasingly inauthentic or profane.[6] Thus tourism is above all a quest, driven by nostalgia, for the authentic or sacred, the increase in tourism paralleling the increasing anxiety of the modern individual that his or her reality is inauthentic. Such a theory is in line with literary theory that sees the work of modernist writers such as Lawrence as driven by a similar crisis. In this, MacCannell also steers close to Baudrillard's concept of the "hyperreal" (there is no reality, just simulacra) and the effects of the anxiety produced by the hyperreal. Baudrillard tells us, "When the real is no longer what it used to be, nostalgia assumes its full meaning. There is a proliferation of myths of origin and signs of reality; of second-hand truth, objectivity and authenticity" (171). MacCannell places tourist practices among this proliferation: "Sightseeing is a kind of collective striving for a transcendence of the modern totality, a way of attempting to overcome the discontinuity of modernity, of incorporating its fragments into a unified experience. Of course, it is doomed to eventual failure: even as it tries to construct totalities it celebrates differentiation" (*The Tourist* 13). Sontag advances a similar argument in her classic treatise *On Photography*: "People robbed of their past seem to make the most fervent picture takers, at home and abroad. Everyone who lives in an industrialized society is obliged gradually to give up the past, but in certain countries, such as the United States and Japan, the break with the past has been particularly traumatic" (10). This traumatic break with the past has been recognized by the tourist industry as an exploitable crisis and has resulted in a lucrative "nostalgia" or "heritage" industry that manufactures the past for the modern tourist, a past that is increasingly located in the Third World. Ricardo Ferré, supervisor of Mexico's Huatulco resort development, says that "[t]ourists try to meet people like peasants around here to acquire some of their innocence, their ingenuity" (quoted in Shacochis 50).

This intense desire by the tourist (who, keep in mind, does nothing but consume and spend discretionary income while in the host country) to find something innocent, traditional, and, above all, authentic, creates a situation in which Third World inhabitants are coerced to live in the past, or, as MacCannell suggests in the long quotation above, are forced to *enact* a "backwardness" for First World tourists (and for well-to-do domestic tourists). The term *backwardness* is loaded with suggestive implications that throw a spotlight onto what the tourist hopes to gain from (post)colonial encounters. From the tourist's point of view, the Third World native is backward in ways that buttress the tourist's sense of superiority: technologically, educationally, economically, and culturally. But the Third World performer is backward in the temporal sense as well: he is staged back in time, a removal that grants him an aura of innocence and authenticity; and it is this removal that enables the only superior position the native is permitted: a prelapsarian state of grace. But, following MacCannell's theory, it is all an illusion, an act, an economic "survival strategy" that provides a "cultural service stop" in exchange for tourist dollars. This "forced traditionalism" or enactment of backwardness in all of its many connotations is one form of what MacCannell calls "staged authenticity."

At first glance *staged authenticity* appears to be an oxymoron, but the term is more accurately a useful redundancy: authenticity is always bestowed, invested, marked, adjudicated, certified, framed, and therefore always staged. Moreover, authenticity is extremely fragile, primarily because the process of authentication depends on the process of replication: MacCannell goes so far as to argue that a site/sight becomes authentic only after the first copy of it is produced (*The Tourist* 47–48). Jonathan Culler neatly articulates this dilemma in an oft-quoted passage: "The paradox, the dilemma of authenticity, is that to be experienced as authentic it must be marked as authentic, but when it is marked as authentic it is mediated, a sign of itself and hence not authentic in the sense of unspoiled" (137). If MacCannell and Culler are right, there is more than a little irony in the suggestion that the tourist seeks the authentic out of a fear that his/her world is inauthentic, while tourist sights can be invested with authenticity only by replicating and marking them, replicas and signs that increase the sense that the world is inauthentic. Or, as Sontag puts it, "It is reality which is scrutinized, and evaluated, for its fidelity to photographs" (87), a fidelity that is increasingly difficult to achieve. Furthermore, the mere presence of a tourist has the potential to undermine a site's authenticity, an idea that can perhaps best be suggested by reworking a familiar conundrum: *If a tree falls in a forest and a tourist is present, does it make an authentic sound?* As a means of elaborating on these theories, I will focus on a particular case of staged authenticity in which the primary tourist attraction is what we might call "staged ethnicity," or what MacCannell calls "forced traditionalism." Specifically, I consider the case of the Tarascan fishermen of Lake Patzcuaro in

Michoacán, Mexico, a group of indigenous Americans who have become increasingly dependent on tourism. To begin, let us examine an attempt by outsiders to represent the Tarascans in a series of photographs and essays.

Through the Colonial Looking Glass: Representing the Tarascans

We have no pictures of the fishermen of Patzcuaro, though we wanted something from this place as much as any tourist with an Instamatic and a guidebook. Some sadness kept the camera still. Sadness that there are no more fish. Sadness that the fishermen now pass a hat. Sadness for all of us who must perform. When the photograph becomes the reality, when the camera records images of images, truth gives way. To take pictures under those circumstances makes one an accomplice.
—Patricia Weaver Francisco, *Village without Mirrors*

Here we can see that Vasco de Quiroga, despite his experience "in the field," had not taken his knowledge of the Indians very far: like Columbus or Las Casas, relying on a few superficial resemblances, he sees them not as they are but as he would like them to be, a variant of Lucian's characters.
—Tzvetan Todorov, *The Conquest of America*

✻

In the context of Mexicanness, the Tarascan Indians of Michoacán have become a paradox. Historically, they have successfully marked themselves off as non-Mexican, yet they have also been represented by others in terms that can be described as quintessentially Mexican. To understand this paradox, one needs to know something of the Tarascans' history. They are an indigenous American group, and many still speak the Purepecha language. Their ancestors were powerful adversaries of the Aztecs and successfully resisted Aztec subjugation. They were less fortunate against the Spaniards, however, and became the focus of attempts by sixteenth-century Spanish missionaries, most notably Vasco de Quiroga, to establish a set of idyllic communities modeled on Sir Thomas More's *Utopia*. Quiroga organized the Tarascans into a group of villages each dedicated to the production of a particular craft, and the influence of this socioeconomic arrangement has been long lasting and profound. Tarascan *artesanias* provoke a high level of contact between the Tarascans and outsiders (including the surrounding Mexicans) and also provide an important source of income. The *artesanias* have been successfully promoted by the Mexican tourist industry (which, not coincidentally, has its roots in the nationalism of the 1920s) as national "Mexican" symbols. Largely through the discourse of tourism and the media supporting it (postcards, brochures, advertisements, etc.) the rebozos, straw decorations, guitars, lacquerware, and masks produced by Tarascan artisans have come to symbolize Mexicanness to outsiders. In a parallel manner, and one with more profound implications, the Tarascans themselves have come to be represented as "Mexican," again largely through touristic discourse. The Tarascans' cultural difference—their non-Mexican status—has made them objects of curiosity, a fact capitalized on by the Mexican tourist industry, which packages and promotes the Tarascans as tourist sights, most famously the Patzcuaro fishermen mentioned above. One can walk into any Sanborns in Mexico and buy a postcard of these fishermen in their legendary dugout canoes—postcards emblazoned with the word *Mexico*. And it is through such widely circulated redefinitions that they become no longer just Tarascans but representatives of *Mexico*. Like Stephen Crane's campesino described in chapter 2, the Tarascans have historically proven "romances, songs, and narratives" constructing Mexicanness to be correct. This is not the same thing as saying that their cultural difference has been erased and supplanted by Mexicanness. On the contrary, both the Tarascans' distinctiveness and their representativeness are deliberately allowed to coexist for reasons of economic gain. In this way, the Tarascans' fishing nets have become entangled in a larger discursive net, one that paradoxically permits them simultaneous non-Mexican and Mexican status. Nor is this the only way the Tarascans have been produced through discourse by and for others. They have also been represented in archetypal, romanticized terms that have roots in Montaigne's noble savage—an archetype whose continued presence underscores its immense power and currency in contemporary Western thought. As a way of illustrating these claims, I will examine a text that purports to document Tarascan culture as unique, but ultimately succeeds only in funneling it back through the narrow parameters of the noble savage, parameters that to a certain extent both regulate and are regulated by those of Mexicanness.

Village without Mirrors is an ambitious collection of photographs and essays about the Tarascans by writer Patricia Weaver Francisco and her husband, photographer Timothy Francisco. Although the Franciscos appear throughout the text to have an acute awareness of the problems involved in representing another culture, they nonetheless continue an artistic tradition with potentially harmful effects for the people they have come to live among, write about, and photograph. They begin their book with a disclaimer—that it is neither ethnography nor documentary—although they do acknowledge that the project was motivated by an "overlapping desire to document our encounter with the Tarascan Indians, the mark they left on our lives, the curious ferocity of our attachment" (10). It quickly becomes apparent that the Franciscos are also motivated by a ferocious curiosity, one that makes it difficult for them to produce the kind of culturally respectful text they envision. This is not to say that the Franciscos are oblivious to the problems their endeavor poses. They are careful to acknowledge the invasive potential and subjective quality of photography. "Photographs have no more objective meaning than a dream," they tell us, adding, "Our intent is to achieve a synthesis between fact and imagination in a way that honors truth. The photographs and essays are meant to be apprehended together, so they may illuminate and beguile one another" (10). They further outline their project as "an attempt to portray and illuminate an encounter" (10). And: "Our subject here is the mirror which 'the Other' holds up to the self, one culture reflecting and informing another" (10). Clever, for one of the Franciscos' methods is to import a full-length mirror (since few in their host village have one), invite the Tarascans to pose before it, and photograph the subjects' reactions to their reflections. Already the reader begins to feel uncomfortable.

Despite their obvious respect for the Tarascans and their rigorous vigilance against condescension, the Franciscos have produced a collaborative text (beautiful, to be sure, and remarkable in many ways) that reveals more than anything else their urgent desire to perceive the Tarascans in fixed terms (pastoral, noble, and innocent). When the Tarascans are perceived to be outside these acceptable categories, the artists' disappointment is obvious. They, like Vasco de Quiroga, see the Tarascans as they want to see them. Or more accurately, they choose not to see and not to represent photographically the aspects of Tarascan culture that contradict their own Utopian vision of what Tarascan society should be. The irony is never greater than when they criticize Edward Curtis's use of costumes, wigs, and cosmetics with his Native American subjects to photograph an idealized vision of the Indians, "the real as a medium for portraying an ideal" (64), a critique that precisely describes the Franciscos' own venture.

The fishermen Weaver Francisco refers to in the passage quoted above are from Janitzio Island in Lake Patzcuaro. Years ago, the Tarascans fished the *pescado blanco* of the lake in dugout canoes with nets shaped like wings. During the twentieth century, as the fish population decreased due to pollution, introduction of foreign flora, and overfishing, the Tarascans of Janitzio found there was more money to be made in selling an illusion to tourists (that of the picturesque fisherman) than in the fish themselves. Although certainly not as popular a tourist destination as Cancún or Acapulco, Janitzio nevertheless manages to attract sixty to a hundred tourists every hour to photograph the pretend fishing and then to visit the statue of Mexican hero José Maria Morelos, located at the end of a circuitous route that winds past innumerable souvenir shops and restaurants.

To refuse to photograph this locale because it is too commercialized is to deny Mexico's post–World War II history. Tourism has become one of Mexico's most important industries, and the meandering path bordered on either side by stands and shops, winding its way so apparently haphazardly to the main attraction, is emblematic of the careful attention and planning that permeate every level of Mexican tourism. For example, before deciding to develop the now famous Cancún coastline into a resort area, Mexican analysts spent two years reviewing possible sites and calculating such factors as average weekly hours of sunshine, soil types, and tidal patterns (Shacochis 42).

Regardless of the Franciscos' aesthetic sensibilities or notions of how Tarascans *should* live, tourism is a vital and increasingly important part of their economy and their lives. The Franciscos' decision not to address these aspects of Tarascan society becomes even more puzzling given the epigraph to their book by John Berger, which sets out the following challenge, presumably one the Franciscos intended to meet: "Memory works radially, that is to say with an enormous number of associations all leading to the same event. . . . A radial system has to be constructed around a photograph so that it may be seen in terms which are simultaneously personal, political, economic, dramatic, every day and historic" (6). I would underscore "political," "economic," and, yes, "personal" and "every day," too, and suggest that the Franciscos' memory appears to function not radially but very selectively.

Ironies abound in the text even as Weaver Francisco attempts to be ironic herself. In one vignette she writes about three Tarascan villages, each with a different level of isolation from the dominant Mexican culture. It is the village with the highest degree of contact with the "outside world" that troubles her most: "Prosperous, anonymous, San Juan is connected by bus to Uruapan, a city whose museum enshrines clothes and cooking utensils which the Tarascans still use every day" (14). But how different is her book from that museum? Only the clothes, the utensils, and the pastoral traditions that fall within her preconceived range of what is Tarascan are enshrined by these photographs and this text. This book *is* a museum of sorts, even though the Franciscos do not understand that, although they do eventually proclaim that they have come in the name of history to preserve vanishing traditions (59).

In one of the more revealing essays in the book, "The Photographer," Weaver Francisco suggests that her husband's work is a type of theft, but likens him to Robin Hood and adds, "stealing is holy when it's meant as a gift" (24). She describes his quiet approach toward three men wearing hats, each man with his back to Francisco:

> Suddenly, he sees the three hats, how their brims are arranged in that exquisite order he has come all this way to find. This is the rare bird he has been shadowing through the dry jungle. It poises before him, sunning itself against a wall unaware of its beauty. He takes aim, shoots and in the split second between perfection and life, one hat blurs into a face. The man inside the hat spits. Three men spit. He flushes and slinks away after a bird with white wings disguised as a little girl. How much he is hated for seeing the beauty in hats. (24)

I find it interesting not only that the language in this passage slips into the white hunter/exotic prey mode, but also that the obvious disdain of the men whose privacy is violated is disregarded; it is her husband who receives Weaver Francisco's sympathy and concern.

Another troublesome feature of this text that seeks to illuminate a cultural encounter are the captions the Franciscos write for the photographs. Some of the Tarascans photographed are identified by name, others by physical attributes in ways that suggest the tradition of Western fine art that the Franciscos see themselves working within, reducing the Tarascans to objects;

for example, "Woman with Silver Teeth" (69). The captions that seek to explain the emotions or expressions of the subjects are equally troubling: "Is That Me?" (79). Are the Indians so easily understood? Do their thoughts and emotions open up to the photographer as they pose? Or are they so mysterious to the untrained eye that the viewer requires the help of the more "culturally aware" Franciscos to interpret the photograph?

The essays dealing with the mirror experiment are even more problematic. Weaver Francisco again describes the work of her husband in terms of a hunt: "He has come to capture them, but they cannot be had so easily. An old man insists on posing with a rifle he has never used. The girls take hours changing their clothes and emerge no longer beautiful. Even the babies stop crying when they see him approach" (61). A moment later she registers more surprise and disappointment when the Tarascans appear indifferent and expressionless before the mirror. They do not primp, mug, or squirm before the camera like Americans would, and Weaver Francisco tries unsuccessfully to fathom their composure: "Is this the pose of a culture comfortable in the mask of *machismo*?" (64). She reconciles these contradictions by retreating into one of the oldest stereotypes of all: the inscrutable Indian. "The photographs refuse to tell us more than we know. In the end, the villagers' disinterest in the mirror forces us to take and select photographs expressive of an artistic vision" (64).

What the Tarascans are demonstrating here is that they are not a homogeneous group. The Franciscos are put off by the Tarascans who wish to primp (the girls who change clothes) or pose with a symbolic possession (however unusual it might be), but they are equally disappointed by the fact that the mirror does not produce a more emotional response. What conclusions can be drawn? None. The Tarascans are not a people without an awareness of self-presentation or vanity; nor are they unemotional; nor are they primitives who can be dumbfounded or astonished by their own reflections. In the end, despite their good intentions, the Franciscos' project is frustrated by their preconceived ideas of how Tarascans should live, work, act, and respond to stimuli. Like Vasco de Quiroga, the Franciscos choose to see the Tarascans as they want them to be. And like so many books about Mexico, they reinforce old and damaging stereotypes about its indigenous peoples and cultures. Their project becomes one of many that etch ever deeper the imaginary line between modern and primitive, for as MacCannell tells us: "The solidarity of modernity, even as it incorporates fragments of primitive social life, the past and nature, elevates modernity over the past and nature. There is nothing willful in this; it is automatic; it is a structure *sui generis.* Every nicely motivated effort to preserve nature, primitives and the past, and to represent them authentically contributes to an opposite tendency—the present is made more unified against its past, more in control of nature, less a product of history" (*The Tourist* 83).

Ethnicity as Tourist Attraction

By now it should be obvious that the Tarascans are key players in what Pierre van den Berghe and Charles Keyes call "ethnic tourism": a situation "wherein the prime attraction is the [perceived] cultural exoticism of the local population and its artifacts" (344).[7] MacCannell's theories give us much insight into the Franciscos' response to the fishermen. If we return again to his remarks about the dramatization of backwardness while reconsidering the Franciscos' attempts to represent the Tarascans, we begin to see that indeed their text does contribute to a "museumization of [Tarascan] quaintness" that puts them fundamentally at odds with the openly performative nature of the Tarascans' attempt to dramatize their "backwardness" for economic and cultural survival. I believe that what MacCannell calls the "traditional folks' difficulty in attempting to live someone else's version of their life" has as much to do with the fluid nature of cultural identity as it does with the transformative power of the tourist-host relationship, both of which are at the crux of the Franciscos' "nervous concern" over authenticity.

Is such nervous concern or anxiety over authenticity always part of the Third World tourist setting? The Franciscos' words are an attempt to mark themselves as somehow different (less touristy and more sophisticated) than the other passengers on the ferry to Janitzio. Regardless of their rhetoric, however, the Franciscos *are* tourists, and it seems plausible that if they can recognize the encounter with the fishermen as a staged performance, so can the other tourists. Such recognition would create a situation that Maxine Feifer and John Urry term "post-tourist." According to Urry, post-tourism has three main features: easy access through technology to a multitude of tourist attractions, a rapid shifting through responses to a single tourist attraction, and, most important, self-consciousness: "[T]he post-tourist knows that they [*sic*] are a tourist and that tourism is a game, or rather a whole series of games with multiple texts and no single, authentic tourist experience" (100). Urry continues, "The post-tourist thus knows that . . . the apparently authentic local entertainment is as socially contrived as the ethnic bar, and that the supposedly quaint and traditional fishing village could not survive without the income from tourism" (100). It is precisely this self-consciousness and recognition of artifice that is the source of the post-tourist's satisfaction. Since we are dealing with a supposedly quaint and traditional fishing village, let's consider the possibility that the Franciscos are not the only outsiders to recognize the situation as contrived or staged (and thus inauthentic) and that post-tourists actually take satisfaction in the knowledge that the encounter is contrived and that they are audience members at a show. Such an argument could certainly be supported by the behavior of the Tarascan fishermen and tourists that Francisco describes: after a few brief moments of staged authenticity (the pretend fishing), the pretense is dropped and the canoes circle the tourist boats while the fishermen pass a hat. Regardless of the Franciscos' disappointment with the show, the overt staging of this spectacle has not diminished its attraction for the other tourists, who applaud and continue to take pictures. There are three possible explanations for this discrepancy: (1) unlike the Franciscos, the other tourists do not recognize the interaction as staged; (2) the other tourists are post-tourists who recognize the encounter as staged and take pleasure in the act of recognition as well as in the flattering belief that the performance is for them; or (3) the site of authenticity has been successfully relocated from the fishing to another site.[8] All three possibilities are applicable to this case and to other Mexican tourist attractions. After all, it would be impossible to argue that all visitors to Mexico are post-tourists; it is quite common to hear tourists in Mexico reject a visit to a particular site because "it's too touristy"—in other words, inauthentic. Such decisions may tell us more about social class than anything else, but they also point to the fact that many tourists still desire some form of authentic Mexican experience. Nor can we assume that tourists are unable to recognize staged authenticity, or, as in the case of the Franciscos, that such recognition somehow prevents one from being a tourist. But it is the third possibility that I find most interesting, namely, that authenticity can be strategically manipulated by the host population. This possibility can be borne out by considering a fourth: that in the postmodern or post-tourist age, the indigenous hosts no longer feel it necessary to conceal the staging area. Again, this is suggested by the willingness of the Tarascans to present their fishing performance as an economic transaction. On the other hand, it is possible to find evidence to suggest that the hosts believe that some information is best kept hidden from the guests (MacCannell, *The Tourist*). For example, in July 1993, the *Voz de Michoacán*, the largest newspaper in the state, reported that a severe cholera outbreak on the island of Janitzio had been concealed from authorities for at least a month because the Tarascans there feared that public knowledge of it would disrupt tourist traffic to the island. In this case, economic concerns outweighed those of public health. Made public, the information is damaging to the tourist trade not only as a physical prohibition, but also because it reinforces popular adages ("Don't drink the water") and conceptions about Mexico as a physically dangerous place that the Mexican government has worked hard to erase.

What I want to suggest is this: while it may be true that the sophistication of travelers has increased in terms of their ability to recognize tourist constructs, so has the ability of the hosts to successfully stage authenticity. In other words, what has come to be recognized as authentic and inauthentic is, like cultural identity itself, in a continuous state of flux. When hosts can incorporate the underlying economic elements as part of the attraction, they will. Although there are those like the Franciscos who view the openly profit-oriented nature of such tourist spectacles with disdain, there are other tourists who find the *manner* in which the transaction is conducted "authentic" and thus attractive. The passing of the straw hats from circling canoes can be viewed as just as quaint and picturesque as the pretend fishing. We could go so far as to argue that the passing of the hats is done in such a way that it becomes even more authentic, and thus more pleasing, than the fishing itself. After all, one doesn't mind being presented with the magician's bill when it is pulled from behind one's ear. So while we may have reached a postmodern moment when we are able to recognize some tourist displays as constructs and either reject them as such (as the Franciscos do) or take pleasure in their very constructedness, the ability to conceal—to effectively stage—has evolved at a parallel rate. While tourists may be more sophisticated in recognizing certain attractions as constructs, new constructs continue to beguile. The pretend fishing of Janitzio may be viewed as inauthentic, but not the passing of the hat. Ironically, the economic transaction itself has been successfully transformed by the Tarascans into an "authentic" and thus touristworthy attraction. All of which leads to the inescapable conclusion that the greatest tourist construct of all time is none other than the concept of authenticity.

Earlier I suggested that not only is the coercive nature of tourism in the Third World fundamentally at odds with one of its major objectives (ethnic or cultural authenticity), but that the fluid nature of cultural identity also makes cultural authenticity difficult to fix. Interaction with tourists may initially provoke unconventional behavior, (e.g., learning how to pose picturesquely rather than actually fishing), but such behavior can always be reintegrated into the community's sense of identity. It is not hard to imagine the Tarascans of Janitzio as making their current occupations as tourist attractions an integral part of who they are—tourist performer may over time come to be viewed as a very traditional Tarascan quality. Such a transformation of cultural identity was documented by Oriol Pi-Sunyer in his study of a Catalan fishing village. Initially a source of resentment for local residents, tourism eventually became so important to the local economy that the inhabitants came to think of themselves as a tourist community rather than a fishing community. The extent of this transformation was starkly dramatized in 1987 when the community actively protested commercial fishing as a threat to the environment and the tourist trade. No doubt the protests also had much to do with differences between small- and large-scale fishing operations, but the repeated and specific mention of tourism as something worthy of the community's protection is indicative of a major shift in community identity. This phenomenon is also visible in the transformation of indigenous Mexican crafts from traditional items valued for their practical function to tourist souvenirs valued for their exotic appearance; the transformed crafts are gradually reincorporated into the host cultures as new types of traditional art. Furthermore, tourists' demand for authenticity can also stimulate renewed interest in dormant or abandoned cultural traditions on the part of the host communities, as in the case of Louisiana Cajun communities and in the Tarascan region.[9] Regarding the latter, Robert Kemper notes that tourism and urban encroachment have had

> the curious effect of strengthening certain aspects of traditional life, in particular fiestas and rituals like the Night of the Dead or the Holy Week celebrations in the Lake Patzcuaro region. In one sense the foreigners now "consume" these experiences as if they were

items for sale. Although many of the benefits derived from these developments fall to intermediaries and other outsiders, *there is no doubt that the local residents and returning migrants see the external interest in local tradition as a reaffirmation of the actual value of the community's culture.* (85; emphasis added)

Kemper's argument is borne out by Stanley Brandes's fascinating case study of the Night of the Dead festival in Tzintzuntzan, Michoacán (another Lake Patzcuaro community). Here, in 1971, state intervention expressly for the purpose of increasing tourism to the region methodically transformed what had been an intimate religious observance for family members into a full-blown spectacle ("practically a theatrical performance") that now attracts droves of tourists and a nationwide television audience. Although the tourism campaign has greatly increased the community's self-esteem, it seems also to have transformed a once solely religious ritual into a more secularized one. Even more intriguing is Brandes's observation that the citizens of Tzintzuntzan now look forward with great anticipation to viewing the tourists, a phenomenon that to date has received insufficient attention by tourism theorists: the extent to which tourists who come to see exotic sights themselves become exotic sights for the local residents. We should also consider that the Tzintzuntzan case is exceptional in that its main attraction is an annual event that occurs over a limited period—thus minimizing the strain on the local community in comparison with host communities that experience a year-round tourist influx (Brandes 88–109).

Finally, we cannot assume that authenticity is inherently desired by the tourist. There are tourists who assiduously avoid the authentic, depending on what it connotes, as in the tourist who visits Cancún but does not want to venture outside the tourist bubble because the "real" Mexico is somehow all too authentically dangerous. There are also tourist attractions that are popular precisely because they house nothing but replicas (e.g., Walt Disney World and Madame Tussaud's Wax Museum), sights/sites suggesting the necessity for the oxymoron "authentic replicas."

That authenticity ultimately proves to be so elusive should not surprise us. It is a concept that can be apprehended and authorized only by semiotic markers, markers that, MacCannell argues, are culturally variable and continually in flux: "[T]he point is that tourist attractions are [malleable]: the eventual shape and stability they have is, like signs, socially determined. . . . And society, not the individual, divides reality into what is to be taken as a sight and what is to be taken as information about a sight" (*The Tourist* 132–33). Urry provides an excellent illustration of this point in his history of Niagara Falls, a tourist sight that first commanded attention in the eighteenth century as an awesome display of natural power, then came to be valued in the nineteenth century as a sublime romantic symbol, and now, in the latter twentieth century, has come to symbolize American kitsch (62).

MacCannell's groundbreaking work raises questions that are difficult to answer. For him, the modern is a juggernaut producing a malaise, a nostalgia for the authentic premodern that drives tourism and has created what Bob Shacochis calls the Third World as tourist theme park. In this giant theme park the premodern or traditional is staged for the tourist even as the country rapidly modernizes in order to provide the infrastructure necessary to maximize tourism profits. At first glance, there would appear to be a tremendous tension between these two industry dynamics: the more modern the Third World becomes—the more it resembles the tourist's own world—the more difficult it becomes to stage authenticity. Or, as Shacochis puts it, "By this time, my questions had essentially narrowed to one: What amid all the developing— all the massive hotels and computer stores and video bars— would there be to remind a gringo that he was in Mexico?" (49).

Mexican Theme Parks/Mexico as Theme Park

In examining the implications of Shacochis's question it is useful to first consider the way Mexico is represented in the world's most famous theme park. One of Walt Disney World's most popular sectors is the Epcot Center, which features a select group of international "settings." Mexico is one of the chosen few. The mini-Mexican theme park is housed, of course, within a giant "Mayan" pyramid and contains only the most familiar of Mexican markers. The entrance to the exhibit is dark and museumlike and has a decidedly pre-Columbian emphasis: the walls are covered with a mural depicting Palenque at its supposed zenith (including a gory human sacrifice), while the room itself contains replicas of Mesoamerican artifacts from different pre-Columbian periods. From the dark pre-Columbian era the visitor exits into an "enlightened" colonial setting: a plaza surrounded by pseudo-colonial architecture. Mexican crafts are for sale here, and a mariachi band plays before a backdrop of a Mayan pyramid and smoldering volcano. But the main attraction of Disney's Mexico is the "River of Time" boat ride. Visitors climb into small vessels that whisk them back in time, emerging first in a steamy jungle surrounded by pyramids, then moving into a brightly lit room where animatronic puppets of Mexican children sing, dance, and break piñatas while, overhead, sombrero-clad skeletons play guitars. Next the boats pass beside video screens that project Mexican vendors trying to sell arts and crafts to the visitors, reappearing on each subsequent screen in order to give the impression of relentless pursuit. Their images are then replaced by a resort setting, which in turn is replaced by images of Mexico City.[10]

What does such a shamelessly predictable collection of stereotypical Mexican markers have to do with Mexican tourism? Well, for one thing, Disney's Mexican exhibit also houses an office of the Mexican Secretariat of Tourism where visitors can pick up brochures on Mexican tourist destinations and ask questions of the representatives. But more important, the success of theme parks like Disney World has forced the Mexican Secretariat of Tourism to adopt theme park strategies in its planning and promotion, particularly in the design of the so-called megaresorts (or, to use official terminology, "integrally planned beach centers"), tourist parks designed and built completely from the ground up (Hall 98).[11] Cancún, the prototype for these megaresorts, was selected in 1968 after computers had sifted through two years' worth of research on Mexico's coasts (Shacochis 45). Perhaps the first "city" ever built exclusively for tourists, Cancún has succeeded beyond the Mexican government's wildest expectations, surpassing Acapulco in 1990 as Mexico's most visited seaside resort (Hall 98), and spurring a spate of copycat projects, including the even more grandly conceived Huatulco on the Pacific coast. The palimpsest is once again a useful metaphor for understanding the effects of such resort developments. As Shacochis's question intimates, these completely modern, carefully designed, and sanitized tourist resorts so totally transform the landscape that they effectively erase most of the markers that the Infernal Paradise tradition has trained outsiders to read as authentically Mexican (like those at Disney's Epcot Center), creating a bizarre situation in which the tourist developers must selectively reconstruct Mexicanness—or, to use MacCannell's theory, must strategically stage "authentic" Mexicanness. Thus, in its official brochure promoting Huatulco, the Mexican Secretariat of Tourism proudly announces, "There is even an authentic Mexican village that is a charming focal point for the resort's activity," an authentic village that Veronica Long tells us was created for local fishermen after the government expropriated their beachfront property (210). The secretariat learned the hard way how important such staged authenticity is when its infrastructural makeover of Loreto in Baja California left the town with no identifiable "authentic" Mexicanness whatsoever, and a profound lack of tourist interest (Hall 154). A less subtle response to staging Mexicanness has been the creation of Disney-type theme parks within the tourist parks themselves: Cancún now boasts a Mexican theme park called México Mágico.

In short, the literary myth of the Infernal Paradise has been reified as a chain of Infernal Paradise theme parks built by Mexico's own government—using the texts that created the myth as blueprints. To support this argument I will briefly reconsider the famous passage by Malcolm Lowry quoted at the beginning of chapter 2, juxtaposing it with a description of Mexico from the secretariat's official "overview" brochure sent to me in May 1994. First Lowry's passage:

> The scene is Mexico, the meeting place, according to some, of mankind itself, pyre of Bierce and springboard of Hart Crane, the age-old arena of racial and political conflicts of every nature, and where a colorful native people of genius have a religion that we can roughly describe as one of death, so that it is a good place, at least as good as Lancashire or Yorkshire, to set our drama of a man's struggle between the power of darkness and light. Its geographical remoteness from us, as well as the closeness of its problems to our own, will assist the tragedy each in its own way. We can see it as the world itself, or the Garden of Eden, or both at once. Or we can see it as a kind of timeless symbol of the world on which we can place the Garden of Eden, the Tower of Babel and indeed anything else we please. It is paradisal: it is unquestionably infernal. It is, in fact, Mexico . . . (*Selected Letters* 67)

Now the secretariat's description:

> Mexico is a land of contrasts. From the vibrant color woven into our textiles to the stunning hues of our landscape. From mountain ranges that run right up to the ocean edge to lush tropical jungles and high, snowcapped volcanos. It is Aztec pyramids that stand like sentinels over modern subway stations. And Mayan ruins that decorate luxury resorts. Above all, it is a proud people in whom runs the blood of the Spanish, the French, and over 150 native peoples who have called Mexico home. As visitors have found, a trip to Mexico is a trip like no other. Yes, Mexico is a 20th century playground. But one with a rich and glorious past. When Rome was falling, when Paris was still just an island in the Seine, Mexico's civilization was already flourishing. Here the original people of Mexico already had advanced knowledge of science, mathematics, astronomy and medicine. They had well-established social and legal systems. And they lived in urban centers that would make today's

city planners jealous. That past still permeates this land. You'll find it in the traditions that have been passed down from generation to generation. It lives on in the arts and music. And in the peculiar philosophy about life and death that make the Mexican people so unique—and so charming. It is something to be experienced, something that works its way into your soul. So whether you are coming to explore our archaeological treasures, wander through our colonial cities, or simply relax on one of our beautiful beaches, rest assured. You will take home memories. But you will take home some of the magic of Mexico as well. (*Mexico Mexico* 1–2)

That these passages echo one another so resonantly is a reminder that Lowry was utilizing advertising rhetoric to promote his as yet unpublished novel about Mexico. More important, however, the two passages demonstrate the degree to which advertising rhetoric relies on Infernal Paradise tropes to promote Mexican tourism. The relationship between such literary production and tourism's impact on developing nations cannot be overstated. Literature and other discourses produced outside the Third World determine what will be perceived by the tourist as culturally authentic, and with tourism appearing more and more as an economic panacea to developing nations, there is tremendous pressure to adapt their cultures to the discursive constructs created of them by the First World. It is in this way that tourism is very much a colonizing force and a form of imperialism. François Ascher points out that travel reports—literary, pictorial, photographic, and cinematographic—produced by First World writers, artists, and intellectuals unwittingly play a crucial role in the development of the tourist industry by creating charismatic and exotic images of developing nations that become instant reference points for tourist organizers: "But the absurdity is not that [tourists] end up by seeing countries more or less as they had already imagined them, but that as a result of the actual measures taken by [tour operators], the countries visited end up by corresponding to the tourists' expectations, at least as far as certain landscapes are concerned" (63). Thus, I want to emphasize not only the important link between literary discourse and the successful maintenance of tourism in developing nations, but also the importance of the Infernal Paradise myth as one of the key frames of reference for Mexican tourist propaganda.

Why worry about the impact of such propaganda? To answer that question, we should consider the degree to which tourism has been centralized, bureaucratized, and systematized in Mexico and the importance it has achieved not only for the nation's economy but in the national psyche as well. In comparison with most developing nations, Mexico's approach has been exceptional. Government planning dating back to 1929 has to some degree enabled the Mexican government to circumvent the closed system of transnational tourism corporations that limits economic benefit to the host country.[12] In fact, many of the recommendations outlined in Ascher's 1985 UNESCO report (for developing nations interested in developing tourism without becoming dependent on transnational corporations) have long been in place in Mexico (81–82). Nevertheless, foreign investment in tourist projects in Mexico, particularly through the lending of international credit, has meant that a considerable portion of tourist revenue flows out of the country.[13] And even though Mexico may be less dependent on transnational corporations than other Third World nations, it is nonetheless dependent on tourist income, and without it would crumble economically. Tourism is, as Shacochis comments, "an economic detonator . . . , a magnet for foreign currency, [and] an alternative destination for landless migrants flooding urban centers, especially Mexico City" (44). As for systemization, consider that between 1968 and 1988 Mexico successfully carried out an endogenous twenty-year plan in which tourist "communities" at Cancún, Ixtapa, and Los Cabos (the integrally planned megaresorts I spoke of earlier) were built from the ground up. By now it should come as no surprise that the emphasis on developing tourist theme parks has required a thematic marketing approach. In 1990, FONATUR—the development and finance arm of the secretariat—spent $20 million to promote

Mexico as a tourist destination, an intense advertising campaign that bears directly on the production of Mexicanness.

Mexican Tourist Propaganda and Mexicanness

> So come, play in our warm waters. Relax on some of the most beautiful beaches in the world. Climb the steps of a pyramid and go back to a different time, when incredible civilizations ruled this land. Then chat over a cold margarita with some of the direct descendants of those people. Stroll along the cobblestone streets of a colonial town. Gaze up at the spires of a baroque cathedral. And as the notes of a timeless melody drift from a balcony overhead, let the magic of Mexico carry you away.
>
> Mexico, Secretariat of Tourism, *Mexico Mexico*

✣

The marketing strategy we see emerging from the Mexican tourism industry is a shrewd form of the simultaneous Mexican narratives that Robert Stone presents so well in *Children of Light,* an approach I call—in a very literal sense—Dial-a-Mexico. The Secretariat of Tourism has a toll-free number in the United States that puts potential tourists in touch with a representative who helps them select the kind of Mexican adventure they want to experience.[14] Since 1993, the secretariat has organized tourism marketing around the two central tropes of magic and dreams. Its campaign logo consists of the word *MEXICO* positioned over an emblem made to resemble a Mayan glyph, under which runs one of two slogans: "Everything you ever dreamed of" and "The magic never leaves you." In addition to these two general themes, the secretariat has created six tourist "genres" with which to classify all Mexican tourist attractions: sun and surf, pre-Columbian civilization, ecotourism adventure, the Spanish colonial period, the "art and soul" of Mexico, and sports and recreation. With perhaps the exception of the sports and recreation category, each of these tourist genres is derived directly from motifs popularized by the texts of the Infernal Paradise tradition. For example, increasingly popular ecotours are but the most recent incarnation of the idea of spiritual renewal through a journey into the wilderness, an archetypal motif we have seen to be at the core of many of the Infernal Paradise novels. Moreover, each of the six categories is further thematized. The secretariat's 1993 sun and surf brochure, for example, creates a distinct mystique for each of its major beach resorts. Acapulco is characterized as "the boisterous Riviera of the West"; Cancún as a "tropical paradise"; Cozumel as a "spectacular natural aquarium"; Huatulco as an "undiscovered, secluded gem"; Ixtapa/Zihuatanejo as a resort with a modern/premodern "split personality"; La Paz as Mexico's "uncommercialized" resort; Loreto is the "desert by the sea" (somewhat ironic, since as noted above, it is more properly "deserted" by the sea); Los Cabos is a resort designed for fishing and sports enthusiasts; and so on. (A 1990 government-sponsored report generated to encourage foreign investment in its tourism projects refers to the development of Mexico's northwest coast as centered on the themes "The Next Mediterranean" and "The World's Largest Aquarium.") But while the thematic grouping of Mexican tourist attractions aids the industry by creating easily recognizable fantasies from which tourists may select, it's important to keep in mind that the strategy is not to separate the themes but to allow the consumer to rearrange them in any combination he or she might desire. This is consistent with Mexico's ultimate marketing goal: to portray Mexico as infinitely malleable, a place that can be, in the industry's catchphrase, "everything you ever dreamed of," or, to paraphrase Lowry, a place on which the tourist can place anything he or she pleases. It is not uncommon to find ads for Mexican tourism that picture Aztec or Mayan pyramids juxtaposed against spotless white beaches, reinforcing the idea that these different themes can be experienced simultaneously. Paradoxically, the claims of infinite variety rest on variations on a limited number of predominant Mexican themes, themes that significantly and deliberately accrue elements of Mexicanness created by the Infernal Paradise texts: the exotic,

the primitive, the ancient, the magical, the mysterious, the colorful. These thematic Mexicos coexist like the different sectors of
Disney World, a similarity that industry ads have even begun to
self-consciously acknowledge in post-tourist gestures. A recent
government ad, for example, prominently features the famous
Mayan temple El Castillo under the heading "The Original Magic
Kingdom." Nor is such Disneyfication of a Mexican tourist attraction an isolated event. Rosemary Lee notes that during the
1970s, the "restoration" of archaeological sites in the Yucatán
peninsula included the addition of sound and light shows with
recorded narrations by Charlton Heston (182). The theme park
has come full circle. Originally a means of presenting simulacra
of famous global tourist attractions in close proximity to one another (the theme park, after all, is a descendant of the World's
Fair), the success of theme parks like Disney World has forced
the Mexican tourist industry to repackage its attractions in ways
that mimic their replicas, underscoring Sontag's observation that
it is reality that is increasingly scrutinized for its fidelity to simulacra (87).[15]

National Rhetoric

It's interesting to contrast the propaganda circulated outside the
country with the national rhetoric about the industry directed at
Mexicans themselves. As tourism has come to play an increasingly important role in the national economy, the claims for its
benefits to the Mexican people have increased proportionately.
Since World War II, Mexican administrations have consistently
vowed that they would develop tourism in ways that would respect Mexican customs and beliefs, strengthen international understanding between cultures, and strengthen the cultural identity of the Mexican people (Shacochis 45–46). For example, in
1967, President Gustavo Díaz Ordaz of Mexico asserted that

tourism represents a very important source of revenue which contributes toward the financing of the economic and social development of our country. But it signifies, besides, something much more
important: an understanding of the Mexican's way of life, of his
virtues, of his history and art, of his ancient culture and folklore, of
his land and gentle climate, of his aspirations and achievements.
All this fosters closer ties of friendship among Mexicans themselves
and with other nations of the world, and shows Mexico to them as
it really is, with its historical and cultural realities, thus increasing
in the consciousness of the world the prestige and respect our country inspires. (Quoted in Mexico, Department of Tourism, *Tourism
as a Medium of Human Communication* 16)

Such rhetoric can be better understood by considering the parallels between Mexican nationalism of the 1920s and contemporary tourist propaganda. Both have to a certain extent relied on
a celebration of Mexico's indigenous cultures, in particular its
pre-Columbian indigenous cultures. In fact, the murals of the nationalist period that were instrumental in shifting national consciousness from Spain to Mesoamerica have become among the
most popular tourist attractions in Mexico. But just as the height-
ened sense of community generated by nationalism did not necessarily go hand in hand with economic and political reform (in
fact, it became nothing more than a cover for the corruption of
new power brokers), neither does the income generated by tourist
propaganda do much to heighten a sense of national Mexican
community. In many ways the problems of nationalist and tourist concerns over authenticity parallel each other; both ultimately
fail because they rely on monolithic and fixed conceptions of cultural identity.[16]

Earlier I suggested that the different narratives comprising the
Infernal Paradise were superimposed on each other without completely obliterating earlier texts, as in a palimpsest, a discursive
formation that appears to have suggested not only the predominant strategy of the Mexican tourist industry (the development of

multilayered theme parks) but the very themes of those parks as well. Different Mexican myths coexist and are promoted simultaneously. Before ever leaving home the visitor to Mexico selects a Mexican narrative he or she will experience, and then, once in Mexico, becomes the reader of a palimpsest, shifting rapidly from narrative to narrative—"exploring" ancient ruins in the morning, bartering with natives at noon, sipping piña coladas in the afternoon, being serenaded by mariachis in the evening—until the texts blur together. A trip to Chichen Itza may be experienced simultaneously as pleasure, education, work, adventure, and time travel. Again, as in Stone's novel, the tourist site/sight may be simultaneously a resort, a religious shrine, a museum, an hacienda, and a pig farm. Using a model like the palimpsest allows us to account for the concurrence of these different but interwoven narratives. Moreover, the increasing popularity of ecotours in which the tourist pays to participate in ecological cleanup, scientific research, archaeological digs, or the chance to live with an indigenous family—in other words, a new kind of tourism that intentionally fuses activities not previously associated with tourism—confirms the necessity for and usefulness of a model that is built on notions of hybridity and multiple narratives.

Postscript: The Impact of Tourism on the Third World

By this time, my questions had essentially narrowed to one: What amid all the developing—all the massive hotels and computer stores and video bars—would there be to remind a gringo that he was in Mexico?
—Bob Shacochis, "In Deepest Gringolandia"

✶

That Shacochis can ask such a question and have it make perfect sense is perhaps the best and most alarming indication of the extent to which a discursive network has fashioned and authorized particular versions of Mexicanness as authentic. After all, one of the implications of his question is that technology (computers, video bars) is somehow inauthentic and un-Mexican. His question also crystallizes the issue over which tourism theorists are most likely to diverge. Proponents point to the modernization tourism generates and its subsequent benefits to the local population in terms of improved infrastructure, education, and health care—all in addition to an improved local economy. Opponents argue that such modernization is also a frequently unwanted Westernization, and that the benefits are highly restricted while tourism actually exacerbates and introduces new social problems (e.g., increased crime). Moreover, critics charge, to the extent that poverty and subservience can be made into tourist attractions, so too will tourism exert pressure to prevent those social ills from being addressed. This brings us to an interesting question: To what extent can a developing nation manage tourism to maximize benefits to its populace while protecting them from its accompanying destructive effects?

Let's consider the pros and cons a bit further. At one extreme is Ascher's view that the transnational corporations headquartered in First World nations form closed systems that effectively circumvent local economies. I would add that in the case of Mexico, the federal government and foreign debt siphon off most of the tourism revenue; little of it reaches local economies. Ascher's argument is echoed by Rosemary Lee, who concludes that the modern tourist industry does not foster economic development because it initially reinforces the power of a local elite and then inevitably moves toward foreign domination. She adds that as certain ethnic types and traditions increase in popularity as tourist attractions (e.g., the Tarascans, or the Maya in Yucatán), so too does pressure to keep those communities underdeveloped. Such pressure, I would add, can be generated from within the community—even to the point of putting itself at risk—as it becomes more dependent on tourist income, as in the case of the Tarascans who concealed a cholera epidemic for fear of disrupting the tourist-based economy.

Unlike Ascher and Lee, Valene Smith argues that tourism can in fact benefit indigenous communities by stimulating local economies and providing avenues of upward mobility for the indigenous population. Moreover, she argues, such benefits outweigh potential harmful effects (including increases in crime, prostitution, and drug sale and use). Smith contends that concern over the colonizing nature of tourism is to some extent moot, since the mass media function as a more pervasive, invasive, and homogenizing cultural force. Perhaps most provocatively, she disputes theorists such as Lee who argue that tourism ultimately inhibits modernization rather than enables it. Smith insists that continuing modernization in the Third World, in part brought about by tourism, will gradually diminish conflict between tourists and hosts, and that the "worldwide cultural homogenization" under way makes it necessary to preserve traditional cultures in theme parks and museums, or what she calls "model cultures"—models that should reduce the pressure to keep traditional cultures underdeveloped (6–17). Another theorist reluctant to portray tourism as primarily a disruptive, negative force is David Harrison, who argues that linking vices to tourism is misleading because the roots of the problem usually extend deeper into the culture than host-guest relations go. While tourism may encourage economic dependency of a "less developed country" on developed countries, he says, economic dependency is not always followed by political dependency. He also (correctly, I think) points out that the hosts are not powerless in the relationship and often adapt to the social upheaval tourism brings about (19–34).

Despite their many important contributions to tourism theory, I am fundamentally at odds with Smith's argument and troubled by Harrison's defense of tourism even as he recognizes its links to serious social problems in less developed nations. Smith's views attribute far too much faith in a trickle-down distribution of benefits generated by tourism than is borne out by case studies such as Lee's and Kemper's. More convincing are Ascher's observations that the development of infrastructure and other types of modernization are carried out selectively in ways that enhance tourist facilities while neglecting the surrounding areas. And again, as Hall notes, the success of megaresorts provides little incentive to a centralized tourist industry like Mexico's to pursue smaller-scale joint ventures with local communities. I believe that unless tourism is negotiated at a grassroots level in the host community, its effects will always be destructive to some degree—despite the hosts' practice of oppositional tactics, to paraphrase de Certeau, or their ability to adapt, as Harrison emphasizes. Even in Mexico, where the national government has worked hard to circulate tourist revenue within the national economy, local communities are rarely consulted regarding tourist planning and receive a minimal share of tourism income. To return to the Tarascan case for a moment, Kemper notes that in 1987, 125,000 tourists visited the Lake Patzcuaro region: "At the local level, Patzcuaro suffers from the control of an elite tourist sector, while hampered by a bureaucratic government at state and national levels. While the local population has benefited from tourism, it continues to be relatively powerless to influence the course of tourist development" (77; my translation). This is also precisely the case described by Lee in Yucatán. As for Harrison, his astute observations seem somewhat limited. After all, tourism may not be the root cause of social problems such as prostitution and drug abuse, but it has certainly been shown to exacerbate them, as the growing body of scholarship documenting the sex tourism industry in the Asian Pacific attests. And contrary to his argument that economic dependency does not necessarily create political dependency, Linda Richter has shown that the economic dependency engendered by tourism may encourage oppressive reprisals by Third World governments against political dissidents in order to convey to potential tourists an image of political stability, a perception Richter has shown to be crucial to international tourism (45). I echo her recommendation that the political security necessary for tourism to generate economic benefits should be ensured not by oppressive, centralized control, but by

direct consultation with and active involvement of local communities in tourism planning. This is also the conclusion reached by
Veronica Long in her study of the Huatulco development (218).

Although such attempts to work with local communities,
called "social impact mitigation" by FONATUR, are increasingly
advocated by government planners, problems continue to arise,
not the least of which are skepticism and resentment among the
local population. For example, FONATUR routinely creates a
"community development team" to work with local communities affected by large-scale tourist developments. The team's primary mission is to prepare the community for the transition to a
new economy by providing such things as job training and English language courses.[17] Studies have shown that such training is
rarely adequate, however, and that much of the team's time is
spent arbitrating land expropriation issues, with the result that
most of the jobs generated by tourist development go to migrant
workers from other areas. For example, in the Ixtapa case, experienced hotel workers migrated from Acapulco to claim the best
jobs. Therefore, the frequent claim by tourism proponents that it
increases employment to host communities glosses over the fact
that skilled labor is often imported from other parts of the country (Long 211). Furthermore, the sudden influx of large numbers
of temporary workers increases inflation dramatically, usually
with a severe impact on the local population, and overloads the
new infrastructure, resulting in serious problems of health, sani-
tation, and electricity. Finally, when local residents do attempt to
exert some measure of control over touristic development, the
central planning agencies may assume a defensive posture. Long
has documented such a case in Huatulco in which local residents
petitioned FONATUR and the courts for the right to develop their
village into a tourist attraction (as an authentic fishing village!)
that they, the local residents, would control, but their petition
was rejected (216). The relative lack of success of "social impact
mitigation" strategies to date underscores the fact that ultimately
they are designed to facilitate resort development, and not the

host community's transition to a dramatically different economy. In fact, such strategies are nothing more than coercion masked by a kinder face, and that makes them all the more insidious. Is it any wonder that local Mexican communities have reacted with great skepticism toward the federal government's claim that there are great benefits to be derived from tourism?

I close this chapter by mentioning an example of successful grassroots development and control of a tourist economy in a developing nation: the Kuna Indians of San Blas, Panama.[18] The Kuna wrested control of the tourist trade away from foreign and national interests through such strategies as the formation of co-operatives that give them greater bargaining power in selling Kuna arts and crafts, and the creation of an ecological preserve adjacent to their islands that both serves as a buffer against en-croachment by other cultures and also attracts ecotourists, whose numbers the Kuna can regulate. It is sobering to note, however, that local autonomy was granted to the Kuna by the Panamanian government only after violent conflict and resistance to foreign attempts to cultivate a tourist trade using the Kuna as attractions (hotels were burned, hotel owners attacked). The Kuna experi-ence may stand as a model example of what Margaret Swain calls indigenous tourism ("tourism based on the group's land and cul-tural identity and controlled from within by the group" [85])— but it also underscores the reluctance of national and interna-tional agencies to allow it and the violence that may result when endogenous tourist economies at the local level are not pursued as a matter of policy.

Epilogue

I was drinking beer to kill time, the erotic and sensitive Mexican time
which is so different from the clean-packaged, well-kept time of the Americanos. Time in Mexico can be cruel and punishing, but it is never indifferent. It permeates everything, it changes reality. Einstein would have loved
Mexico because there time and space are one. I stare more often into empty
space when I'm in Mexico. The past seems to infuse the present, and in the
brown, wrinkled faces of the old people one sees the presence of the past.
In Mexico I like to walk the narrow streets of the cities and the smaller
pueblos, wandering aimlessly, feeling the sunlight which is so distinctively
Mexican, listening to the voices which call in the streets, peering into the
dark eyes which are so secretive and proud. The Mexican people guard a
secret. But in the end, one is never really lost in Mexico. All streets lead to
a good cantina. All good stories start in a cantina.
—Rudolfo Anaya, "B. Traven Is Alive and Well in Cuernavaca"

✿

In this book I have attempted to show that Mexico is more than a
geographic and political entity; it is also the product of an interdependent array of discourses that form a discursive network.
The Mexicanness produced by the various discourses forming
this network is generated by political and economic interests and
has significant social impact. For example, we have seen that in
the decades prior to the Mexican American War, English-language
literature produced a Mexicanness that supported the ideology of
Manifest Destiny. In the twentieth century, Chicano movement
leaders produced a form of Mexicanness that galvanized Mexican
Americans during the civil rights struggle but ultimately proved
to be too narrowly conceived to sustain a Chicano coalition. We

have also seen that certain forms of Mexicanness, such as the myth of the Infernal Paradise, have become particularly influential through their historical reinscription in the discursive network (a reinscription to which Mexican Americans have contributed as avidly as Anglo writers). In other words, the power of certain forms of Mexicanness depends on the repetition of key elements in a variety of discourses that mutually support and reinforce one another. I was recently reminded of the dominance of the Infernal Paradise myth at a lecture I gave to undergraduates in the Mexican-American Studies program at the University of Arizona. When I presented them with the Rudolfo Anaya passage above and asked for their reactions to it, all of the students said that they felt it was an accurate description of Mexico and Mexicanness; no one questioned its characterization of Mexicans as mysterious, sensual beings living in an erotic, timeless land; nor did they question the implications of such a characterization. I attribute their unquestioning acceptance of the Infernal Paradise to its repeated reinscription and distribution by way of the discursive network I have articulated in this study. As I suggested in chapter 2, the Mexican images produced in the service of various political interests at different historical moments have become a filter through which we view Mexico, and have, through repetition, become so ingrained in our conception of what Mexico is, that most Americans never question them.

I have also argued that the best way to apprehend and examine the production of Mexicanness is by conceptualizing the network producing it as a palimpsest: a multilayered text that by definition implies the suppression of other texts created at earlier historical moments. Such a conceptualization allows us to identify the counterhegemonic voices that challenge the prevailing assumptions of dominant Mexican constructs. That challenge should, in turn, provoke an investigation of the interests supporting competing Mexican constructs and provoke a consideration of the repercussions of that production. Perhaps most important, using the palimpsest as a theoretical model foregrounds cultural identity as an object of study and insists on an understanding of cultural identity as fluid and provisional, thereby resisting monolithic conceptualizations of cultural identity and providing space for intracultural differences.

Notes

Introduction

1. I'm indebted to Stephanie Athey, Stetson University, for the latter observation.

2. From the Greek *palimpsestos*, literally, "scraped again."

3. Whenever I use the term *discourse* in this study I mean specifically a semiotic system that is inextricably bound up with a broad array of social institutions that govern the distribution of power within that society.

4. To this point I have placed the term *Mexico* within quotation marks to indicate that it is something more than a geographic or political entity, a convention I will now drop for readability even though I continue to connote its status as discursive construct. When I need to make this status explicit I will do so with the term *Mexicanness.*

5. Pratt notes that the term was first coined by Fernando Ortiz in a 1947 study of Afro-Cuban culture (228, n. 4). I would add that her discussion of how marginalized groups respond to domination bears remarkable similarities to Michel de Certeau's ideas of oppositional tactics articulated in *The Practice of Everyday Life*, trans. Stephen F. Rendall.

6. Aztlán was the Aztecs' mythical, paradisal homeland. I discuss its evolution and political uses extensively in chapter 1. As for the Chicano movement (a.k.a. the Chicano Power movement, the Chicano nationalist movement, and el Movimiento), scholars disagree as to its precise chronology, but I have (generously) fixed its boundaries at 1965 and 1975. The best history of the movement is still *Youth, Identity, Power,* by Carlos Muñoz, Jr.

7. I owe a tremendous debt to each of these authors: Robinson for breaking new scholarly ground; Keen for his masterful discussion of how the representation of Aztec culture by Mexicans as well as non-

Mexicans responded to and influenced important political and philosophical movements; Walker for identifying the prominence and importance of the Infernal Paradise trope, as well as for excellent discussions of the English modernists; and Gunn for his thorough and precise history of the literary tradition. See Cecil Robinson, *With the Ears of Strangers*; Benjamin Keen, *The Aztec Image in Western Thought*; Ronald Walker, *Infernal Paradise: Mexico and the Modern English Novel*; and Drewey Wayne Gunn, *American and British Writers in Mexico, 1556–1973*.

Chapter 1. Toward a New Understanding
of Aztlán and Chicano Cultural Identity

1. Several theorists have been instrumental in helping me conceive of the palimpsest as a useful analytical tool and a theoretical trope. José Rabasa's and Davíd Carrasco's work on Mesoamerican history, Sandra Messinger Cypess's exploration of la Malinche, Annette Kolodny's proposal for a new approach to American literary history, and Michel de Certeau's examination of oppositional practices all use the palimpsest to vividly convey the complicated nature of their areas of inquiry. See José Rabasa, *Inventing America: Spanish Historiography and the Formation of Eurocentrism*; Davíd Carrasco, *Quetzalcoatl and the Irony of Empire: Myths and Prophecies in the Aztec Tradition*; Sandra Messinger Cypess, *La Malinche in Mexican Literature: From History to Myth*; Annette Kolodny, "Letting Go Our Grand Obsessions: Notes toward a New Literary History of the American Frontiers"; and Michel de Certeau, *The Practice of Everyday Life*.

2. Not initially!

3. Padilla is drawing on the work of Franz Fanon. See Genaro M. Padilla, "Myth and Comparative Cultural Nationalism: The Ideological Uses of Aztlán"; for Anzaldúa's position, see Patti Blanco, "Interview with Gloria Anzaldúa."

4. See, for example, Enrique Florescano, *Memoria mexicana* and *El nuevo pasado mexicano*; and Susan D. Gillespie, *The Aztec Kings: The Construction of Rulership in Mexica History*.

5. By Eurocentric, I mean the common tendency to study Mesoamerican cultures with the goal of explaining the Spanish Conquest (as, e.g., in

the work of Octavio Paz and Tzvetan Todorov). The inevitable result of these studies obsessed with the Conquest is to portray all of the Mesoamerican cultures as inferior, the product of a people destined to be conquered. See Paz, *The Other Mexico;* and Todorov, *The Conquest of America: The Question of the Other.*

6. I thank Larry Evers, University of Arizona, for suggesting this observation to me.

7. See, for example, Mario Barrera, *Beyond Aztlan: Ethnic Autonomy in Comparative Perspective* 3–44.

8. For another example of a failed attempt to define Chicano ethnicity based on commonalities, see Alice H. Reich, *The Cultural Construction of Ethnicity: Chicanos in the University.*

9. "Indeed, a crucial but neglected area of research is the historical geography of the Chicano population" (Saragoza 45). Sergio D. Elizondo and Gilberto Cardenas also criticize the southwestern focus; see Elizondo, "ABC: Aztlán, the Borderlands, and Chicago"; and Cardenas, "Who Are the Midwestern Chicanos: Implications for Chicano Studies."

10. Alarcón points toward further investigation of this interrelationship when she comments, "It must be noted, however, that each woman of color cited here, even in her positing of a 'plurality of self,' is already privileged enough to reach the moment of cognition of a situation for herself. This should suggest that to privilege the subject, even if multiple-voiced, is not enough" (Alarcón, "The Theoretical Subject(s) of *This Bridge Called My Back* and Anglo-American Feminism" 366).

11. It is interesting to note the ironic reversal of the controversial theory that the Aztecs believed Cortés to be Quetzalcoatl in Durán's belief that the Mesoamerican culture hero was really Saint Thomas. Nor was Durán the only Spaniard to believe that an early Christian missionary had come to the New World. This is a point often missed by those who suggest that the Aztecs' concern for prophecies was a unique cultural attribute that facilitated the Conquest. See Fernando Horcasitas and Doris Heyden, "Fray Diego Durán: His Life and Works" 23–31.

12. There were other reasons, to be sure, including Europeans' intense curiosity about the New World. For a fuller discussion of the motives behind these historical recovery efforts, see Carrasco, *Quetzalcoatl and the Irony of Empire* 15.

13. Jorge Klor de Alva argues that because of the dialogical methods

employed by Sahagún in compiling his *Historia general,* authorship and authority must be primarily attributed to the indigenous informants and scholars; see "Sahagún and the Birth of Modern Ethnography: Representing, Confessing, and Inscribing the Native Other" 34.

14. Todorov's argument that the Aztecs were defeated because they lacked the ability to improvise has also been effectively challenged by Gananath Obeyesekere and Inga Clendinnen. Clendinnen's essay is far and away the most important reassessment of the Conquest to have appeared in years. See Obeyesekere, *The Apotheosis of Captain Cook: European Mythmaking in the Pacific* 16–22; and Clendinnen, " 'Fierce and Unnatural Cruelty': Cortés and the Conquest of Mexico." I'm grateful to my colleague Joan Dayan, University of Arizona, for bringing Obeyesekere's work to my attention. See also S. Gillespie, *The Aztec Kings* 4–120; and Todorov, *The Conquest of America.*

15. For the former observation, see Benjamin Keen, *The Aztec Image in Western Thought.* For an example of the latter, see Sandra Messinger Cypess, *La Malinche in Mexican Literature: From History to Myth.*

16. "El Plan Espiritual de Aztlán," in *Aztlán: Essays on the Chicano Homeland* 1–5. The plan was first delivered at the Chicano National Liberation Youth Conference in Denver in March 1969, and was first published in *Documents of the Chicano Struggle* (New York: Pathfinder, 1971). Attributing specific authorship to the plan is problematic, as I discuss later in the chapter. For the critique that Aztlán/cultural nationalism divides more than it unifies, see Klor de Alva, "Aztlán, Borinquen, and Hispanic Nationalism" 147; and Barrera, *Beyond Aztlan* 45–63.

17. See also Leal, "In Search of Aztlán" 11.

18. Leal, "In Search of Aztlán" 11; Forbes, *Aztecas del Norte: The Chicanos of Aztlan* 17. It is significant both that the term is reputed here to have been brought to the attention of Chicanos by the Native American movement and that Aztlán as a Chicano homeland was located in the Southwest—significant because both issues remain controversial and insufficiently addressed. The use of Aztlán to promote the Southwest as the legitimate homeland of a particular ethnic group has a most ironic predecessor, as research by Ramón Gutiérrez has uncovered: In 1885, Aztlán was used in propaganda written and published by the secretary of the Territory of New Mexico for the purpose of attracting Anglo settlers to the region in order to establish an Anglo majority vis-à-vis the

Hispano population prior to statehood. See Gutiérrez, "Aztlán, Montezuma, and New Mexico: The Political Uses of American Indian Mythology" 172–90.

19. Norma Alarcón, for example, offers an excellent critique of cultural movements that are based on theories of common denominators; see "The Theoretical Subject(s) of *This Bridge Called My Back* and Anglo-American Feminism" 359.

20. Attributing authorship to "El Plan Espiritual" is a complicated matter. Muñoz attributes the specific language of the document to four movement leaders: Alurista, Luis Valdez, Jorge Gonzales, and Juan Gómez-Quiñones (97, n. 3). He is careful to point out, however, that "El Plan Espiritual" reiterates resolutions that were developed by conference participants within the context of the nationalist ideology espoused by Rodolfo Gonzales (76). This is supported by Alurista, who attributes authorship of the plan to the conference delegates (222). Therefore, when I speak of the authors of the plan, I mean both the principal conference leaders who drafted the actual document and the conference participants who developed the ideas and resolutions on which the plan was based.

21. See, for example, Eric Wolf, *Sons of the Shaking Earth* 119–20.

22. This is a popular story with Mesoamerican historiographers. See, for example, Florescano, *Memoria mexicana* 85–89.

Chapter 2. Mexico as Infernal Paradise

1. Ronald Walker was the first critic to delineate the prominence of this trope and its implications; see *Infernal Paradise: Mexico and the Modern English Novel.*

2. Traven expert Karl S. Guthke speculates that Traven himself may not have been sure who his parents were. For a fascinating discussion of the Traven mystery, see Guthke's essay "In Search of B. Traven, Mystery Man," in his book *Trails in No-Man's Land: Essays in Cultural and Literary History* 114–32.

3. With the exception of film and journalism, I discuss each of these discourses elsewhere in this book. Those interested in examining the portrayal of Mexicanness in film should consult Juan R. García, "Hollywood and the West: Mexican Images in American Films, 1894–1983." I would also briefly point out that the Infernal Paradise motifs are a staple

of Hollywood films set in Mexico; three well-known examples are Orson Welles's *Touch of Evil*, Sam Peckinpah's *The Wild Bunch*, and Oliver Stone's *Born on the Fourth of July*.

4. Mary Maples Dunn, introduction to Alexander von Humboldt, *Political Essay on the Kingdom of New Spain* 3–18.

5. For the influence of Vasconcelos on Porter, see Thomas F. Walsh, *Katherine Anne Porter and Mexico: The Illusion of Eden*. For his influence on Lawrence, see Alesia García's unpublished manuscript "'And It Is Told' from D. H. Lawrence to Rudolfo A. Anaya: Quetzalcoátl and Utopian Mesoamerica" (1993).

6. Taken from a facsimile of the title page of the 1648 first edition of Gage's text, reproduced in *Thomas Gage's Travels in the New World*, ed. J. Eric S. Thompson, xv.

7. As Gunn observes, "Such accounts have proliferated in the twentieth century; almost every Mexican visitor seems to think about publishing his impressions, and a large number succeed" (*American and British Writers in Mexico, 1556–1973* 3). Some well-known examples are Carl Lumholtz, *Unknown Mexico*; D. H. Lawrence, *Mornings in Mexico*; Graham Greene, *The Lawless Roads*; and Mary and Fred del Villar's *Where the Strange Roads Go Down*. One can note characteristics of the Infernal Paradise embedded even in the titles: Mexico is unknown, lawless, and strange. See also the excellent article by Carlos Monsiváis, "Travelers in Mexico: A Brief Anthology of Selected Myths."

8. Ironically, a similar vacuum has been created within Latin American studies in the United States during the twentieth century, largely through overemphasis on the Conquest. J. Jorge Klor de Alva comments:

It bears mentioning here that English sources on colonial Latin America during most of this century have generally focused on the age of conquest and early exploration with minimal attention paid to the centuries that followed. The net result has been that, until very recently and then only in certain texts, schools in the United States have tended to skip or gloss over the southwestern colonial period; that is, everything between the initial Spanish exploration in Latin American and the Caribbean and the landing of the English on the Atlantic shores has been elided. This common practice has led to the frequent omission of a full century of Hispanic occupation of the (future) U.S. Southwest, thereby helping to maintain the idea that U.S. history is strictly an east to west phenomenon, with Mexicans playing only a very minor role as (the permanent) foreigners. ("The Postcolonization of the (Latin) American Experience: A Reconsideration of 'Colonialism,' 'Postcolonialism,' and 'Mestizaje'" n. 38)

9. According to both Dunn and Pratt, Humboldt's Mexican work singlehandedly produced a British investment boom in the mining of Mexican silver (Pratt, *Imperial Eyes* 131); for Dunn's remarks, see her introduction to Humboldt's *Political Essay* 13.

10. Drawing on Robinson, Gunn cites Timothy Flint's *Francis Berrian, or the Mexican Patriot* (1826) as the first American novel set partly in Mexico. See Gunn, *American and British Writers in Mexico, 1556–1973* 18; and Robinson, *With the Ears of Strangers* 22–24. There were, of course, Anglo travel narratives and chronicles that antedated Flint's work.

11. See Mary Louise Pratt, "Scratches on the Face of the Country; or, What Mr. Barrow Saw in the Land of the Bushmen," and *Imperial Eyes*, especially chapters 3 and 4.

12. It's also characteristic of the romantic style of sightseeing that emerged in the nineteenth century. For an excellent discussion of the evolution of sightseeing and changes in the conventions of European travel narratives, see Judith Adler, "Origins of Sightseeing."

13. Eric Wolf notes that this is in part due to the chronicles produced by the Spaniards themselves, which Prescott had researched:

The entire enterprise of the Spanish Conquest seems shrouded in a curious air of unreality. . . . Actors, acts, and motive seem superhuman: their lust for gold and for salvation, their undivided loyalty to a distant monarch, their courage in the face of a thousand obstacles seem to defy simple psychological explanations. They not only made history; they struck poses against the backdrop of history, conscious of their role as makers and shakers of this earth. The utterances of a Cortés, a Panfilo Narváez, a Garay, are replete with references to Caesar, Pompey, and Hannibal. Cortés plays not only at being himself; he is also the Amadis of Gaul celebrated in the medieval books of chivalry. They were not satisfied with the simple act; they translated each act into a symbolic statement, an evocation of a superhuman purpose. Struck with admiration of their deeds and postures, their chroniclers took them at their word. In the pages of the history books these men parade in the guise of their own evaluation of themselves: half centaurs, pawing the ground with their hoofs and bellowing with voices like cannon, half gods, therefore, and only half men. (Wolf, *Sons of the Shaking Earth* 153–54)

14. Vicki Broach, conversation with the author.

15. Todorov theorizes that the Aztecs were so bound by ritual that they were unable to improvise to counter the Spanish invasion, a theory that, as Clendinnen notes, harkens back to Prescott's portrayal of a "fatally indecisive" Montezuma. As I suggested in my first chapter, Spanish colonial histories offer plenty of evidence to refute Todorov's theory, as does Clendinnen's persuasive essay.

16. Although such providential interpretations of the events of the Conquest are typical of Spanish accounts prior to the nineteenth century, they are not axiomatic. See, for example, the excellent essay by David A. Boruchoff, "Beyond Utopia and Paradise: Cortés, Bernal Díaz and the Rhetoric of Consecration."

17. See Bernal Díaz del Castillo, *The Conquest of New Spain*, trans. J. M. Cohen, 220–24.

18. As Juan R. García puts it, "In most [dime novel] story lines Mexicans became gross caricatures who ran the gamut from the sandal-footed peon to the proud but impoverished hidalgo who clung tenaciously to a by-gone era. Between these two extremes were a host of other stock characters, including the evil and scheming priest; the beautiful and strong-willed señorita; the dark and lascivious female half-breed; the jealous but inept Latin lover; and the ruthless and treacherous bandido" ("Hollywood and the West: Mexican Images in American Films, 1894–1983" 78). See also Arthur G. Pettit, *Images of the Mexican American in Fiction and Film* xx.

19. For a discussion of the expatriate community in Mexico, see Gunn, *American and British Writers in Mexico, 1556–1973* 76–101.

20. My citations refer to the 1934 version as reprinted in *The Collected Stories of Katherine Anne Porter*.

21. David T. Peterson, "Inspired Truth? Images of Mexico in Katherine Anne Porter's 'Hacienda'" 17–18 (unpubl. MS, 1993). I'm grateful to David for permission to quote from his essay.

22. The important exception here is Greene, whose whiskey priest is Mexican. It should also be noted that Anglo characters play crucial roles throughout the novel.

23. For a fuller discussion of the symbolic role of the Mexican landscape in these novels, see Douglas Veitch, *Lawrence, Greene and Lowry: the Fictional Landscape of Mexico.*

24. I might add that Cather herself was not above using such stereotypes. One of her earliest stories, "The Dance at Chevalier's" (published in 1900 under the pseudonym Henry Nicklemann), features as sinister a Mexican as any who ever appeared in a dime novel. The story has been republished in *North of the Rio Grande: The Mexican-American Experience in Short Fiction,* ed. Edward Simmen, 27–38.

25. D. H. Lawrence, *Selected Essays* 191. The essay, "Indians and an Englishman," first appeared in *Dial* in 1923.

26. "In his affirmation of blood and violence, Lawrence resembles here [in *The Plumed Serpent*] strands of European thought he criticized elsewhere: the proto-fascist Futurists, with their celebration of 'war as the sole true hygiene,' and Bataille" (Marianna Torgovnick, *Gone Primitive: Savage Intellects, Modern Lives* 169). The quote within the quote is attributed by Torgovnick to Lawrence from one of his letters (278, n. 20).

27. Lawrence, "America, Listen to Your Own," *New Republic* (December 1920), reprinted in *Phoenix* 90.

28. My colleague Stephanie Athey suggested to me the very plausible idea that Lowry, ironically, could not see that his novel of spiritual adventure is not so different from the adventure genre he parodies.

29. This gap is true only for literature. Other discourses comprising the Infernal Paradise, most notably cinema, continued circulating the familiar images during this period. Among the best known of the Infernal Paradise films produced during this time are Orson Welles's *Touch of Evil* (1959), John Sturges's *Magnificent Seven* (1960), and Sam Peckinpah's *Wild Bunch* (1969).

30. Stone's title is a biblical allusion that has three possible sources, each resonant with his text. The best known is the parable of the unjust steward (Luke 16:8), often problematic because it appears to recommend dishonesty: "And the Lord commended the unjust steward, because he had done wisely: for the children of this world are in their generation

wiser than the children of light." The phrase appears again in Ephesians 5:8 following Paul's admonition to avoid fornication, uncleanness, and covetousness: "For ye were sometimes darkness, but now are ye light in the Lord: walk as children of light; (For the fruit of the Spirit is in all goodness, and righteousness, and truth;) proving what is acceptable unto the Lord." Finally, the phrase appears in 1 Thessalonians in perhaps its most suggestive resonance with Stone's text: "But ye, brethren, are not in darkness, that day should overtake you as a thief. Ye are all the children of light, and the children of the day: we are not of the night, nor of darkness. Therefore let us not sleep, as do others; but let us watch and be sober. For they that sleep, sleep in the night; and they that be drunken are drunken in the night. But let us, who are of the day, be sober, putting on the breastplate of faith and love; and for an helmet the hope of salvation" 1 Thessalonians 5:4–8. As Robert Solotaroff points out and as will become apparent in my analysis, both of Stone's central characters have trouble functioning while sober, and the allusion to Ephesians and Thessalonians suggests that the resulting tragedy in the novel is the meting out of divine justice. The reference to the parable of the unjust steward, on the other hand, is problematic in much the same way as Stone's denouement: Walker, like the steward, is apparently rewarded for his irresponsible behavior. I thank my colleague Herbert Schneidau not only for helping me locate the biblical references but also for his helpful observations regarding the Luke passage. All citations here are from the King James version.

31. John A. McClure points out that the movement from a metropolitan center to a colonial periphery is characteristic of Stone's work, with the exception of *Dog Soldiers*, in which the movement is deliberately reversed. I thank my colleague Jeremy Green for bringing McClure's work to my attention.

32. Bob Shacochis, "In Deepest Gringolandia: the Third World as Tourist Theme Park"; conversation with Robert Stone, May 1, 1992.

33. This interpretation appears borne out by Stone himself, who in a conversation with Solotaroff is critical of Walker's actions: "Above all, I got into the notion of a relationship between two people who know that nothing good can happen to them from each other and who know that they have nothing but trouble and even potential destruction to give to each other but who willfully—*and one of them more willfully than the*

other—out of nostalgia, out of weakness, out of perversity, out of a desire for generalized destruction, for his own destruction, out of a combination of self-destructiveness and selfishness, make this pilgrimage" (Solotaroff, *Robert Stone* 116; emphasis added).

34. See, for example, George M. Spangler, "Kate Chopin's *The Awakening*: A Partial Dissent." A portion of this article is reprinted in the 1976 Norton critical edition of Chopin's text. See Chopin, *The Awakening*; and also Solotaroff, *Robert Stone* 127.

35. What I mean by postmodern play is a kind of self-indulgent pleasure in escapist role playing that has been elaborated and criticized by Dean MacCannell as a practice that alienates the individual from communities and serves oppressive corporate institutions. See, in particular, his essay "Postmodern Community Planning," in *Empty Meeting Grounds: The Tourist Papers*.

36. See *The Hero with a Thousand Faces*.

Chapter 3. "Where Do You Get Your Ideas about Mexico?"

1. The obligatory note regarding terminology: in the past, I scrupulously used the term *Chicano* only when referring to people or groups who shared a political affiliation with the Chicano Power movement of the late 1960s and its principles, reserving the term *Mexican American* for umbrella applications that would include all people or groups in the United States of Mexican descent. Over the years I've become less of a stickler on this point, primarily because I believe the term *Mexican American* to be as ideologically loaded as *Chicano*. Acknowledging this, I use the two interchangeably here, mostly for readability. When referring specifically to aspects and advocates of the movement, I continue to use *Chicano*. I might add that the fact that this question over terminology invariably provokes heated debate seems to me another example of the need to conceive of cultural identity as provisional and fluid.

2. For example, Bruce-Novoa points out that the work of John Rechy is frequently absent from formulations of the Chicano literary canon because he focuses on sexual, rather than ethnic, identity. See Juan Bruce-Novoa, "Canonical and Non-Canonical Texts," in *RetroSpace* 132–45.

3. Paredes remarks of the heroic border corrido that the genre inevitably emphasizes the Mexicanness of the heroic protagonist so that

the two terms *Mexican* and *heroic* become synonyms. Corridistas of the border region could then use the term *Mexican* as a kind of shorthand for an entire set of heroic attributes (intelligent, sly, brave, etc.) admired by the local community.

4. For example, Ramón Saldívar says,

Pocho has always been somewhat of an embarrassment to Chicanos. Even the preface to the Anchor paperback edition attempts to apologize for the novel. Richard's rejection of his father's values . . . , his statements that "codes of honor are stupid" [108], his rejection of the Catholic faith . . . , and, finally, his departure at the novel's end to join the United States armed forces in the months after Pearl Harbor are seen as assimilationist tendencies, indicating an uncritical acceptance of "melting pot" theories of American immigration. (*Chicano Narrative* 65)

Saldívar goes on to argue, as I do here, that the novel is more complicated in its stance toward immigration than such a simplistic interpretation allows. As for the shift in political ideology and method brought about by the movement, reference the excellent history by Carlos Muñoz, Jr., *Youth, Identity, Power: The Chicano Movement.*

5. For example, Villarreal writes, "Although he loved his mother, Richard realized that a family could not survive when the woman desired to command, and he knew that his mother was like a starving child who had become gluttonous when confronted with food. She had lived so long in the tradition of her country that she could not help herself now, and abused the privilege of equality afforded the women of her new country" (*Pocho* 134).

6. In a well-known interview with Bruce-Novoa, Villarreal commented, "Much of our prose is little better than mediocre. Much of our poetry is even worse, and the only area where the output is first rate, because there is so little of it, is drama." He goes on to attribute this mediocrity to the assessment of Chicano literature on political grounds rather than some other set of criteria. Bruce-Novoa, *Chicano Authors: Inquiry by Interview* 47.

7. Mario's story draws on the tradition of the border corrido in its documentation of racial injustice with conventional corrido figures: the Mexican American male sharecropper, the greedy Anglo landowner, the corrupt Anglo sheriff. It inverts the corrido formula by omitting all

heroic action on the protagonist's part. For a different take on *Pocho's* debt to the corrido tradition, see Ramón Saldívar's study of the novel in *Chicano Narrative*, in which he argues that Juan Rubio's character and values are firmly rooted within the tradition of heroic corridos (61).

8. The lone exception here is Renato Rosaldo, who notes that the novel's opening is like a parody of a clichéd Mexican movie ("Fables of the Fallen Guy" 86).

9. See, for example, Ramón Saldívar, "Romance, the Fantastic, and the Representation of History in Rudolfo A. Anaya and Ron Arias," in *Chicano Narrative*; and Jane Rogers, "The Function of the La Llorona Motif in Anaya's *Bless Me, Ultima*."

10. Although never identified by name, the god's description as a plumed serpent suggests this association.

11. See, in particular, Anaya's essay, "Aztlán: A Homeland without Boundaries."

12. The best biographical work on Traven has been done by Karl S. Guthke. See his *B. Traven: The Life behind the Legends*, and *Trails in No-Man's-Land: Essays in Literary and Cultural History*. See also Philip Jenkins and Ernst Schürer, eds., *B. Traven: Life and Work*.

13. The association here of the working class and Traven makes sense, since he was well known for a series of social protest novels often referred to as the "jungle" novels, books depicting the exploitation of the Indians and the working class in southern Mexico.

14. I am indebted here to my student Alesia García, Ph.D. candidate in American literature at the University of Arizona, who has written an excellent analysis of the many similarities between the work of Anaya and Lawrence called "'And It Is Told' from D. H. Lawrence to Rudolfo A. Anaya: Quetzalcóatl and Utopian Mesoamerica."

15. My thanks to Amy Kaminsky, University of Minnesota, for this observation.

Chapter 4. If a Tree Falls . . . Tourism and Mexicanness

I especially thank my Tío, Octavio Morelos, for supplying me with much of the historical background on Mexico's tourist industry.

1. These statistics are drawn from research by Bob Shacochis, Sylvia Chant, and Veronica H. Long; see the Bibliography for references.

2. On ecotourism, see Beverly Dirks, "New Breed of Traveler."

3. Nelson Graburn, as quoted in James Lett, Epilogue to *Hosts and Guests* 276.

4. This, as Urry says later and as I've noted above, is more true of societies making the transition from industrial to service economies. In the postmodern era, the separation between work and leisure is blurring.

5. Despite the growing consensus on this point, I am concerned that the emphasis on the visual obscures other aspects of the social practice of tourism. Although gazing may be the most common tourist activity, it is only one part of a broader experience that includes other senses.

6. MacCannell defines the modern as postindustrial society: "Postindustrial or modern society is the coming to consciousness of industrial society, the result of industrial society's turning in on itself, searching for its own strengths and weaknesses and elaborating itself internally. The growth of tourism is the central index of modernization so defined" (*The Tourist* 182).

7. Van den Berghe and Keyes use the term *exotic* rather loosely, and I think it bears keeping in mind that its basic meaning is "something foreign," although its more popular connotations usually imply an appealing excess of novelty or color.

8. As my colleague Stephanie Athey pointed out, the flattery that goes hand in hand with a post-tourist self-consciousness is frequently overlooked. The post-tourist knows that he or she is witnessing a performance, but it is a performance for him or her. Like other tourists, the post-tourist enjoys being catered to.

9. For the Cajun case, see van den Berghe and Keyes, "Tourism and Re-Created Ethnicity" 351.

10. My thanks to Stephanie Athey and Alesia García for suggesting that I visit Epcot.

11. A 1990 government report defines megaresorts as large-scale, multiuse, multipurpose developments. See *Tourism Investment in Mexico* 7.

12. Mexico's federal government has officially overseen tourism since 1929. A concise chronology of Mexican tourism is provided in Alvarez, *Enciclopedia de México* 13:7863–71.

13. For an excellent discussion of the impact of foreign investment in Mexico, see Rosemary Louise Lee, *The Tourist Industry in Yucatán: A*

Case Study in the Interaction between Class Structure and Economic Development.

14. Such marketing practices are not unique to the Mexican tourist industry and result in large part from advertisers' increasing reliance on demographic research and marketing. For example, the state of California's 1994 tourism ad campaign uses an approach similar to the Mexican.

15. A recent example of this phenomenon in the United States is the debate over the Disney company's proposal to build a U.S. history theme park near the Civil War battlefield at Manassas, Virginia. Arguments for and against the project neatly encapsulate many of the issues outlined in this chapter. Local proponents touted increased jobs and revenue; Disney claimed the park would increase U.S. citizens' understanding of their country's history; opponents argued that the park ("Disney's America") would lessen interest in and ultimately obliterate "authentic" historical sites. In the words of David McCullough, president of the Society of American Historians, "We have so little left that is authentic, that is real, and to replace it with plastic history, mechanized history, is a sacrilege" (from a report by Anne Groer in the *Orlando Sentinel*, May 12, 1994). In the face of such opposition, Disney ultimately abandoned the Virginia site and is searching for a new location.

16. This parallel was suggested to me by Peter Wollen's observation that not only have the nationalist murals become tourist attractions but that the Mexicanness they promote is "now seen as mythic and folkloric in a problematic sense" ("Tourism, Language and Art" 47).

17. See Long, "Government—Industry—Community Interaction in Tourism Development in Mexico"; see also Agustin Reynoso y Valle and Jacomina P. de Regt, "Growing Pains: Planned Tourism Development in Ixtapa-Zihuatanejo."

18. My description of Kuna tourism is drawn from Margaret Byrne Swain's excellent case study, "Gender Roles in Indigenous Tourism: Kuna Mola, Kuna Yala, and Cultural Survival," in *Hosts and Guests* 83–104.

Bibliography

Adler, Judith. "Origins of Sightseeing." *Annals of Tourism Research* 16.1 (1989): 7–29.

Alarcón, Norma. "The Theoretical Subject(s) of *This Bridge Called My Back* and Anglo-American Feminism." In *Making Face, Making Soul: Haciendo Caras,* ed. Gloria Anzaldúa. San Francisco: Aunt Lute, 1990. 356–69.

Alurista [Alberto Baltazar Urista Heredia]. "Myth, Identity and Struggle in Three Chicano Novels: Aztlán . . . Anaya, Méndez and Acosta." In *Aztlán: Essays on the Chicano Homeland,* ed. Rudolfo A. Anaya and Francisco Lomelí. 1989. Albuquerque: University of New Mexico Press, 1991. 219–29.

Alurista, Juan Gómez-Quiñones, Jorge Gonzales, and Luis Valdez. "El Plan Espiritual de Aztlán." 1969. In *Aztlán: Essays on the Chicano Homeland,* ed. Rudolfo A. Anaya and Francisco Lomelí. 1989. Albuquerque: University of New Mexico Press, 1991. 1–5.

Alvarez, José Rogelio, ed. *Enciclopedia de México.* Mexico City: Secretaría de Educación Pública, 1988. 13:7863–71.

Anaya, Rudolfo A. "Aztlán: A Homeland without Boundaries." In *Aztlán: Essays on the Chicano Homeland,* ed. Anaya and Francisco Lomelí. 1989. Albuquerque: University of New Mexico Press, 1991. 230–41.

———. "B. Traven Is Alive and Well in Cuernavaca." In *Cuentos Chicanos,* ed. Anaya and Antonio Márquez. 1984. Albuquerque: University of New Mexico Press, 1991. 1–13.

———. *Bless Me, Ultima.* Berkeley: Quinto Sol, 1972.

———. *Heart of Aztlán.* 1976. Albuquerque: University of New Mexico Press, 1990.

———. *The Silence of the Llano.* Berkeley: Quinto Sol, 1982.

———. *Tortuga.* Berkeley: Justa, 1979.

Anaya, Rudolfo A., and Francisco Lomelí, eds. *Aztlán: Essays on the Chicano Homeland.* 1989. Albuquerque: University of New Mexico Press, 1991.

Anzaldúa, Gloria. *Borderlands/La Frontera: The New Mestiza.* San Francisco: Aunt Lute, 1987.

———, ed. *Making Face, Making Soul: Haciendo Caras.* San Francisco: Aunt Lute, 1990.

Ascher, François. *Tourism: Transnational Corporations and Cultural Identities.* Paris: UNESCO, 1985.

Bardeleben, Renate von, Dietrich Briesemeister, and Juan Bruce-Novoa, eds. *Missions in Conflict: Essays on U.S.-Mexican Relations and Chicano Culture.* Tübingen: Narr, 1986.

Barrera, Mario. *Beyond Aztlan: Ethnic Autonomy in Comparative Perspective.* 1988. Notre Dame: University of Notre Dame Press, 1990.

Barrio, Raymond. *The Plum Plum Pickers.* 1969. Binghamton, N.Y.: Bilingual, 1984.

Baudrillard, Jean. *Selected Writings.* Ed. Mark Poster. Stanford: Stanford University Press, 1988.

Blanco, Patti. "Interview with Gloria Anzaldúa." *University of Arizona Poetry Center Newsletter* 16 (1991): 4–5.

Boorstin, Daniel J. *The Image: A Guide to Pseudo-Events in America.* New York: Harper, 1961.

Boruchoff, David A. "Beyond Utopia and Paradise: Cortés, Bernal Díaz and the Rhetoric of Consecration." *MLN* 106 (1991): 330–69.

Brandes, Stanley. *Power and Persuasion: Fiestas and Social Control in Rural Mexico.* Philadelphia: University of Pennsylvania Press, 1988.

Bruce-Novoa, Juan. *Chicano Authors: Inquiry by Interview.* Austin: University of Texas Press, 1980.

———. "Mexico en la literatura chicana." *Revista de la Universidad de Mexico* 29.5 (1975): 13–18. Reprinted as "Mexico in Chicano Literature" in *RetroSpace.* Houston: Arte Público, 1990. 52–62.

———. *RetroSpace.* Houston: Arte Público, 1990.

Calderón, Héctor, and José David Saldívar, eds. *Criticism in the Borderlands: Studies in Chicano Literature, Culture, and Ideology.* Durham: Duke University Press, 1991.

Calderón de la Barca, Frances. *Life in Mexico.* 1842. Berkeley: University of California Press, 1982.

Campbell, Joseph. *The Hero with a Thousand Faces.* 1949. Princeton: Princeton University Press, 1973.

Cardenas, Gilberto. "Who Are the Midwestern Chicanos: Implications for Chicano Studies." *Aztlán* 7 (1976): 141–52.

Carrasco, Davíd. *Quetzalcoatl and the Irony of Empire: Myths and Prophecies in the Aztec Tradition.* Chicago: University of Chicago Press, 1982.

Cather, Willa. "The Dance at Chevalier's." 1900. In *North of the Rio Grande: The Mexican-American Experience in Short Fiction,* ed. Edward Simmen. New York: Penguin, 1992. 28–38.

———. *Death Comes for the Archbishop.* 1927. New York: Vintage-Random, 1971.

Chabram, Angie, and Rosa Linda Fregoso. "Chicana/o Cultural Representations: Reframing Alternative Critical Discourses." *Cultural Studies* 4 (1990): 203–12.

Chant, Sylvia. "Tourism in Latin America: Perspectives from Mexico and Costa Rica." In *Tourism and the Less Developed Countries,* ed. David Harrison. London: Belhaven, 1992. 85–101.

Chávez, John R. *The Lost Land: The Chicano Image of the Southwest.* 1984. Albuquerque: University of New Mexico Press, 1991.

Chopin, Kate. *The Awakening.* 1899. New York: Norton, 1976.

Cisneros, Sandra. *The House on Mango Street.* 1984. New York: Random, 1991.

———. *Woman Hollering Creek and Other Stories.* New York: Random, 1991.

Clendinnen, Inga. "'Fierce and Unnatural Cruelty': Cortés and the Conquest of Mexico." *Representations* 33 (1991): 65–100.

Cortés, Hernando. *Five Letters: 1519–1526.* Trans. J. Bayard Morris. New York: Norton, n.d.

Cripps, Michael. "*Under the Volcano*: The Politics of the Imperial Self." *Canadian Literature* 92 (1982): 85–101.

Culler, Jonathan. "Semiotics of Tourism." *American Journal of Semiotics* 1.1–2 (1981): 127–40.

Cypess, Sandra Messinger. *La Malinche in Mexican Literature: From History to Myth.* Austin: University of Texas Press, 1991.

Dana, Richard Henry. *Two Years before the Mast.* 1840. New York: Random, 1936.

de Certeau, Michel. *The Practice of Everyday Life.* Trans. Steven F. Rendall. Berkeley: University of California Press, 1984.

de Kadt, Emanuel, ed. *Tourism—Passport to Development?* New York: Oxford University Press, 1979.

del Villar, Mary, and Fred del Villar. *Where the Strange Roads Go Down.* 1953. Tucson: University of Arizona Press, 1991.

Díaz del Castillo, Bernal. *The Conquest of New Spain.* Ed. and trans. J. M. Cohen. New York: Penguin, 1963.

———. *True History of the Conquest of New Spain.* 4 vols. Trans. Alfred Percival Maudslay. London: Hakluyt Society, 1908–16.

Dirks, Beverly. "New Breed of Traveler." *Northwest Airlines World Traveler* 12 (1993): 66.

Doerr, Harriet. *Consider This, Señora.* New York: Harcourt, 1993.

———. *Stones for Ibarra.* New York: Viking, 1984.

Durán, Diego. *The Aztecs: The History of the Indies of New Spain.* Trans. Doris Heyden and Fernando Horcasitas. New York: Orion, 1964.

———. *Book of the Gods and Rites and the Ancient Calendar.* Ed. and trans. Fernando Horcasitas and Doris Heyden. Norman: University of Oklahoma Press, 1971.

Elizondo, Sergio D. "ABC: Aztlán, the Borderlands, and Chicago." In *Missions in Conflict: Essays on U.S.-Mexican Relations and Chicano Culture,* ed. Renate von Bardeleben, Dietrich Briesemeister, and Juan Bruce-Novoa. Tübingen: Narr, 1986. 13–23.

Ernest, John. "Reading the Romantic Past: William H. Prescott's *History of the Conquest of Mexico.*" *American Literary History* 5.2 (1993): 231–49.

Feifer, Maxine. *Tourism in History: From Imperial Rome to the Present.* New York: Stein and Day, 1986.

Flores, Juan, and George Yudice. "Living Borders/Buscando America: Languages of Latino Self-formation." *Social Text* 24 (1990): 57–84.

Florescano, Enrique. *Memoria mexicana: Ensayo sobre la reconstrucción del pasado: época prehispánica–1821.* Mexico City: Editorial Joaquín Mortiz, 1987.

———. *El nuevo pasado mexicano.* Mexico City: Cal y Arena, 1991.

Forbes, Jack D. *Aztecas del Norte: The Chicanos of Aztlan.* Greenwich, Conn.: Fawcett, 1973.

Ford, Richard. *The Ultimate Good Luck*. 1981. New York: Vintage-Random, 1986.

Francisco, Patricia Weaver, and Timothy Francisco. *Village without Mirrors*. Minneapolis: Milkweed, 1989.

Gage, Thomas. *The English-American his Travail by Sea and Land: Or, a New Survey of the West-India's*. 1648. London: Routledge, 1928.

———. *Thomas Gage's Travels in the New World*. 1958. Ed. J. Eric S. Thompson. Norman: University of Oklahoma Press, 1985.

García, Alesia. "'And It Is Told' from D. H. Lawrence to Rudolfo A. Anaya: Quetzalcóatl and Utopian Mesoamerica." Unpublished essay, 1993.

García, Juan R. "Hollywood and the West: Mexican Images in American Films, 1894–1983." In *Old Southwest/New Southwest: Essays on a Region and Its Literature*, ed. Judy Nolte Lensink. Tucson: Tucson Public Library, 1987. 75–90.

Gillespie, Nick, and Virginia Postrel. "On Borders and Belonging: A Conversation with Richard Rodriguez." *Reason* (August 1994). Reprinted in *Utne Reader* (March 1995): 76–79.

Gillespie, Susan D. *The Aztec Kings: The Construction of Rulership in Mexica History*. Tucson: University of Arizona Press, 1989.

Greene, Graham. *The Lawless Roads*. 1939. New York: Penguin, 1982.

———. *The Power and the Glory*. 1940. New York: Penguin, 1986.

———. *A Sort of Life*. London: Bodley Head, 1971.

Gunn, Drewey Wayne. *American and British Writers in Mexico, 1556–1973*. Austin: University of Texas Press, 1974.

Guthke, Karl S. *B. Traven: The Life behind the Legends*. Chicago: Lawrence Hill, 1991.

———. *Trails in No-Man's-Land: Essays in Literary and Cultural History*. Columbia, S.C.: Camden, 1993.

Gutiérrez, Ramón. "Aztlán, Montezuma, and New Mexico: The Political Uses of American Indian Mythology." In *Aztlán: Essays on the Chicano Homeland*, ed. Rudolfo A. Anaya and Francisco Lomelí. 1989. Albuquerque: University of New Mexico Press, 1991. 172–90.

Haggard, H. Rider. *Montezuma's Daughter*. London: Longmans, 1893.

Hall, Ron. "Great Beaches of the World." *Condé Nast Traveler* (December 1993): 96–107, 152–55.

Harrison, David, ed. *Tourism and the Less Developed Countries*. London: Belhaven, 1992.

Heath, Ernie, and Geoffrey Wall, eds. *Marketing Tourism Destinations: A Strategic Planning Approach*. New York: Wiley, 1992.

Horcasitas, Fernando, and Doris Heyden. "Fray Diego Durán: His Life and Works." In *Book of the Gods and Rites and the Ancient Calendar*. Ed. and trans. Horcasitas and Heyden. Norman: University of Oklahoma Press, 1971. 23–31.

Hulme, Peter. *Colonial Encounters: Europe and the Native Caribbean, 1492–1797*. New York: Methuen, 1986.

Humboldt, Alexander von. *Political Essay on the Kingdom of New Spain*. 1811. Trans. John Black. Ed. Mary Maples Dunn. Norman: University of Oklahoma Press, 1988 [1 vol.].

Huxley, Aldous. *Beyond the Mexique Bay*. New York: Harper, 1934.

Jenkins, Philip, and Ernst Schürer, eds. *B. Traven: Life and Work*. University Park: Pennsylvania State University Press, 1986.

Joyce, James. *A Portrait of the Artist as a Young Man*. 1916. New York: Viking, 1964.

Keefe, Susan E., and Amado M. Padilla. *Chicano Ethnicity*. Albuquerque: University of New Mexico Press, 1987.

Keen, Benjamin. *The Aztec Image in Western Thought*. 1971. New Brunswick: Rutgers University Press, 1990.

Kemper, Robert V. "Urbanizacion y desarrollo en la region Tarasca a partir de 1940." In *Antropologia social de la region purepecha*, ed. Guillermo de la Peña. Zamora, Michoacan: Colegio de Michoacan, 1987. 67–96.

Klor de Alva, J. Jorge. "Aztlán, Borinquen, and Hispanic Nationalism in the United States." In *Aztlán: Essays on the Chicano Homeland*, ed. Rudolfo A. Anaya and Francisco Lomelí. 1989. Albuquerque: University of New Mexico Press, 1991. 135–71.

———. "The Postcolonization of the (Latin) American Experience: A Reconsideration of 'Colonialism,' 'Postcolonialism,' and 'Mestizaje.'" In *After Colonialism: Imperial Histories and Postcolonial Displacements*, ed. Gyan Prakash. Princeton: Princeton University Press, 1995. 241–75.

———. "Sahagún and the Birth of Modern Ethnography: Representing, Confessing, and Inscribing the Native Other." In *The Work of Bernardino de Sahagún: Pioneer Ethnographer of Sixteenth-Century Aztec*

Mexico, ed. Klor de Alva, H. B. Nicholson, and Eloise Quiñones Keber. Albany: Institute for Mesoamerican Studies, 1988. 31–52.

Kolodny, Annette. "Letting Go Our Grand Obsessions: Notes toward a New Literary History of the American Frontiers." *American Literature* 64 (1992): 1–18.

Lattin, Vernon E., ed. *Contemporary Chicano Fiction: A Critical Survey.* Binghamton, N.Y.: Bilingual, 1986.

Lawrence, D. H. *Mornings in Mexico.* New York: Knopf, 1927.

———. *Phoenix: The Posthumous Papers of D. H. Lawrence.* Ed. Edward D. McDonald. London: Heinemann, 1936.

———. *The Plumed Serpent.* 1926. New York: Vintage, 1959.

———. *Selected Essays.* New York: Penguin, 1981.

———. *Selected Letters.* Ed. Diana Trilling. New York: Farrar, 1958.

Leal, Luis. *Aztlán y México: Perfiles literarios e históricos.* Binghamton, N.Y.: Bilingual, 1985.

———. "In Search of Aztlán." Trans. Gladys Leal. In *Aztlán: Essays on the Chicano Homeland,* ed. Rudolfo A. Anaya and Francisco Lomelí. 1989. Albuquerque: University of New Mexico Press, 1991. 6–13. First published in *Denver Quarterly* 16 (1981): 16–22.

Lee, Rosemary Louise. *The Tourist Industry in Yucatan: A Case Study in the Interaction between Class Structure and Economic Development.* Ph.D. diss., University of California, Irvine, 1977. Ann Arbor: University Microfilms International, 1981. Catalogue no. 78-1458.

Lett, James. Epilogue to "Touristic Studies in Anthropological Perspective," by Theron Nuñez. In *Hosts and Guests: The Anthropology of Tourism,* ed. Valene L. Smith. Philadelphia: University of Pennsylvania Press, 1989. 275–79.

Limón, José. *Mexican Ballads, Chicano Poems: History and Influence in Mexican-American Social Poetry.* Berkeley: University of California Press, 1992.

Lincoln, Bruce. *Discourse and the Construction of Society: Comparative Studies of Myth, Ritual, and Classification.* New York: Oxford University Press, 1989.

Long, Veronica H. "Government—Industry—Community Interaction in Tourism Development in Mexico." In *The Tourism Industry: An International Analysis,* ed. M. Thea Sinclair and M. J. Stabler. Wallingford, England: CAB International, 1991. 205–22.

Lowry, Malcolm. *Selected Letters of Malcolm Lowry.* Ed. Harvey Breit and Margerie Bonner Lowry. New York: Capricorn, 1969.

———. *Under the Volcano.* 1947. New York: Penguin, 1986.

Lumholtz, Carl. *Unknown Mexico.* 2 vols. New York: Scribner's, 1902.

MacCannell, Dean. *Empty Meeting Grounds: The Tourist Papers.* London: Routledge, 1992.

———. *The Tourist: A New Theory of the Leisure Class.* 1976. New York: Random, 1989.

Marcus, Joyce. *Mesoamerican Writing Systems: Propaganda, Myth, and History in Four Ancient Civilizations.* Princeton: Princeton University Press, 1992.

Marquez, Antonio. "A Discordant Image: The Mexican in American Literature." *Minority Voices* 5 (1981): 41–51.

McCarthy, Cormac. *All the Pretty Horses.* 1992. New York: Random, 1993.

McClure, John A. *Late Imperial Romance.* London: Verso, 1994.

Mexico. Department of Tourism. *Tourism as a Medium of Human Communication.* Mexico City: Mexican Tourism Department, 1967.

Mexico. Secretariat of Tourism. *Like a Dream, Southern Mexico.* Mexico City: Mexico Tourism, 1990.

———. *Mexico Beaches.* Mexico City: Mexico Tourism, 1993.

———. *Mexico Mexico.* Mexico City: Mexico Tourism, 1993.

Monsiváis, Carlos. "Travelers in Mexico: A Brief Anthology of Selected Myths." Trans. Jeanne Fergusson. *Diogenes* 125 (1984): 48–74.

Muñoz, Carlos, Jr. *Youth, Identity, Power: The Chicano Movement.* London: Verso, 1989.

Nash, Denison. "Tourism as a Form of Imperialism." In *Hosts and Guests: The Anthropology of Tourism,* ed. Valene L. Smith. Philadelphia: University of Pennsylvania Press, 1989. 37–52.

Obeyesekere, Gannath. *The Apotheosis of Captain Cook: European Mythmaking in the Pacific.* Princeton: Princeton University Press, 1992.

O'Connor, Richard. *Ambrose Bierce: A Biography.* Boston: Little, 1967.

Padilla, Genaro M. "Myth and Comparative Cultural Nationalism: The Ideological Uses of Aztlán." In *Aztlán: Essays on the Chicano Homeland,* ed. Rudolfo A. Anaya and Francisco Lomelí. 1989. Albuquerque: University of New Mexico Press, 1991. 111–34.

Paredes, Américo. *With His Pistol in His Hand: A Border Ballad and Its Hero.* 1958. Austin: University of Texas Press, 1990.

Paredes, Raymund. "Mexican-American Literature: An Overview." In *Recovering the U.S. Hispanic Literary Heritage,* ed. Ramón Gutiérrez and Genaro Padilla. Houston: Arte Público, 1993. 31–51.

Pastor Bodmer, Beatriz. *The Armature of Conquest: Spanish Accounts of the Discovery of America, 1492–1589.* Trans. Lydia Longstreth Hunt. Stanford: Stanford University Press, 1992.

——. "Silence and Writing: The History of Conquest." In *1492–1992: Re/discovering Colonial Writing,* ed. René Jara and Nicholas Spadaccini. Minneapolis: Prisma Institute, 1989. 121–63.

Paz, Octavio. *The Labyrinth of Solitude.* Trans. Lysander Kemp. 1950. New York: Grove, 1985.

——. *The Other Mexico.* Trans. Lysander Kemp. New York: Grove, 1972.

Pearson, Sheryl S. " 'Is There Anybody There?': Graham Greene in Mexico." *Journal of Modern Literature* 9.2 (1982): 277–90.

Peterson, David T. "Inspired Truth? Images of Mexico in Katherine Anne Porter's 'Hacienda.' " Unpublished essay, 1993.

Pettit, Arthur G. *Images of the Mexican American in Fiction and Film.* College Station: Texas A&M University Press, 1980.

Pina, Michael. "The Archaic, Historical and Mythicized Dimensions of Aztlán." In *Aztlán: Essays on the Chicano Homeland,* ed. Rudolfo A. Anaya and Francisco Lomelí. 1989. Albuquerque: University of New Mexico Press, 1991. 14–48.

Pi-Sunyer, Oriol. "Changing Perceptions of Tourism and Tourists in a Catalan Resort Town." In *Hosts and Guests: The Anthropology of Tourism,* ed. Valene L. Smith. Philadelphia: University of Pennsylvania Press, 1989. 87–99.

Porter, Katherine Anne. *The Collected Essays and Occasional Writings of Katherine Anne Porter.* New York: Delacorte, 1970.

——. *The Collected Stories of Katherine Anne Porter.* New York: Harcourt, 1979.

——. *Outline of Mexican Popular Arts and Crafts.* Los Angeles: Young and McAllister, 1922.

Portis, Charles. *Gringos.* New York: Simon, 1991.

Pratt, Mary Louise. "Arts of the Contact Zone." *Profession* (1991): 33–40.

———. *Imperial Eyes: Travel Writing and Transculturation*. London: Routledge, 1992.

———. "Scratches on the Face of the Country; or, What Mr. Barrow Saw in the Land of the Bushmen." In *"Race," Writing and Difference*, ed. Henry Louis Gates, Jr. Chicago: University of Chicago Press, 1986. 138–62.

Prescott, W. H. *History of the Conquest of Mexico*. 1843. New York: Random, n.d.

Rabasa, José. "Dialogue as Conquest: Mapping Spaces for Counter-Discourse." *Cultural Critique* 6 (1987): 131–59.

———. *Inventing America: Spanish Historiography and the Formation of Eurocentrism*. Norman: University of Oklahoma Press, 1993.

Reich, Alice H. *The Cultural Construction of Ethnicity: Chicanos in the University*. New York: AMS Press, 1989.

Reynoso y Valle, Agustin, and Jacomina P. de Regt. "Growing Pains: Planned Tourism Development in Ixtapa-Zihuatanejo." In *Tourism: Passport to Development?* ed. Emanuel de Kadt. New York: Oxford University Press, 1979. 111–34.

Richter, Linda K. "Political Instability and Tourism in the Third World." In *Tourism and the Less Developed Countries*, ed. David Harrison. London: Belhaven, 1992. 35–46.

Robinson, Cecil. *No Short Journeys: The Interplay of Cultures in the History and Literature of the Borderlands*. Tucson: University of Arizona Press, 1992.

———. *With the Ears of Strangers: The Mexican in American Literature*. 1963. Tucson: University of Arizona Press, 1969.

Rodriguez, Richard. *Days of Obligation: An Argument with My Mexican Father*. New York: Viking, 1992.

Rogers, Jane. "The Function of the La Llorona Motif in Anaya's *Bless Me, Ultima*." In *Contemporary Chicano Fiction: A Critical Survey*, ed. Vernon E. Lattin. Binghamton, N.Y.: Bilingual, 1986. 200–205.

Rosaldo, Renato. "Fables of the Fallen Guy." In *Criticism in the Borderlands: Studies in Chicano Literature, Culture, and Ideology*, ed. Héctor Calderón and José David Saldívar. Durham: Duke University Press, 1991. 84–93.

Sahagún, Bernardino de. *Florentine Codex: General History of the Things of New Spain*. 13 vols. Trans. Arthur J. O. Anderson and Charles E.

Dibble. Santa Fe: Monographs of the School of American Research and the University of Utah, 1975.

Said, Edward W. *Orientalism.* 1978. New York: Vintage-Random, 1979.

Saldívar, Ramón. *Chicano Narrative: The Dialectics of Difference.* Madison: University of Wisconsin Press, 1990.

Sánchez, Rosaura. "Ideological Discourses in Arturo Islas's *The Rain God.*" In *Criticism in the Borderlands: Studies in Chicano Literature, Culture, and Ideology,* ed. Héctor Calderón and José David Saldívar. Durham: Duke University Press, 1991. 114–26.

Sandoval, Chela. "Feminism and Racism: A Report on the 1981 National Women's Studies Association Conference." 1982. In *Making Face, Making Soul: Haciendo Caras,* ed. Gloria Anzaldúa. San Francisco: Aunt Lute, 1990. 55–71.

Saragoza, Alex M. "Recent Chicano Historiography: An Interpretive Essay." *Aztlán* 19.1 (1988–90): 1–77.

Shacochis, Bob. "In Deepest Gringolandia: Mexico and the Third World as Tourist Theme Park." *Harper's* (July 1989): 42–50.

Simmen, Edward, ed. *North of the Rio Grande: The Mexican-American Experience in Short Fiction.* New York: Penguin, 1992.

Smith, Valene L., ed. *Hosts and Guests: The Anthropology of Tourism.* Philadelphia: University of Pennsylvania Press, 1989.

Solotaroff, Robert. *Robert Stone.* New York: Twayne, 1994.

Sontag, Susan. *On Photography.* 1977. New York: Doubleday, 1989.

Soto, Gary. *Living up the Street: Narrative Recollections.* San Francisco: Strawberry Hill, 1985.

Spangler, George M. "Kate Chopin's *The Awakening*: A Partial Dissent." *Novel* 3 (1970): 249–55.

Spurr, David. *The Rhetoric of Empire: Colonial Discourse in Journalism, Travel Writing and Imperial Administration.* Durham: Duke University Press, 1993.

Stephens, John L. *Incidents of Travel in Central America, Chiapas and Yucatan.* 2 vols. 1841. New York: Dover, 1963.

Stone, Robert. *Children of Light.* 1986. New York: Random, 1992.

Suarez, Mario. "Kid Zopilote." 1947. In *North of the Rio Grande: The Mexican-American Experience in Short Fiction,* ed. Edward Simmen. New York: Penguin, 1992. 111–18.

Swain, Margaret Byrne. "Gender Roles in Indigenous Tourism: Kuna

Mola, Kuna Yala, and Cultural Survival." In *Hosts and Guests: The Anthropology of Tourism*, ed. Valene L. Smith. Philadelphia: University of Pennsylvania Press, 1989. 83–104.

Todorov, Tzvetan. *The Conquest of America: The Question of the Other.* Trans. Richard Howard. 1982. New York: Harper, 1984.

Torgovnick, Marianna. *Gone Primitive: Savage Intellects, Modern Lives.* Chicago: University of Chicago Press, 1990.

Tourism Investment in Mexico. San Diego: San Diego State Institute for Regional Studies of the Californias, 1991.

Traven, B. *The Treasure of the Sierra Madre.* 1927. New York: Farrar, 1988.

Urry, John. *The Tourist Gaze: Leisure and Travel in Contemporary Societies.* London: Sage, 1990.

Valdez, Luis. "La Plebe." In *Aztlan: An Anthology of Mexican American Literature*, ed. Valdez and Stan Steiner. New York: Vintage-Random, 1972. xiii–xxxiv.

———. "Zoot Suit." *Zoot Suit and Other Plays.* Houston: Arte Público, 1992.

van den Berghe, Pierre L., and Charles F. Keyes. "Tourism and Re-created Ethnicity." *Annals of Tourism Research* 11 (1984): 343–52.

Veitch, Douglas W. *Lawrence, Greene and Lowry: The Fictional Landscape of Mexico.* Waterloo, Ont.: Laurier University Press, 1978.

Villarreal, José Antonio. *Pocho.* 1959. New York: Anchor-Doubleday, 1970.

Walker, Ronald G. *Infernal Paradise: Mexico and the Modern English Novel.* Berkeley: University of California Press, 1978.

Walsh, Thomas F. *Katherine Anne Porter and Mexico: The Illusion of Eden.* Austin: University of Texas Press, 1992.

Waters, Frank. "Quetzalcoatl versus D. H. Lawrence's *Plumed Serpent.*" *Western American Literature* 3 (1968): 103–13.

Wolf, Eric. *Sons of the Shaking Earth.* Chicago: University of Chicago Press, 1959.

Wollen, Peter. "Tourism, Language, and Art." *New Formations* 12 (1990): 43–59.

Woodcock, George. "Mexico and the English Novelist." *Western Review* 21 (1956): 21–32.

Index

About the Author

Daniel Cooper Alarcón was born and raised in Menasha, Wisconsin. He worked as a newspaper reporter before pursuing graduate studies at the University of Minnesota and is currently a member of the English Department at the University of Arizona. Cooper's scholarship has appeared in the journal *Aztlán* (1992) and in the critical anthology *Subjects and Citizens* (1995), and his short fiction has been published in the anthologies *New Chicana/Chicano Writing* (1992) and *New World: Young Latino Writers* (1996). *The Aztec Palimpsest* is the culmination of six years of study and research.

DATE DUE
